The Structural Change of Knowledge and the Future of the Social Sciences

This book is a compendium of pragmatism in the social sciences. While addressing several distinct spheres, it carries a common message: the future of the social sciences depends on a shared understanding of society based on the knowledge of various disciplines and transcending the currently forbidding borders between scientific knowledge and the other forms of knowledge. Looking back at the social science traditions this is nothing new. To ensure a fruitful future for the social sciences a paradigm shift is unavoidable. The consequence of the increase of knowledge in the last two centuries was the specialization of the sciences. The nineteenth century saw the separation of humanities and social sciences; the twentieth century is even characterized by specialization within the disciplines and the occurrence of competing schools of thought. This book tries to overcome the barriers that are built between and within the disciplines, and to counteract the unnecessary barriers created by the emergence of "schools of thoughts" that distrust each other and the social sciences as a whole.

This book was originally published as a special issue of *Innovation: The European Journal of Social Science Research*.

Ronald Pohoryles is Research Director of the ICCR and President of the European Association of the Advancement of the Social Sciences. He is the founder and editor-in-chief of *Innovation: The European Journal of Social Science Research*. He is also Visiting Senior Lecturer at the Institute of Political Science at the University of Vienna, Austria, where he teaches classical liberal scholars.

Andrew Sors is Head of Science and Technology for the European Commission's Delegation to India. He was previously Head of Social Sciences and Humanities Research at the European Commission. He has been a visiting professor at Manchester University, UK, and spent three years as Rector of the Collegium Budapest Institute for Advanced Study, Hungary.

The Structural Change of Knowledge and the Future of the Social Sciences

Edited by
Ronald Pohoryles and Andrew Sors

Routledge
Taylor & Francis Group

LONDON AND NEW YORK

First published 2018 by Routledge

2 Park Square, Milton Park, Abingdon, Oxfordshire OX14 4RN
52 Vanderbilt Avenue, New York, NY 10017

Routledge is an imprint of the Taylor & Francis Group, an informa business

First issued in paperback 2019

British Library Cataloguing in Publication Data
A catalogue record for this book is available from the British Library

ISBN 13: 978-1-138-06595-6 (hbk)
ISBN 13: 978-0-367-23392-1 (pbk)

Typeset in TimesNewRomanPS
by diacriTech, Chennai

Publisher's Note
The publisher accepts responsibility for any inconsistencies that may have arisen
during the conversion of this book from journal articles to book chapters, namely
the possible inclusion of journal terminology.

Disclaimer
Every effort has been made to contact copyright holders for their permission to
reprint material in this book. The publishers would be grateful to hear from any
copyright holder who is not here acknowledged and will undertake to rectify any
errors or omissions in future editions of this book.

Contents

CONTENTS

Citation Information

The chapters in this book were originally published in *Innovation: The European Journal of Social Science Research*, volume 30, issue 1 (March 2017). When citing this material, please use the original page numbering for each article, as follows:

Introduction
On the future of social sciences and humanities – a pragmatic perspective
Ronald J. Pohoryles and Andrew Sors
The European Journal of Social Science Research, volume 30, issue 1 (March 2017)
pp. 1–4

Chapter 1
Back to the future? From pragmatic approaches in the social sciences to the development of the patchwork theory
Ronald J. Pohoryles
The European Journal of Social Science Research, volume 30, issue 1 (March 2017)
pp. 5–23

Chapter 2
Social scientists as technicians, advisors and meaning producers
Nico Stehr and Alexander Ruser
The European Journal of Social Science Research, volume 30, issue 1 (March 2017)
pp. 24–35

Chapter 3
Society as an ethical system
John Crowley
The European Journal of Social Science Research, volume 30, issue 1 (March 2017)
pp. 36–46

Chapter 4
Travelling concepts and crossing paths: a conceptual history of identity
Liana Giorgi
The European Journal of Social Science Research, volume 30, issue 1 (March 2017)
pp. 47–60

CITATION INFORMATION

Chapter 5

Knowledge, International Relations and the structure–agency debate: towards the concept of "epistemic selectivities"
Alice B.M. Vadrot
The European Journal of Social Science Research, volume 30, issue 1 (March 2017)
pp. 61–72

Chapter 6

The creative economy: invention of a global orthodoxy
Philip Schlesinger
The European Journal of Social Science Research, volume 30, issue 1 (March 2017)
pp. 73–90

Chapter 7

In search of experiential knowledge
Stuart Blume
The European Journal of Social Science Research, volume 30, issue 1 (March 2017)
pp. 91–103

Chapter 8

Seeing the wood for the trees: Social Science 3.0 and the role of visual thinking
Joe Ravetz and Amanda Ravetz
The European Journal of Social Science Research, volume 30, issue 1 (March 2017)
pp. 104–120

Chapter 9

Maps of the uncertain: a new approach to communicate scientific ignorance
Christoph Henseler and Hans-Liudger Dienel
The European Journal of Social Science Research, volume 30, issue 1 (March 2017)
pp. 121–136

Obituary

A thank you note and a farewell to our colleagues to whom we owe our success
Ronald J. Pohoryles
The European Journal of Social Science Research, volume 30, issue 1 (March 2017)
pp. 137–139

For any permission-related enquiries please visit:
http://www.tandfonline.com/page/help/permissions

Notes on Contributors

Stuart Blume is Emeritus Professor of Science and Technology Studies, Department of Anthropology, University of Amsterdam, the Netherlands.

John Crowley is Chief of Section at the UNESCO Division of Social Transformations and Intercultural Dialogue, Paris, France.

Hans-Liudger Dienel is the Director at the Centre for Technology and Society, Berlin, Germany.

Liana Giorgi is a psychologist, sociologist, and political scientist with more than twenty years' work experience in public policy analysis and regulatory assessment at European Union level.

Christoph Henseler is based at the Department of Vocational Education and Employment, TU Berlin, Germany.

Ronald Pohoryles is Research Director of the ICCR, Vienna, Austria, and President of the European Association of the Advancement of the Social Sciences.

Amanda Ravetz is Senior Research Fellow at the Manchester School of Art, Manchester Metropolitan University, UK.

Joe Ravetz is Co-Director of the Centre for Urban Resilience and Energy, School of Environment and Development, Manchester Metropolitan University, UK.

Alexander Ruser is representative Professor for Cultural Theory and Analysis, and Zeppelin University Chair for Cultural Theory and Analysis, Zeppelin, Germany.

Philip Schlesinger is Professor of Cultural Policy at the Centre for Cultural Policy Research, University of Glasgow, Scotland.

Andrew Sors is Head of Science and Technology for the European Commission's Delegation to India.

Nico Stehr is Karl-Mannheim Chair for Cultural Studies, Zeppelin University, Germany.

Alice B.M. Vadrot is an Erwin Schrödinger Fellow of the Austrian Research Fund (FWF) at the University of Cambridge, UK.

INTRODUCTION

On the future of social sciences and humanities – a pragmatic perspective

The mission of the journal *Innovation: The European Journal of Social Science Research*, whose 30th anniversary we are celebrating in this volume is to provide a unique forum for discussing European issues in an interdisciplinary and transdisciplinary manner. The Journal welcomes articles which contribute to the improvement of social science knowledge and to the setting of a policy-focused European research agenda. Hence, the editorial board of the journal decided to entrust the editorship to Ronald Pohoryles, an experienced social scientist, and to Andrew Sors, a former senior science official at the European Commission. The reason for this particular combination of editors was already defined by Stehr in at the beginning of the third millennium: "One can define knowledge as 'the capacity to act,' as the potential to 'start something going'" (2001, 89). This is particularly true for production and dissemination of social sciences knowledge.

Still, the reader of this journal might be surprised: at the first sight, they come from "different worlds". Ronald Pohoryles is since its existence research director of the ICCR that is publishing the journal over the last 30 years, and the founder and editor-in-chief of this journal; Andrew Sors has between 1982 and 2008 worked at the European Commission, Head of "Social Sciences and Humanities Research" till 2005 to thereafter become Head of Science and Technology at the European Commission's Delegation to India. He has been a visiting professor at Manchester University and spent three years as rector of the Collegium Budapest Institute for Advanced Study. With a Ph.D. in Materials Science and early career as a research engineer in the chemical industry, Andrew has acquired direct experience of the pitfalls as well as the benefits of crossing disciplines and professional boundaries.

Arguably, social science research and research programming are two sides of the same coin; although this metaphor might be misleading as there are important differences between the two sides in terms of their perspectives, priorities, and expectations. However, research communities need funding and there are legitimate expectations from those who fund the research – especially in the public sector. This, in turn, creates some tensions with respect to the necessary autonomy and the creativity of research that might not always have a "successful" outcome. Innovation is by definition a new way of designing structures and actions; they might be successful or lead to fail – the latter being a somewhat frustrating for both the researchers and the research funders. At the same time, without creativity, commitment, imagination and a degree of risk taking the social sciences cannot fulfill their mission (Løchen 1994). For the social sciences and the humanities likewise this not trivial. The societal challenges are quite complex by nature. Let us take the example of the ecological problems the humanity is facing. Merely technological solutions do not suffice, as solutions necessitate an adequate policy answer and to a certain extent the change of behavior of the people. This in turn calls for public participation, which is a complex issue as well as the different stakeholders have different interests and follow different strategies to defend their interests. Or another example: everybody would agree that the fight against poverty is just. However, there are different views on the causes of poverty and the extent of acceptable social inequality. To find an acceptable compromise interdisciplinary research to understand the context is as necessary as the inclusion of non-scientific knowledge. For the social sciences and the humanities, the challenge is to define a new epistemology and new research strategies.

The late Peterson has defined the highest demands made of our journal: "Innovation has offered rare opportunities to break down the rigors of orthodox academic boundaries and reach across disciplines and faculties. (…) Innovation has always attracted those who wanted to try out new angles to established topics" (2012, 9). Of course we cannot always fulfill these demands. However, in the current issue we hope to make an original contribution.

Let us turn to the articles in this issue:

Ronald Pohoryles contends that the future of the social sciences depends on taking a step back to the classics. At first sight, this contention might seem to be contradicted by the growing complexity of society, economy, and policies. However, the social science disciplines themselves are experiencing a greater degree of specialization, as well as by different approaches according to the national traditions and frameworks and finally different schools of thoughts. Looking back at the classical literature, among thinkers such as Adam Smith, Karl Marx, or Max Weber the paradox becomes quite obvious: they were confronted with less complex contemporary societies, but produced a more complex view on social structures and actors. The mission of the social sciences is to contribute knowledge to societal development. Of course, the social sciences cannot address current societal challenges by producing "general theories". Societies have become so complex that simple answers cannot be provided; nor can satisfactory results be produced by theoretical types of thinking aiming to find a single pathway towards a just, safe, secure, and wealthy future for the societies on the global level. The author discusses the pragmatist theories as a possible solution to the dilemma and bases his idea of "patchwork theories" on this tradition.

In their contribution, *Nico Stehr and Alexander Ruser* argue that social scientists produce three types of practical knowledge following the "model of technician", the "model of advisor", and the "model of meaning producers". The role of this knowledge is commonly seen in capturing the complex social reality. However, social scientists quite often complain about the limited impact of their research on society and politics as compared to the natural sciences and technology. The authors hold that an algorithmic model does not apply to the social sciences and see their role (and power) rather as "meaning producers".

John Crowley points to a quite central issue for the social sciences, that of ethics. Interestingly enough he goes beyond the usual debate of ethics in the social sciences, but argues that societies are ethical in their own right. He describes societies as structured patterns of interactions and independencies within common communication spaces. Each such space is guided by rules that are the precondition for defining societies as an ethic system: an intrinsic "mode of self-understanding" that is not imposed externally. To argue his case, he uses the example of inequality. Inequality has both practical and normative aspects. In a global political perspective, the UN has developed the "Agenda for Inclusive and Sustainable Development" that the author explains in detail. This underlines the crucial importance of the relationships between the social sciences and the humanities.

In her contribution, *Liana Giorgi* shows the relevance of psychoanalysis for the social sciences as a whole. Since the late 1980s she has been working in the social sciences and dealing with quite a lot of different types of identities and ethnical minorities in a social science perspective. As psychoanalyst she is confronted in her practical work with the complex issue of identities, which however does not impede her to publish regularly in various journals. Whilst continuing social science research she publishes now mostly in psychoanalytical journals. She reminds us that the concept of identity – one of the core issues in sociology and political science – remains in a strange manner quite imprecise and nebulous. In order to clarify the concept, she proposes to look at the history of the concept. Liana Giorgi has strong social science background in cognitive science, where she graduated at the MIT and obtained a Ph.D. in social and political sciences from Cambridge University and is currently working as psychoanalyst, she is especially well placed for undertaking the challenging issue of an interdisciplinary journey.

Alice Vadrot started her academic career with research in biodiversity politics and policies by looking extensively at the "Intergovernmental Science-Policy Platform on Biodiversity and Ecosystem Services (IPBES)". She had the opportunity to observe the development of the IPBES *ab ovo* and has analyzed the process of its implementation and its functioning. As a science-policy interface that was initiated by a group of scientists facing some resistance from policy-makers the institutionalization of the platform created processes of inclusion and exclusion. For these processes she developed the concept of "epistemic selectivities" to describe the role and social construction of knowledge. In her article, she looks at the theoretical underpinning of the concept and discusses it in relation to the structure-agency debate in international relations.

Philip Schlesinger criticizes the shift from the notion of culture to the concept of the "creative economy" which is strongly supported by the contemporary political system, the media and what he calls "current orthodoxy on academic institutions and research". He holds that the concept of the "creative economy" was originally developed in the UK and was taken over by the European Union, and even by the United Nations. Schlesinger attributes this to the first British New Labour government in 1997–1998 coining the term of "creative industries" that became since hegemonic. The core of the cultural policies since has been to aggregate 13 distinct fields of cultural practice and defining these as "industries" and hence as an industrial policy domain for deriving economic benefits on the domestic as well as the global markets. The growing importance of intellectual property rights has led to a subordination of the cultural complexity to mere economic values. The UK has strongly institutionalized the concept both in cultural support bodies as well in the BBC. Schlesinger deplores the lack of resistance from cultural milieus despite the necessity of a new thinking on the field.

The "economization" of societal issues does not only concern the cultural sphere: As *Stuart Blume* argues, the social sphere is increasingly confronted by the dominance of the strategy of cost cutting in the health care sector over societal needs. Resistance against this development comes from organization of patients, but from the health professions as well. Patient organizations call for the use of "experiential knowledge", that is, the knowledge of those who live with chronic diseases. Blume discusses the content of this knowledge and how it is related to individual experiences. He understands the role of social scientists in the integration of the diverging experiences based stakeholder knowledge and discusses the challenges social scientists are need to address in this regard in their work.

To address the major challenges with which the contemporary social sciences are confronted *Joe Ravetz and Amanda Ravetz* call for a major paradigm shift towards transdisciplinary thinking. In their complexity, the social and political challenges deal with subjects that show no clear boundaries, and hence are quite fuzzy objects to be studied. Meaningful results cannot be expected from specific disciplines within the traditional academic systems alone. Barriers to novel approaches are, however, both the traditional academic career path and the funding structures. Still, attempts for "Science 3.0" are emerging from the work on complex systems and design thinking. Visualization offers the opportunity to mobilize tacit knowledge, creativity and form a bridge from analysis to synthesis for complex inter-connected problems and offer an interface to combine scientific knowledge and other forms of rationality.

Hans-Liudger Dienel and Christoph Henseler share the view of J and A Ravetz on the complexity of social phenomena and the related uncertainties in science. Among (social) scientists there seems to be a widespread consensus about accepting uncertainty and nescience, that is, lack of knowledge. However, the scientists themselves seem to assume that the public at large expects clear and unambiguous results from scientific research. This problem calls for a shift in science communication. In order to bridge the gap between the scientific debates and the somewhat biased interaction with the society the authors propose a new methodology, the "Maps of Uncertainty", as a solution and give some examples of the successful use of the instrument.

As editors, we have taken the liberty of calling this issue of Innovation a compendium of pragmatism in the social sciences. While addressing several distinct spheres, the edition as a whole carries a common message: the future of the social sciences depends on a shared understanding of society based on the knowledge of various disciplines and transcending the currently forbidding borders between scientific knowledge and the other forms of knowledge. Looking back at the social science traditions this is nothing new. To ensure a fruitful future for the social sciences a paradigm shift is unavoidable. The consequence of the increase of knowledge in the last two centuries was the specialization of the sciences. The nineteenth century saw the separation of humanities and social sciences; the twentieth century is even characterized by specialization within the disciplines and the occurrence of competing schools of thought. This issue tries to overcome the barriers that are built between and within the disciplines, and to counteract the unnecessary barriers created by the emergence of "schools of thoughts" that distrust each other and the social sciences as a whole.

References

Løchen, Yngvar. 1994. "Commitment and Imagination in the Social Sciences: A Concern for the Future State of Sociology." *Innovation: The European Journal of Social Science Research* 7 (4): 405–412. doi:10.1080/13511610.1994.9968420.

Peterson, Martin. 2012. "Innovation: One Step Ahead of the Research Community." *Innovation: The European Journal of Social Science Research* 25 (1): 9. doi:10.1080/13511610.2012.655962.

Stehr, Nico. 2001. "A World Made of Knowledge." *Society* 39 (1): 89–92. doi:10.1007/BF02712625.

Ronald J Pohoryles
ICCR Foundation, Vienna, Austria

Andrew Sors
Brussels, Belgium

Back to the future? From pragmatic approaches in the social sciences to the development of the patchwork theory

Ronald J. Pohoryles[a,b]

[a]ICCR Foundation, Wällischgasse, Vienna, Austria; [b]European Association for the Advancement of Social Sciences, Vienna, Austria

The debate on the function of the social sciences in complex societies, and more generally of the role of knowledge, leads necessarily to a discussion on pragmatism. The gap between theoretical approaches and empirical research still exists and has even widened, in part as a result of the use and abuse of social science knowledge in politics and by the media. However, the academic system is equally to blame for this. Mutual ignorance and scholastic fights are barriers against openness, creative and imaginary thinking. The structures and the practices of the academic system reinforce this trend. Pragmatism aims at overcoming these cleavages by looking at commonalities between different approaches rather than by disputing their validity. It aims at a comprehensive understanding of the process of knowledge production and at the productive use of results. Defining itself in this tradition, the patchwork theory goes beyond the traditional pragmatic approaches: it catches part of the reality of social phenomena from a certain perspective that allows for an overview without having the full picture. Methodologicall, the approach guided by patchwork theory emphasizes the relevance of stakeholders' knowledge and citizen science, and calls for public participation and democratic access to the production and use of knowledge in a discursive manner.

There is no royal road to logic, and really valuable ideas can only be had at the price of close attention. But I know that in the matter of ideas the public prefer the cheap and nasty. (Peirce, 1878, "How to Make Our Ideas Clear")

Introduction

In many European academic systems, the habilitation – in Latin "venia legendi" or "venia docendi" – is the entry point for an academic career and continues to constitute a prerequisite for attainment of academic status. In the 1980s this was the case not only for universities but also for private research organizations. I always understood this tradition as a form of gate-keeping: in order to produce a habilitation many young researchers carry out research on conventional topics using conventional methods as this is what is expected of them. Insofar as a habilitation takes three to five years of research and writing, this particular form of initiation rite is unlikely to stimulate creative thinking and innovation among young researchers.

In Austria, the procedure for acquiring a habilitation is quite complex. The candidate is expected to submit to the faculty a still unpublished book. After submission, the faculty assigns a committee of full professors, assistant professors and student representatives. The committee invites at least two faculty members and external referees for the evaluation of the work submitted. The final step is a public presentation in the presence of the committee. The procedures are similar to those for a Ph.D. but more formal and more ritualized.

The book I chose to write for this purpose had to do with reform policies in Europe; the 1970s and my approach was influenced by pragmatism. The manuscript included a fresh look at various theoretical approaches and relied on empirical data, some of which came from my own research, some from secondary sources (Pohoryles 1985). Both referees submitted positive reports, however I had the impression that my approach was not fully understood. I was accused for eclecticism. To quote one of the reports: "The text provided is quite eclectic […] His thesis is based on system theory, which is a male approach. However, if you do system theory you should do it like Pohoryles *(own translation)*".[1]

I would still hold that my book was not eclectic but rather written with reference to the pragmatic tradition, and I cannot find a reference to system theory in my book, which, of course, does not mean that I do not recognize the latter's merits.

The focus of my article is the future of the social sciences as a mode of thinking that contributes to the development of society. The future of the social sciences depends on its ability to serve societies' needs. This remark is not trivial: it opens up a series of questions. What are the needs of societies and what is the potential of the social sciences to respond to these needs?

In what follows I will shortly discuss the different pragmatic approaches in the Social Sciences and the Humanities to thereafter develop the idea of a Patchwork Theory. I am aware of the possible objections against the concept of a patchwork theory, both because of the ambiguous connotation of the term and for epistemological reasons. Furthermore, there might be a concern whether the approach I propose needs to be coined by a new name. I will address these objections and give some examples from my own research, and research carried out at the institute I am leading since 1987. Against this background I will discuss the future options for the social sciences in the conclusion.

Pragmatism in the social sciences

The limits of a journal article do not allow me to elaborate on the development of, and the different approaches, of pragmatism in full detail. Rather I will concentrate on those ideas of pragmatism that are relevant for the development of the patchwork theory.[2]

The origins of pragmatism date back to the nineteenth century. Charles Sanders Pierce was the first scholar to elaborate the basic principles of pragmatism, though in the language of philosophy of the nineteenth century:

> The very first lesson that we have a right to demand that logic shall teach us is, how to make our ideas clear; and a most important one it is, depreciated only by minds who stand in need of it. To know what we think, to be masters of our own meaning, will make a solid foundation for great and weighty thought. (Peirce 1878, 288)

From a science ethics perspective, Pierce's approach implies that the sciences must be prepared to present their ideas in clear manner allowing for open debates with the aim of consensus building. Peirce is aware of the reasons that might lead *prima facie* to different results. However, an open discourse between scholars following different paths in their research may lead to agreement:

> All the followers of science are animated by a cheerful hope that the processes of investigation, if only pushed far enough, will give one certain solution to each question to which they apply it. […] They may at first obtain different results, but, as each perfects his method and his processes, the results are found to move steadily together toward a destined centre. So with all scientific research. […] This great hope is embodied in the conception of truth and reality. That is the way I would explain reality. (Peirce 1878, 297)

But, as Peirce notes himself, such a result is highly unlikely. Even if scholars are willing to overcome personal vanities and professional snobbery, they are hardly ever in the position to obtain full knowledge about a certain subject, or about the full range of impacts that influence the properties of the object of a study. Even if one assumes that all of the approaches to a certain object under investigation are valid and diversity can be resolved by an open discourse, reliability remains doubtful:

> Though in no possible state of knowledge can any number be great enough to express the relation between the amount of what rests unknown to the amount of the known, yet it is unphilosophical to suppose that, with regard to any given question (which has any clear meaning), investigation would not bring forth a solution of it, if it were carried far enough. (Peirce 1878, 301)

In the view of early pragmatism, while the lack of reliability has to be taken into account, it should not undermine creative thinking. Creative thinking contributes equally to the progress of scientific thinking and to the development towards a more just society. As an illustration of this, Abbott (2010) looked at the contribution of pragmatist scholars of the early "Chicago School" to public debates on social justice by way of articles for the "Chicago Tribune". Abbott refers especially to Charles Richmond Henderson, who became professor of sociology and chaplain of the university in 1892, where he remained until his death in 1915. Henderson was deeply rooted in his religious beliefs, and his academic performance was explicitly related to these beliefs. As liberal protestant he aimed at bridging the gap between Protestantism and Catholicism yet, at the same time, he never tired from underlining that other religious beliefs, and even atheism, have to be respected on their own right. Drawing normatively on his religious beliefs and his philosophical work, Henderson actively engaged with civil society besides supporting various charities (Abbott 2010). Other pragmatists from the "Chicago School" took a more secular approach but were equally committed to social justice both in word and deed Walter Lippman, for instance, was among the most influential thinkers for modern social liberalism (Lippmann 1938).[3]

A prominent example of a social researcher with a normative approach in Europe is Paul Lazarsfeld. Before he had to flee Austria from the Nazis, Paul Lazarsfeld entertained a close relationship to the Austrian social democratic party. The famous Marienthal study on the social impact of unemployment, which he carried out together with Marie Jahoda and Hans Zeisel, was in fact financed by the Austrian Trade Union (Jahoda, Lazarsfeld, and Zeisel 1932). His later appointment at the University of Chicago was made in recognition not only of his excellent theoretical knowledge and empirical skills but also of his normative approach. The same applied to Merton, with whom Lazarsfeld closely collaborated upon his arrival in the USA (Abott and Gaziano 1999).

In modern sociology there are many methodological applications of pragmatist thinking. Pragmatist thinking allows for the use of quite different methods according to the respective object of observation and, furthermore, for innovative methodological developments. Henrik Kreutz, following Karl Mannheim's understanding of the role of social sciences as contemporary diagnostics, applied various methodologies to analyse the current development of societies. In a special issue dedicated to various qualitative approaches one finds a compendium of the use of photographs, texts in literature and other documents for the social sciences (1987). Further developing his idea of quasi-experimental questions (Kreutz 1972). Kreutz also explored the application of computer simulation models as well (Kreutz and Bacher 1991).

In the literature there are prominent examples of pragmatist thinking. Respecting the space limits of a journal article I confine myself to elaborate briefly on the ideas of Jürgen Habermas. Coming from a creative interpretation of Marxism in the tradition of the *Frankfurt School* Habermas oriented himself towards pragmatism in the late 1960s. In his epistemological turn he displayed a growing interest in knowledge (adding under brackets the original German notion of "Erkenntnis" as the English translation could be misunderstood).[4]

In "Knowledge and Human Interests" he deplores the widening of the gap between the natural sciences and the social sciences since the nineteenth century. He insists, however, on the epistemological differences between the natural sciences, on the one hand, the humanities and the social sciences, on the other hand. Habermas claims that these differences are based on different knowledge interests ("Erkenntnisinteresse"): the natural sciences display a practical knowledge interest; humanities have a hermeneutic interest; and the social sciences an emancipatory interest (Habermas 1973, English translation: Habermas 1987). In his earlier work on the logic of the social sciences, Habermas was also critical of the division between the different schools within the social sciences (Habermas 1967, English translation Habermas 1988).[5]

Feenberg (1996) criticizes Habermas from a specific angle. Whilst he appreciates most of Habermas' ideas he criticizes his "defence of modernity": in Feenberg's interpretation, Habermas sees natural science and technology as being too strongly related to a mere instrumental form of rationality without reflecting the social construction of technology (Feenberg 1996). This specific critique is not fully justified since Habermas elsewhere criticizes technology as an ideology. With reference to Weber's idea of the different elements of social actions, that is, "zweckrational" and "wertrational" (1971),[6] Habermas distinguishes between purpose-driven and culturally driven actions (1970). However what Habermas has indeed not adequately explored is the transfer of paradigms from the natural sciences to social science theories. Whilst he recognizes that the three different models of rationality in the natural sciences, in the social sciences and in the humanities are all similarly legitimate and valid, he does not discuss the potential of transferability of knowledge from one field to another.

In French sociology Luc Boltanski and Laurent Thévenot are among the most renowned scholar to have used a pragmatic approach in their sociological thinking. Let us return to the discussion of Peirce's work. To reiterate: Although Pierce considers the relation between the known and unknown a major obstacle with respect to determining the "eternal truth" of an argument, he is willing to accept that a consensus achieved by way of may lead to a common agreement on the object under observation, which comes close to truth. In the same vein, but dealing with societal disagreements, Boltanski and

Thévenot argue that such an agreement is possible if the dimension of disagreement is reduced. This thought provides a link to Habermas' theory about the existence of several levels of discourse ultimately leading to rational consensus (2007). The argument reads as follows:

> Just as we shall seek to understand the way the polity model is structured by the requirement that the plurality of principles of agreement must be reduced, we shall attempt to show that the model is similarly informed by the way the tensions inherent in a universe embracing multiple natures – tensions between reason and practice, between generality and contingency, and between justice and equity – constrain judgment while allowing it a certain latitude. Our work will thus be devoted to the study of the procedures that make it possible to bring disputes to a close. (Boltanski and Thévenot 2006, 42)

Boltanski's and Thévenot's starting point is that the natural and social sciences share a common theoretical base. They both follow a similar logic while analysing "very diverse beings – persons, institutions, tools, machines, rule governed arrangements, methods of payment, acronyms and names, and so forth" (2006, 41). What all these objects have in common is that it is possible to test them thus accounting for their efficiency. As I will show in the next section this is a major difference between pragmatism and the patchwork theory: whilst insisting on the transferability of model of thoughts the patchwork does not claim a universal logic of knowledge.

A later analysis of Thévenot is more convincing: He deals with a specific topic, that is, power and oppression. Looking at the theoretical approaches of Dewey and Bourdieu he offers an alternative perspective, a "sociology of engagements". In the analysis of power and oppression Thévenot characterizes Dewey's approach as based on an actors' perspective, whereas Bourdieu deals with social structures. The claim of the theory of engagement is to overcome this dualism:

> [The sociology of engagements considers] how human beings engage with their environment, investing in forms of guarantee which would appease their inquietude. The analysis of regimes of engagement demonstrates how the same forms of guarantee that support confidence are also those which give rise to doubt and even criticism of the abuse of power. The dynamics of each regime unfolds the two sides of the guarantee: closing one's eyes when relying with blind faith on the marker of the guarantee; opening one's eyes to what is sacrificed. This twofold characterisation enables us to understand reifying reductions of engagements and to unveil mechanisms through which devices contributing to assurance lead to abusive or oppressive power. (Thévenot 2011, 36)

Again, this quote shows the very essence of pragmatism: not to deny any approach its validity, but combine different elements in order to obtain a synthetic view on a specific subject.

From a perspective of critical sociology Delanty looks at different approaches to critical theory: he examines the notion of critique as used by the Frankfurt School. Bourdieu's critical sociology and critical realism, Foucault's genealogical critique, and various notions of critical practice, most notably the work of Boltanski and Thévenot (Delanty 2011).

Analysing the notion of critique in these theories, Delanty concludes that a comprehensive theory must include elements of all of these approaches:

> Critique as a methodologically grounded approach entails four – or, if necessary, five – dimensions, which can be derived from the general epistemological framework of immanent transcendence in so far as this concerns the identification of society's immanent possibilities for

transcendence. The four core features of critique concern: diagnostic analysis of a problem or crisis situation, reconstructive critique of social actors' communication and action, explanatory critique of the objective structures or mechanisms, and disclosing critique of practically realisable normative possibilities. These roughly correspond to the moments of description, interpretative reconstruction, explanation, and normatively connecting with practice. The fifth feature, namely genealogical critique, enters in conjunction with the second phase, if necessary, to test the status of the normative principles interpretatively reconstructed from communication and action. (Delanty 2011, 86 f)

Delanty observes a shift from the Hegelian-Marxist approach in the tradition of the Frankfurt School towards interpretative conceptions of critique. He appreciates such a shift, opts, however, for a pragmatic approach that is methodologically feasible. In his view while such a theory might not turn out to be satisfying at the macro-level and has just a limited capacity to discover long-term trends on the micro-level, it allows for a better understanding of social conflicts and narrows the gap between a theory of critique and social practices. Delanty summarizes the advantages of such an approach to theory building as follows:

> The model proposed here has […] the advantage of making critique relevant to macro-analysis as well as to social praxis and corrects the tendency towards a constructivist view of social reality as constituted in practices or discourses needing only interpretation. The position advanced here ties practice to a stronger normative purpose built on the foundations of empirical and theoretical analysis of a social reality. (Delanty 2011, 90)

Delanty's claims are well grounded and go fairly beyond the traditional pragmatism. However, the methodological consequences remain vague and do not explain what Delanty means by social praxis. And this brings me to the concept of patchwork theories.

Towards the development of a patchwork theory

As I could show in the last section of this article the transferability of research approaches and theory models between disciplines is meaningful – this is the essence of pragmatism, and, as I will show, the more so of patchwork theory, or, possibly patchwork theories. The idea behind the patchwork is that there exists no fully elaborated theory in the strict sense. This is why I leave it open whether we should speak about the patchwork theory, or rather about patchwork theories. But this is quite adequate given the complexity of the object we are dealing with. And such an open approach is nothing new: in that I am following Merton's advice about the importance of middle-range theories (Merton 1949).

Like pragmatism, the patchwork theory aims at defining a framework in which the existing knowledge can be integrated in a systematic manner. The problem with the existing research is the isolated way in which scientific knowledge is created. This is even more the case for knowledge creation that would benefit from work in other disciplines, or the inclusion of citizens' and stakeholders' knowledge. A comprehensive framework contributes better to the understanding of the society and for responding to societies' needs.

The legitimacy problem of the social sciences

The call for a further development of patchwork theories is related to the role of the social sciences knowledge and its potential to contribute to social and political developments. Although the situation certainly has improved since the early days of August Comte, the social sciences are not yet fully accepted as "scientific", and hence social science knowledge is still not used to its full potential by decision-makers and the society at large. There are reasons for this "legitimacy deficit" of the social sciences. The representation of the social sciences in the media is quite superficial. The media uses the social sciences in many ways that do not necessarily reflect the ideas developed within the disciplines. When it comes to economics the media reports on short-lived economic forecasts that offer precise figures that are periodically revised and hence lack credibility. As the media have a clear gate-keeping function this influences the public attitudes *vis-à-vis* the social sciences.

- The *media coverage* concentrates on public opinion research, especially so during elections. The information and forecasts delivered about voters' preferences are usually rather superficial and entail a high degree of uncertainty. Rather than informing such data often assume a manipulative function.
- *Economic forecasts* are short-lived and based on mathematical models that use plausible assumptions but limited input data regarding the possible impact of policy measures. Thus such forecasts do not cover the complexity of interactions between economic actors and their strategies, policy measures and the growing impact of society by way of participatory actions.
- Invited "experts"[7] *by the media* are limited to short statements on recent political developments that are by default superficial.
- *Politicians* use social science knowledge according to their interests: as there are different schools of thoughts in the social sciences politicians choose experts that are close to their political strategies. This by no means an accusation: I do not here claim there is moral or financial corruption taking place. This is rather a process "mutual alignment", to borrow Lindblom's term from his analysis of the interactions between economic and political actors (Lindblom 1977). Lindblom argues that this dualism is a mode of governance by which dominant social actors share power and exclude other actors from influencing policies. As shown by different studies, Lindblom's approach delivers accurate results in other areas as well (with respect to the media: Pohoryles 1987; with respect to science-policy interfaces: Vadrot 2014).

All of the above contributes to the afore-mentioned legitimacy problem of the social sciences. There are, however, internal reasons as well. There is a long dispute tradition between different schools of thoughts within the social sciences. There are, as we all know, fights over paradigms, theories, and methodologies. These debates are detrimental for the social sciences for two reasons: first, epistemological debates tend to become stagnant fairly quickly, as relations between different scientific communities focus more on separation than on collaboration; second, by contrast to the natural sciences, social sciences, and humanities are not only fragmented by conflicting epistemologies, but also by national traditions as well (Dienel, Hammerlund, and Peterson 2002). These fragmentations further weaken the social science disciplines.

The Norwegian sociologist Yngvar Løchen summarizes the situation as follows:

> The question has been raised whether the conditions under which science is done, are conducive to cooperation between colleagues and healthy competition against the problems under investigation or whether these conditions on the contrary rather stimulate aggression and destructive conflicts among rivals and enemies on the battlefields of science. (1994, 413)

Towards the development of patchwork thinking

Løchen's strong statement does not only speak to the pitfalls of scholarly games. Løchen is keen to highlight the necessity of a "healthy competition between researchers. Andrew Abbot argues in similar manner: in the tradition of pragmatism he insists that the idea of a single method to solve problems is inappropriate and leads subsequently to sterile thinking within narrow borders" (Løchen 1994, 405). In order to justify the own approach researchers stabilize the borders within and without their disciplines (Abbott 2001). The diversity of approaches and methods is not necessarily destructive: Abbott calls for a heuristic approach in the social sciences benefiting from the wealth of thoughts in generating innovative research. Such an approach necessitates an understanding of the contents and the underlying motives of the competing schools of thoughts and the appropriation of the knowledge generated in the respective research. In an open spirit the creation of appropriate methods beyond dogmatism can lead to useful results (2004).

I refer to such an approach as "patchwork thinking". Objections against "patchwork thinking" can come from different perspectives, terminological perspectives and epistemological perspectives.

The first objection might be merely terminological: For instance, the Oxford online dictionary offers the following example for the term patchwork: "The landscape was just a patchwork of fields". The Cambridge online dictionary proposes the same example, but with a different connotation: "We looked out of the aircraft window down onto the patchwork of fields below".

The difference is not trivial: Using the word "just", like the Oxford example does, it means something pejorative. The spectator sees the patchwork of fields as something quite uninteresting that is not what he expects from a nice landscape to look like. By contrast, the Cambridge example is open to further reasoning: the appearance of landscape might lead the spectator observes to reflect on the underlying causes of the shape of this particular landscape, which is clearly caused by human intervention. Hence, the spectator can look at the phenomenon from a specific perspective without having an overview over the shape of the entire planet, the economic, social, and political structures of the country to which the landscape belongs, etc. The spectator (to use Smith's term) might still develop hypotheses on how, by human intervention, the landscape got this specific shape.

More importantly, there are epistemological objections. Some traditional scholars might criticize the open approach of patchwork theories: The traditional disciplinary research is carried out under a strict framework of standards, rules and methodologies and insist on conventional methods of checking for validity and reliability. By contrast, the approach of patchwork theory is more open to interdisciplinary research. This is critique was already voiced against pragmatism, and still this is wrong. Adorno and Horkheimer quote a *bonmot* of a Swedish sociologist who reportedly answered to such a critique: "Do you want to by and large right, or absolutely wrong?" This may sound polemic; however, this reflects Pierce's argument in favour of pragmatism: as shown above, he insists on the relation between the known and the unknown that does not challenge the validity of research, but its reliability.

A less valid argument against interdisciplinary research, but rather a suspicion is voiced by traditional scholars. Some claim that such an approach would be rather be motivated by a lack of disciplinary qualifications than by a search of the truth. This suspicion is based on the career path of many interdisciplinary researchers who studied different subjects and even graduated in different disciplines. This, however, does not mean that these scholars would not be able to deliver high-quality research respecting scientific norms and values.

Finally, and this is an objection against research in a patchwork approach, in an "ivory tower perspective" traditional scholars might criticize the inclusion of stakeholders' knowledge and citizen participation as "unscientific". Such a critique ignores the development of the societies in the twenty first century. Much knowledge is produced outside the traditional academia and the level of education allow us to speak about the "knowledge economy" and the "knowledge society". True, the knowledge gained outside the traditional academia differ from ideal type of traditional knowledge production, both in terms of the methodology and the knowledge interest. But does this justify the exclusion of these types of knowledge, or does strengthening the border between the different sources of knowledge rather widen the gap between unfruitful academic discourse in the ivory tower and the contemporary developments in society and economy and thus in turn make scholarly research irrelevant?

The possible objections might explain why the concept of "Patchwork Theory" in the social sciences or the humanities is not developed to a satisfying extent. Still, some scholars have worked in this direction. By combining juridical approaches and philosophical ones, Altman used patchwork thinking to differentiate between blackmail and forms of hard bargaining. He rightly so notes:

> We might more easily solve the legal and moral puzzles if we stop insisting that one principle must explain every aspect of blackmail. I recommend abandoning the search for a unified explanation […]The legal ban (like most rules) is probably both overinclusive and underinclusive compared to the moral arguments supporting it. (Altman 1993, 1639)

I have dealt with the issue of corruption in the same vein (Pohoryles 1989). In an earlier article I showed that corruption in legal terms is quite clearly defined; however, its interpretation varies across time: the same behaviour might be today understood as successful economic behaviour and later condemned as corruption.

Another example for the patchwork approach is the transfer of models, or a thought experiment, from one discipline to another: In my contribution to a *Festschrift* in honour of Martin Peterson (Hammarlund and Nilson 2006) I discussed the meaning of "Knowledge Society and Knowledge Economy". For my analysis I used the famous example of Schrödinger's Cat (Schrödinger 1935; 1983): Schrödinger holds that under specific conditions a cat can be at the same time dead and alive. In the experiment the cat is caged up in a steel chamber that contains a radioactive substance. In the course of one hour one of the atoms decays, or, with equal probability, none. In this hour, the cat is alive, if the decay does not happen; if the decay however, does happen, the cat is dead. According to Schrödinger, the Psi function (a quantum wave function) for the entire system would show this by having in it the living and the dead cat. In my analysis of the "New Economy", another term for "knowledge economy" the cat's state in Schrödinger's example has led me to the following conclusion: "The object is already defined in its premises: New economy is part of the starting point and not part of the study. The question is not whether there is such a thing like the New Economy, The New Economy is taken as given" (Pohoryles and Giorgi 2006).

The philosopher Berys Gaut offers a wider approach to patchwork theories. He criticizes the mainstream theories in philosophical aesthetics and moral philosophy, intentionalism and utilitarism. His definition of the patchwork theory as a series of local theories of interpretation looks at the diversity of the ascription of properties of individual activities:

> I […] propose an alternative view, the patchwork theory, which holds that no global theory of interpretation […] is correct. Instead, one needs a series of local theories of interpretation

(597) […] The process of interpretation involves ascribing an immense variety of radically different properties to works, and the problem with any global account of interpretation is that the constraints on the correct ascription of one type of property may be greatly different from those on another, so that no theory of interpretation will give the grounds for ascription of all of them […] In the case of some of the properties which pose a problem for intentionalism, intentions play a more significant and direct role, but they figure only as one of a variety of potentially conflicting criteria which determine the correct ascription of the properties. In these cases, then, a cluster theory, not intentionalism, gives the correct account of interpretation (602 ff). (Gaut 1993)

Gaut refers to semiotics while the social sciences use different paradigms. But the transferability is obvious. As social phenomena are not "visible" like physical objects, researchers cannot observe them directly, but look at structures, institutions, agencies, or analyse narratives and more generally data that are based on specific assumptions: in quantitative research researchers assume they represent "reality" through indicators constructed based on theories, or chosen based on expectations derived from professional or personal experience; in qualitative research researchers generalize from texts, or interviews, which includes much interpretative work. When it comes to modelling even more interpretation is necessary: researchers have to limit the amount of input variables, which reduces the complexity even more as compared to other methodologies. Economic forecasts show the shortcomings of model building: Due to oversimplification, results gained are short-lived and hardly ever as precise as suggested.

One of the shortcomings of Gaut's approach is that he is inclined to relativism. He himself admits that "the argument advanced here has important consequences for the role of relativism" (p. 597). Gaut has a point in his critique of Grand Theories. This, however, does not necessarily lead to relativism: Robert K. Merton proposed moving away from Grand Theories and looking more modestly at sets of social phenomena in order to develop, middle-range theories. Arguably, Merton's approach can be understood in the tradition of pragmatism: Looking at "such disparate general theorists as Marx and Spencer, Simmel, Sorokin and Parsons" he insists on the validity of the general theories, provided one understands the internal logic of these theories:

> But in fact, as we shall note later in this introduction, comprehensive sociological theories are sufficiently loose-knit, internally diversified, and mutually overlapping that a given theory of the middle range, which has a measure of empirical confirmation, can often be subsumed under comprehensive theories which are themselves discrepant in certain respects. […] Middle-range theory enables us to transcend the mock problem of a theoretical conflict between the nomothetic and the idiothetic, between the general and the altogether particular, between generalizing sociological theory and historicism. (Merton 1949, 451 f)

Merton's methodological proposal is to replace the search for a general sociological theory "by developing special theories from which to derive hypotheses that can be empirically investigated and by evolving, not suddenly revealing, a progressively more general conceptual scheme that is adequate to consolidate groups of special theories" (Merton 1949, 457).

This quote leads us to a very often ignored idea of Merton's thinking: ultimately he believes in the aim and possibility of developing a General Theory. The claim for the development is simply premature:

> But this perspective ignores the fact that between twentieth-century physics and twentieth-century sociology stand billions of man-hours of sustained, disciplined, and cumulative

research. […] We are not ready. Not enough preparatory work has been done. (Merton 1949, 455)

Middle-range theories in this view have only a transitory status towards the development of a general theory. This becomes obvious when Merton comes to the following conclusion:

> Sociological theory, if it is to advance significantly, must proceed on these interconnected planes: (1) by developing special theories from which to derive hypotheses that can be empirically investigated and (2) by evolving, not suddenly revealing, a progressively more general conceptual scheme that is adequate to consolidate groups of special theories. (Merton 1949, 457)

Just to reiterate: Merton's concept of middle-range theories is based on the assumption that there is a gap between sociological theory and empirical research. He does not deny the possibility of the development of a general sociological theory, holds, however, that this claim is premature. He understands the attempts of his contemporary colleagues against the background of what I call the "legitimacy deficit", as explained above in more detail, but offers instead a more modest system that ultimately might lead to the desired result. Furthermore, he is explicitly working as sociologist within a confined discipline. Only reluctantly he concedes that some of his colleagues are successfully looking at similar disciplines like social psychology and anthropology.

I hold that there are two important differences between Merton's approach and the patchwork theory: First, patchwork theories do not necessarily claim to contribute to a unified general theory. Rather, patchwork theories should be understood as a heuristic approach to understand contemporary societies, their aim rather to indicate pathways towards various scenarios as determined by the different norms and values of different social actors. Second, patchwork theories do not confine themselves to a specific discipline, whilst not ignoring the importance of disciplinary rules and academic education within these disciplines. But part of the thinking in terms of patchwork theories is openness and creativity.

In what follows I will show that the research practice based on patchwork thinking must not to be confused with relativism, but has clear structures and sound rules and standards that might differ from the traditional ones, but which offer reliable and valid results nevertheless.

Putting patchwork theories to research

The traditional academic system is often criticized as an "ivory tower", and there are good reasons for this reproach that go beyond institutional barriers against innovative thinking. Luk van Langenhove calls for a "more useable knowledge for society" and a paradigm shift in the social sciences. Such a paradigm shift necessitates a change in the institutional set-up of traditional universities, their evaluation schemes and the career opportunities for young researchers (van Langenhove 2007). Langenhove looks at the history of the relation between the social sciences and the natural sciences whilst also addressing the relation between the natural environment and the societal framework. With respect to our topic the originality of van Langenhove's book is his view on "the way in which the social sciences are organised and the way researching and theorizing is performed" (van Langenhove 2007, 306). He makes a convincing case for transdisciplinary research, that is, the inclusion of citizen knowledge and citizen science into scientific research. One particular relevant observation of van Langenhove is that participatory approaches to social science research cannot be appropriately evaluated within the traditional academic peer-review model, since the latter does not take into account stakeholder views (Pohoryles 2007a, 35).

National research landscapes have an important role to play in this respect. We find in the EU many different traditions of universities and research organizations and these impact on participation in research programmes that necessitate international cooperation and/or the inclusion of stakeholders. This is particularly true for the social sciences. While European collaborative research is carried out mainly by universities in the UK, the role of private research organizations is greater in Central Europe. This is related to the internal organization of the institutions and the career path of young researchers (Pohoryles and Schadauer 2009). The different logic under which these institutions operate favours the role of private research organizations, often not-for-profit associations, in international cooperative non-traditional research (Pohoryles 1993).

Funding structures also play an important role for the type of research that is provided by knowledge producers. Traditional national funding agencies favour the traditional academic research, hence traditional universities with strict border lines between disciplines and the reliance on established methodologies. By contrast, public agencies look for applied research ("expert reports") with clear-cut results that does not always consider the complexity of problems. Private research foundations sometimes offer more freedom for research, their importance for the social sciences is however limited.

Although there are reasons to criticize several aspects of the European Framework Programmes for Research and Development, these are still the most relevant venues for mainstreaming social sciences, and with them stakeholder interests, into technological research (van der Meulen 2002).

One of the criticisms of EU programmes concerns their strict formalism in accordance with the logical framework rules that govern technology, engineering, and management projects. Research proposals are successful when they follow an industrial logic: research has to be organized in work packages, controlled by milestones and documented in deliverables. The outcome is often judged in quantitative terms (time, resource use and allocation, citation index, etc.) rather than in qualitative terms. As a result, many approaches to interdisciplinary research involve simply putting together disciplinary "work packages" and therefore lack a comprehensive vision (Pohoryles and Schadauer 2009, 151). On the other hand, the programme arguably offers the option to carry out research in a non-traditional way outside academic routines. Experience shows that at least within the central European tradition, this necessitates research institutions that are different from traditional universities (van der Meulen 2002).

Despite their technical design, European research projects both support and enable patchwork thinking. I will refer to three examples to demonstrate my case. All three projects were interdisciplinary, the last is both interdisciplinary and transdisciplinary.

My first example is the project "A European Public Space Observatory: Assembling Information that Allows the Monitoring of European Democracy (EUROPUB)" project. Already the name of the project explicates its pragmatic intention. The project is not alone about the development of a methodology. Although a set of monitoring indicators were developed, these were based on a solid theoretical approach linking European politics and policy-making the emergence of a European public space. The context was the legitimacy problem of the European Union as evidenced by the growing Euroscepticism which in 2005 resulted in the rejection of the European Constitutional Treaty by way of referenda in France and in the Netherlands. The project addressed the question whether existing institutional constellations and socio-political practices provide an effective system of political contestation with a genuinely European focus. Starting from a functional concept of a European public space that is in line with both democratic theory and socio-institutional practices, the EUROPUB project dealt with the identification and the assessment of institutional opportunity structures for effective contestation of EU policy-making in selected policy areas. Relevant to the full picture is the analysis of the emergence of a specific European political class. Based on these considerations the researches involved developed a set of data and tested the transferability to various policy fields (Giorgi, von Homeyer, and Parsons 2006).

The project and its publications demonstrate many characteristics of what I understand under "patchwork thinking". In the literature one finds many publications on democracy theory, public participation, and European politics and policies. The researchers working on this project managed to integrate all these different aspects using documents, narratives, and a representative survey study. The project's results based on six policy studies and a survey of the European political class advance a strong argument for the increase and improvement of participatory practices in the framework established by representative democracy.

Another example of patchwork thinking is the EURO-FESTIVAL project, which was one of the first projects to be launched under the social science theme of the Seventh Framework Programme as a small collaborative project. Its objectives were to explore how arts festivals use aesthetic forms to symbolize, represent and communicate social and political life; to study the way in which festivals frame the discourse of identity in relation to the arts; and to analyse how festivals represent sites of competition for access to resources, status and power. The project comprised 13 case studies in different cultural fields and different countries. Arguably, it was the first project to systematically examine the cultural significance of festivals as sites for contestation and democratic debate against the background of aesthetic cosmopolitanism. Once again we have here a very ambitious and creative project being conceptualized as an interdisciplinary collaborative project.

The EURO-FESTIVAL research (Giorgi, Sassatelli, and Delanty 2011) is another good example for the potential entailed in patchwork thinking. The scope of the project is broader than usual cultural sociology studies. It includes not only an investigation on the aesthetics of festivals, or the economic aspects of festivals (as often in the critique of the capitalist transformation of the arts), but relates the issue to political and social life, to identity issues and to the relation of festivals to cosmopolitanism. The pragmatic approach of the study was elaborated as follows:

> Different views of the public sphere are not necessarily to be treated as as inherently contradictory. […] The communicative action approach is a theory of action […] and therefore places the emphasis on agency. By contrast, the field approach is a descriptive-analytical theory, which is more interested in understanding patterns and structures and the power relations between them. Both approaches are valid and both have something to contribute to the understanding of the dynamics of the public sphere, as well as of the cultural public sphere and hence also of festivals. (Giorgi and Sassatelli 2006, 5)

By accepting the validity of competing theoretical approaches as valid and using the essence of both approaches for gaining new insights of the subject at hand the authors follow the pragmatic tradition. What, however, goes beyond is the way in which the subject is approached. The authors do not confine themselves to a specific form of aesthetic manifestations, but look at various case studies of the arts, or more specifically, they explore artistic manifestations within different genres and in different international settings. Following the cultural sociological approach they apply standard sociological methods to the study of festivals as organizations. In parallel they explore the artistic programmes of festivals and how these are used by artists and audiences to connect and create a reflective space. In this way the project delivers many parts of a complex puzzle, or, as I would call it, a patchwork to illustrate the general idea of the project.

As last example I use a transdisciplinary European project, the EURO-COOP project that was coordinated by the ICCR and delivered in the 6th Framework programme. The project "Regional Innovation Policy Impact Assessment and Benchmarking Process: Cooperation for Sustainable Regional Innovation" was designed to develop an innovative methodology to assess the impact of regional innovation policies as a common activity of researchers, regional and local authorities and other stakeholders. The project went beyond traditional policy assessment studies, not only because of the involvement of stakeholders, but also because of the multi-criteria approach that included all aspects of sustainable development, economic aspects, social aspects, ecological aspects, and participation.[8] The methodological framework was developed by the Centre for Urban Resilience and Energy of the University of Manchester. Jointly with the other project partners and the inclusion of local stakeholders the methodology is quite innovative and was successfully implemented:

> A "Regional System of Innovation" has many possible stakeholders; and a Regional Innovation Strategy and/or policy has many possible effects, direct or indirect, in the shorter or longer term. Any impact assessment has to be aware of these possibilities, and particularly those which involve more intangible changes in communications or relationships between stakeholders. Therefore, the Regional Innovation Policy Impact Assessment method does not aim at a single fixed answer to the assessment. It aims more to provide a working template and route map for investigation. This should help to explore the regional innovation agenda, theoretical paths of causes and effects, the relationships of stakeholders, and the organizational learning capacity as a foundation for the innovation process. Therefore, the Regional Innovation Policy Impact Assessment method does not aim at a single fixed answer to the assessment. It aims more to provide a working template and route map for investigation. (Ravetz et al. 2006, 4)

The description of this method gives a very good overview of the possible implementation of a transdisciplinary methodology from a patchwork perspective. Also relevant are those projects working with citizen groups to explore specific themes in policy and research terms. The future of the social sciences depends on the use of this knowledge in combination with a sound methodological approach. This approach promises to deliver a deeper understanding of the complexity of modern societies thus contributing to their development. This is what Karl Mannheim succinctly defined as the responsibility of intellectuals (Mannheim 1940).

Conclusions

In this article I have been referring to my own work and that of my institute more than one should regularly do in a journal article. I have two justifications: firstly, in terms of contents, my own work has all along been oriented towards patchwork thinking. Referring to it has helped me to keep something like a red line in reflecting about a complex issue; secondly, on a more personal note, I draw the reader's attention to the fact that this issue is dedicated to the 30th anniversary of a journal that I founded and which is published by the institute I led for the last third of a century. This has motivated me to look back on my own work.

What I have shown in this article is that the patchwork theory is well grounded in the tradition of the social sciences, but goes beyond existing approaches. Arguably, one might rather speak of a patchwork approach in pragmatism instead of patchwork theory, or patchwork theories. I would not object, however I still favour the notion of "patchwork theory" as the operationalization of a theory as shown in the example of the projects I was referring to above necessitates a particular form of patchwork thinking.

My final remark refers to the title of this article: back to the future. I think that this title is justified. In the tradition of the social sciences, patchwork thinking was the usual way of approaching complex issues. Let us take the example of Adam Smith. In a recent book I made the argument that one cannot understand Adam Smith alone on the basis of his most famous book, *The Wealth of Nations* (Smith 1776). Most authors who refer to Adam Smith hold that the central issue of this book is his plea for free markets. But this is not doing justice to the wealth of the book: it contains many political ideas and discusses social implications as well. Interestingly enough he also insists on the importance of state interventions. Besides, according to Adam Smith, moral behaviour is another prerequisite for functioning markets (Smith 1759). This shows in my view that Smith was analysing economy and society both from a holistic and pragmatic approach. I would even take a step further and argue that his methodology is also quite innovative in the sense advocated by the patchwork theory. In order to support his approach, Smith uses quite deliberately historical examples. This is an issue I have elaborated elsewhere (Pohoryles 2015). Suffice to mention here Heilbroner who wrote in his introduction to the collection of Adam Smith's texts notes: "No economist's name is more frequently invoked than that the one of Adam Smith, and no economist's works are less frequently read" (Heilbroner and Malone 1986).

The same holds for Max Weber. In his *opus magnum* Weber elaborates his theory in a theoretical manner, but backs it with historical examples. One of the frequent misunderstandings of his axiom of "Wertfreiheit" (freedom of values from research and independence from values in the work of the researchers). Weber insists on strict academic rules for the methodology applied in research. However, this does not apply for the selection of (historical) examples the researcher chooses to support the theoretical reasoning. These examples are, given the amount of historical events, out of necessity at the deliberate selection of the researcher (Weber 1971).

The call for a return to the past to ensure a future of the social sciences does not mean we should copy traditional ways of thinking. Our world is far more complex than the past. For one, past societies displayed a more clear-cut class structure. This is no longer the case in modern capitalist societies, the less so in view of globalization. But the future of the social sciences is related to heuristic approaches that combine the answer to concrete social challenges with a view on societal developments on a large scale. And this calls for the inclusion of citizens' knowledge, public participation – in short: democratization of knowledge and access.

Acknowledgements

I am indebted to all my colleagues at the ICCR and its predecessor, the Interdisciplinary Centre for Comparative Research in the Social Sciences. In more than 30 years the ICCR has employed more than 100 researchers, of which around 10 researchers could be seen as core staff. Without their research and the continuous discussions with them the development of the patchwork theory would have been impossible.

My particular gratitude is owed to *Liana Giorgi*. She has run the institute with me over a long time, nearly from its beginning onwards till 2011, when she left the institute for starting a new career as psychoanalyst. Although she is still working as a social scientist as well her new orientation does not allow anymore a full-time engagement in a research institute. Although she never referred to patchwork theories explicitly her research contributed a lot to my own thinking. She has also contributed to the improvement of the manuscript of this article.

Finally, I extend my gratitude to Professor emeritus *Henrik Kreutz*. Although his later thinking has led to a separation in dispute I admit that my academic work is influenced by his approach. He insisted in the necessity of creative thinking and respecting science ethics, which in turn requires independence of researchers from institutional pressures.

Notes

1. My pragmatic approach did not come from the academic teaching at the university. Nearly from the beginning of my studies I had the chance to work at a private research institute of the research-oriented assistant professor (and thereafter professor at the Friedrich Alexander University Erlangen-Nuremberg) Henrik Kreutz who was developing his own approach in the tradition of pragmatism. Pragmatism was at that time not part of the dominant curricula in the social sciences (Pohoryles 1988).
2. It should be noted here that I leave it up to the reader whether he or she understands patchwork theory as theoretical approach in its own right, or whether one should rather speak about a patchwork approach within the pragmatist tradition. In agreement with Merton I hold that such a discussion would create a "mock problem" ((Merton 1949).
3. Walter Lippmann"s writing was of great importance for the European social liberalism. To discuss his famous book "The Good Society" French sociologists invited liberals from across Europe to Paris to discuss his ideas (N.N. 1939). Interestingly enough this meeting was dominated by scholars from the "Freiburg School", a liberal group of intellectuals, of which most of the members joined the resistance against Hitler. During this event the group coined the term "neo-liberalism" to distinguish itself from the then in liberal circles dominant free-market ideology. Interestingly enough, the mainstream contemporary sociology has appropriated the term and use it in the precisely opposite direction (Pohoryles 2015).
4. "Erkenntnis" in German means rather the process of gaining knowledge and the results of this process, whereas "Wissen" is the knowledge itself. "Erkenntnis" is related to epistemology and not to the knowledge as such.
5. It is quite interesting to note that the divide in the social sciences is a global phenomenon, however in different cultural contexts. In the USA Collins and Collins refer to four different traditions in the social sciences (1994). Whilst Habermas deplores the cleavages in the social sciences he contributed to the famous German "Positivismusstreit" and started himself a controversy between Niklas Luhmann and himself (Habermas and Luhmann 1971; Maciejewski and Eder 1973).
6. Actutally, Max Weber is more complex than often represented in the social science literature. In his view, social actions are motivated by four elements, or in his term "Idealtypen" (idealized types) of rationality, "*Zweckrationalität*" (purposeful rationality), and "*Wertrationalität*" (value-orientated rationality). Furthermore, social action can be motivated "*traditionell*" (based on traditions)*, or "affekiv"* (emotional motivation). Note that in Weber"s view the elements do not exclude each other: rather, most social actions are motivated by all of the motivations, or at least on some of them (Weber 1971).
7. The definition of the status of "expert" is not trivial. In a discussion the relation between research and political decision I proposed to define experts straight away as "people who are paid by a third party for their opinions", by which I did not mean that they are corrupt in any sense, but that their status was rather ascribed than achieved in Parsons' terms (Parsons [1951] 1991). Of course, experts are chosen based on their achievements; the assessment of the value of their achievement is, however, assessed by those who appoint the experts. Based on empirical research Vadrot has coined the term "epistemic selectivity" to describe the process of gaining recognition as expert (Vadrot 2014).
8. Unlike most scholars refer to sustainability as triangle I rather prefer to add a fourth dimension to ecological, economic and social aspects, which is public participation. Public participation does not only raise the awareness of the citizens, but allow the inclusion of their local knowledge (Pohoryles 2007b).

References

Abbott, Andrew Delano. 2001. *Chaos of Disciplines*. Chicago, IL: University of Chicago Press.

Abbott, Andrew Delano. 2004. *Methods of Discovery: Heuristics for the Social Sciences*. Contemporary Societies. New York: W.W. Norton.

Abbott, Andrew Delano. 2010. "Pragmatic Sociology and the Public Sphere: The Case of Charles Richmond Henderson." *Social Science History* 34 (3): 337–371. doi:10.1215/01455532-2010-004.

Abott, Andrew Delano, and Emanuel Gaziano. 1999. "Transition and Tradition: Departmental Faculty in the Era of the Second Chicago School." In *A Second Chicago School?* edited by Gary Allen Fine, 221–272. Chicago, IL: University of Chicago Press.

Altman, Scott. 1993. "A Patchwork Theory of Blackmail." *University of Pensylvania Law Review* 141: 1691–1715.

Boltanski, Luc, and Laurent Thévenot. 2006. *On Justification: Economies of Worth*. Princeton: Princeton University Press.

Collins, Randall, and Randall Collins, eds. 1994. *Four Sociological Traditions: Selected Readings*. New York: Oxford University Press.

Delanty, Gerard. 2011. "Varieties of Critique in Sociological Theory and Their Methodological Implications for Social Research." *Irish Journal of Sociology* 19 (1): 68–92. doi:10.7227/IJS.19.1.4.

Dienel, Hans-Luidger, K. G. Hammerlund, and Martin Peterson. 2002. "The Historical Context of the Evolution of National Research Systems and International RTD Collaboration." *Innovation: The European Journal of Social Science Research* 15 (4): 265–278. doi:10.1080/1351161022000042534.

Feenberg, Andrew. 1996. "Marcuse or Habermas: Two Critiques of Technology." *Inquiry* 39 (1): 45–70. doi:10.1080/00201749608602407.

Gaut, Berys. 1993. "Interpreting the Arts: The Patchwork Theory." *The Journal of Aesthetics and Art Criticism* 51 (4): 597. doi:10.2307/431892.

Giorgi, Liana, Ingmar von Homeyer, and Wayne Parsons. 2006. *Democracy in the European Union: Towards the Emergence of a Public Sphere*. London: Routledge.

Giorgi, Liana, and Monica Sassatelli. 2006. "Introduction: Festivals and the Cultural Public Sphere." In *Festivals and the Cultural Public Sphere*, 1–11. Routledge Advances in Sociology. Abingdon: Routledge.

Giorgi, Liana, Monica Sassatelli, and Gerard Delanty, eds. 2011. *Festivals and the Cultural Public Sphere*. Routledge Advances in Sociology. Abingdon: Routledge.

Habermas, Jürgen. 1967. "Zur Logik der Sozialwissenschaften." *Pilosophische Rundschau* Beiheft 5. http://www.vordenker.de/ggphilosophy/habermas_logik-sozialwiss.pdf.

Habermas, Jürgen. 1970. "Technology and Science as 'Ideology'." In *Toward a Rational Society*. Translated by J Shapiro. Boston, MA: Beacon Press.

Habermas, Jürgen. 1973. *Erkenntnis und Interesse: Im Anhang, "Nach dreissig Jahren – Bemerkungen zu "Erkenntnis und Interesse""*. Philosophische Bibliothek, Bd. 589. Hamburg: F. Meiner.

Habermas, Jürgen. 1987. *Knowledge and Human Interests*. Cambridge, MA: Polity Pr.

Habermas, Jürgen. 1988. *On the Logic of the Social Sciences*. Translated by Shierry W. Nicholsen. Studies in Contemporary German Social Thought. Cambridge, MA: MIT Press. https://is.muni.cz/el/1423/jaro2013/SOC911/um/HABERMAS_One_the_logic_of_social_sciences.pdf.

Habermas, Jürgen. 2007. *The Theory of Communicative Action, Volume 1: Reason and the Rationalization of Society*. Translated by Thomas MacCarthy. The Theory of Communicative Action. Boston, MA: Beacon.

Habermas, Jürgen, and Niklas Luhmann. 1971. *Theorie der Gesellschaft oder Sozialtechnologie – Was leistet die Systemforschung?* Frankfurt am Main: Suhrkamp.

Hammarlund, K. G., and Tomas Nilson, eds. 2006. *A Case of Identities: Festschrift in Honour of Martin Petersen, June 22, 2006*. Gothenburg Studies in Modern History 2. Gothenburg: University Press.

Heilbroner, Robert, and Laurence J. Malone, eds. 1986. *The Essential Adam Smith*. New York: Norton & Co. http://www.amazon.com/The-Essential-Adam-Smith/dp/0198772696.

Jahoda, Marie, Paul F. Lazarsfeld, and Hans Zeisel. 1932. *Die Arbeitslosen von Marienthal: ein soziographischer Versuch über die Wirkungen langandauernder Arbeitslosigkeit; mit einem Anhang zur Geschichte der Soziographie*. 24. Aufl. Edition Suhrkamp 769. Frankfurt am Main: Suhrkamp.

Kreutz, Henrik. 1972. *Soziologie der empirischen Sozialforschung. Theoretische Analyse von Befragungstechniken und Ansätze zur Entwicklung neuer Verfahren.* Stuttgart: Ferdinand Enke.

Kreutz, Henrik, ed. 1987. "Pragmatische Analyse von Texten, Bildern Und Dokumenten." *Angewandte Sozialforschung.*

Kreutz, Henrik, and Johann Bacher, eds. 1991. *Disziplin und Kreativität: sozialwissenschaftliche Computersimulation: theoretische Experimente und praktische Anwendung.* Forschungen zur Soziologie und Sozialanthropologie, Bd. 2. Opladen: Leske+Budrich.

van Langenhove, Luk. 2007. *Innovating the Social Sciences: Towards More Useable Knowledge for Society.* Vienna: Passagen. http://www.passagen.at/cms/index.php?id=62&isbn=9783851657487&L=2.

Lindblom, Charles E. 1977. *Politics and Markets: The World's Political-Economic System.* New York: Basic Books.

Lippmann, Walter. 1938. *The Good Society.* London: Billing. https://ia802604.us.archive.org/21/items/goodsociety035221mbp/goodsociety035221mbp.pdf.

Løchen, Yngvar. 1994. "Commitment and Imagination in the Social Sciences: A Concern for the Future State of Sociology." *Innovation: The European Journal of Social Science Research* 7 (4): 405–412. doi:10.1080/13511610.1994.9968420.

Maciejewski, Franz, and Klaus Eder. 1973. *Theorie der Gesellschaft oder Sozialtechnologie: Beiträge zur Habermas-Luhmann-Diskussion.* 1. Aufl. Theorie. Theorie-Diskussion. Supplement 1. Frankfurt (am Main): Suhrkamp.

Mannheim, Karl. 1940. *Ideology and Utopia.* London: Kegan Paul, Trench, Trubner.

Merton, Robert. [1949] 2012. "On Sociological Theories of the Middle Range." In *Classical Sociological Theory,* edited by Calhoun, Craig J., Joseph Gerteis, James Moody, Steven Pfaff, and Indermohan Virk. 3rd ed., Chapter 35, 448–459. Chichester: Wiley-Blackwell, a John Wiley & Sons Ltd.

van der Meulen, Barend. 2002. "Institutional Innovation and Europeanization of Research." *Innovation: The European Journal of Social Science Research* 15 (4): 261–264. doi:10.1080/1351161022000042525.

N.N. 1939. "Colloque Walter Lippmann." *Wikipédia.* https://fr.wikipedia.org/w/index.php?title=Colloque_Walter_Lippmann&oldid=104892448.

Parsons, Talcott. [1951] 1991. *The Social System.* New ed. Routledge Sociology Classics. London: Routledge.

Peirce, Charles S. 1878. "How to Make Our Ideas Clear." *Popular Science Monthly,* In The Essential Peirce, Vol.1, edited by N. Houser and C. Kloesel, 124–141, no. 12(1992). Bloomington, IN: Indiana University Press: 286–302.

Pohoryles, Ronald J. 1985. "Die Goldenen 70er Jahre? : Reformpolitische Optionen Und gesellschaftliche Herausforderungen im Modernisierungskontext."

Pohoryles, Ronald J. 1987. "What Power the Media? The Influence of the Media in Public Affairs: An Austrian Case Study." *Media, Culture & Society* 9 (2): 209–236.

Pohoryles, Ronald J. 1988. "Teaching Social Sciences: Hommage à Henrik Kreutz." *Innovation: The European Journal of Social Science Research* 1 (4–5): 411–420. doi:10.1080/13511610.1988.9968129.

Pohoryles, Ronald J. 1989. "Do Democracies Need Corruption? A Pragmatic View on a Widespread Phenomenon." *Innovation: The European Journal of Social Science Research* 2 (4): 393–399.

Pohoryles, Ronald J. 1993. "Between Society, Politics and the Market: The Structure and Future of Social Scientific Research Against the Background of the Process of Internationalization." *Innovation: The European Journal of Social Science Research* 6 (2): 195–210.

Pohoryles, Ronald J. 2007a. "Do the Social Sciences Need to Be Rethought And, Hence, Innovated?" In *Innovating the Social Sciences: Towards More Useable Knowledge for Society,* edited by Luk Langenhove, 15–48. Vienna: Passagen Verlag.

Pohoryles, Ronald J. 2007b. "Sustainable Development, Innovation and Democracy: What Role for the Regions?" *Innovation: The European Journal of Social Science Research* 20 (3): 183–190. doi:10.1080/13511610701805971.

Pohoryles, Ronald J. 2015. "Zur Aktualität von Adam Smith. Der Beitrag des Liberalismus zu Staat, Wirtschaft und Gesellschaft (The Contribution of Liberalism to the Understanding of State, Economy and Society)." In *Die Aktualität von Adam Smith,* edited by Ronald J. Pohoryles, 13–42. Marburg: Metropolis.

Pohoryles, Ronald J., and Liana Giorgi. 2006. "Knowledge Society and Knowledge Economy: What's New in the New Economy?" In *A Case of Identities*, edited by K. G. Hammerlund and Tomas Nilson, 73–96. Gothenburg Studies in Modern History. Gothenburg: University Press.

Pohoryles, Ronald J., and Andreas Schadauer. 2009. "What Future for the European Social Sciences and Humanities?" *Innovation: The European Journal of Social Science Research* 22 (2): 147–187. doi:10.1080/13511610903112747.

Ravetz, Joe, Elvira Uyarra, Kieron Flanagan, and Tatiana Kluvankova-Oravska. 2006. "Regional Innovation Policy Impact Assessment Scheme." Workpackage 10 of the EURO-COOP project (Regional Innovation Policy Impact Assessment and Benchmarking Process: Cooperation for Sustainable Regional Innovation). Contract No. 517541. Brussels: ICCR.

Schrödinger, Erwin. 1935. *Die Gegenwärtige Situation in Der Quantenmechanik* (Quantum Theory and Measurement). Translated by John D. Trimmer. Original Version: Naturwissenschaften 23.

Smith, Adam. 1759. *The Theory of Moral Sentiments*. Edited by Jonathan Bennet. http://www.earlymoderntexts.com/assets/pdfs/smith1759.pdf.

Smith, Adam. 1776. *The Wealth of Nations: The Economics Classic-A Selected Edition for the Contemporary Reader*. John Wiley.

Thévenot, Laurent. 2011. "Power and Oppression From the Perspective of the Sociology of Engagements: A Comparison with Bourdieu's and Dewey's Critical Approaches to Practical Activities." *Irish Journal of Sociology* 19 (1): 35–67. doi:10.7227/IJS.19.1.3.

Vadrot, Alice. 2014. *The Politics of Knowledge and Global Biodiversity (Hardback) - Taylor & Francis*. Routledge Studies in Biodiversity Politics and Management. London: Routledge. http://www.tandf.net/books/details/9780415729901/.

Weber, Max. 1971. *Wirtschaft und Gesellschaft*. Frankfurt am Main: Unknown ('Raubdruck').

Social scientists as technicians, advisors and meaning producers

Nico Stehr[a] and Alexander Ruser[b]

[a]Karl-Mannheim Chair for Cultural Studies, Zeppelin University, Friedrichshafen, Germany;
[b]Chair for Cultural Theory and Analysis, Zeppelin University, Friedrichshafen, Germany

In this paper, we are addressing three issues that are at the core of scholarly reflections about the societal role of social science knowledge: (1) Social scientists tend to follow – although this is not always a deliberate choice – one of three models that describe their role as the producers of practical knowledge. For the sake of simplicity we have called the three models the "model of the technician", the "model of the advisor" and the "model of the meaning producer". (2) Due to the need for social inquiry to adopt a particular, restrictive perspective of its domain, useful knowledge is a complicated matter. Hence the need to put into question a widely supported notion at least among social scientists: When asked about the reasons for the limited "power" of social science knowledge the response frequently is that the adequacy and practical usefulness of social science knowledge is a function of its capturing the full complexity of what indeed are complex social phenomena. (3) Social scientists often tend to lament the marginal impact their intellectual efforts have on society, and they look with great envy across the divide of the so-called two cultures, wondering how and when they will be able to achieve the same kind of success and prestige the natural sciences and technology appear to enjoy in most societies. However, this unhappy view systematically understates the actual power of social science knowledge, in particular its role as a mind maker or meaning producer.

1.   Introduction

It is a truism that scientific knowledge in general and social science knowledge in particular is generated, disseminated and "processed" within specific socio-historical contexts. Likewise, the notion of "pure scientist" is either an idealization or an outright imposture. It is impossible to separate – both at the point of its production and as it comes to be used – social scientific knowledge from social contexts.

Reflections about the societal role of social scientific knowledge demand particular diligence and prudence because of the often-blurred boundaries between descriptions of what scientists do and a normative prescription of what social science scholars should do.

While scientific authority is frequently and sometimes fiercely contested (the case of climate change provides a prime example) scientific knowledge undoubtedly has power in the knowledge society. Our assertion will be that social science knowledge has power in the form of words such as repression and images such as the planet earth that compel or arrest social action. Such a perspective is of course not new, it has been of interest to many scholars from philosophy to political science to sociology (e.g. Jasanoff 2012, 78–102). World images, ideas and simply "meaning" produced by the social sciences and the humanities and exerting societal influence have, for example, been noted by Max Weber (1946a, 64) who called ideas the "switchmen" on history's track, or John Maynard Keynes (1936, 383) who noted the influence of "defunct economists".

On the other hand H. M. Collins attributes the fact that "'[s]cientific' has become a synonym for 'certain'; scientists' view are *authoritative*" (Collins 1992, 160) to the predominance of the *algorithmic model* of science. The algorithmic model refers to highly formalized and transparent research processes that transform the readers of scientific articles into "virtual witnesses" capable of "see[ing] the validity of the procedures and findings" (Collins 1992, 160).

However, the algorithmic model applies more readily to certain fields within the natural sciences. Formalizing social science research is a much more difficult endeavor and does not necessarily lead to useful results.[1] Readers of social science texts will find it harder to become "virtual witnesses" of the research process. Potential users of social science knowledge will have greater problems in validating the procedures as well as the findings generated by the social sciences. However, these difficulties neither release social scientists from the social roles nor can they imply any dispensation from the necessity to address the complex issue of the genesis and the form of useful social science knowledge from a sociological perspective.

In this contribution, we are addressing three issues that are at the core of reflections about the societal role and the corresponding forms of social science knowledge. From Max Weber's seminal perspective, the respective roles and forms of knowledge should be understood to represent "ideal-types". This reference to ideal-type constructs has two major implications: First, Weber reminds us that "[t]he construction of abstract ideal-types recommends itself not as an end but as a *means*" (Weber 1949, 92). It is in this spirit that our contribution will not provide a system for assigning individual scientists to particular roles. Rather, we will try to develop an analytical framework for understanding the various roles social scientists can play, desire to follow, or are assigned. Second, because ideal-types are heuristic tools rather than representations of an empirical reality "their character as ideal thought constructs should be carefully kept in mind, and the ideal-type and historical reality should not be confused with each other" (Weber 1949, 107). This implies that the three roles and the respective forms of knowledge generated under the auspices of these role conceptions are hardly ever encountered in their "pure" forms. What is more likely, in an empirical setting, is an overlap between two or even all three of these models.

(1) Social scientists have a propensity to follow – although this is not always a deliberate choice – one of three models that describe their role as the producers of (practical) knowledge. For the sake of simplicity we have called the three models the model of the technician (instrumentality model), the model of the advisor (capacity model) and the model of the meaning producer.

(2) With respect to their domain of inquiry, social scientists tend to either follow or reject positions also best described by Max Weber. Tenbruck (1984) follows and extends Max Weber's (1949, 72) idea that social scientists are invariably forced to adopt a particular perspective that guides their curiosity about social action. Thus, Weber and Tenbruck reject the otherwise widely supported notion that the adequacy and practical usefulness of social science knowledge is a function of its capturing the full complexity of what indeed are complex social phenomena

(cf. Stehr 1992; Grundmann and Stehr 2012). Hence Weber and Tenbruck can only adhere to what we call the capacity (advisor) or meaning producer model of social science knowledge.

(3) Social scientists are inclined to lament the marginal impact their intellectual efforts have on society, and they look with enormous envy across the divide of the so-called two cultures, wondering how and when they will be able to achieve the same kind of useful success and societal prestige the natural sciences and technology enjoy in most societies.

The common reference of all these reflections is, of course, knowledge. The most useful definition shared by each of our three models would thus seem to be that knowledge is a capacity to act. Knowledge not only extends to accomplishing practical tasks such as driving a car but also serves as a means of orientation for members of society "with regard to the world in which they find themselves, and with it, to themselves" (Elias 1973, 381). Therefore, the model of social science desiring to generate symbolic "meaning" is a function social science research does actually serve at times (see Adolf and Stehr 2014), if not most of the time.

In an essay written more than a century ago, Veblen (1919, 4) addresses the question of the "place of science in modern civilization": "Whatever the common-sense of earlier generations may have held in this respect, modern common-sense holds that the scientist's answer is the only ultimately true one."[2] While Veblen's assertion of the social role of science still holds sway among certain segments of the public and policy-makers, the peculiar social role of the social sciences continues to puzzle social scientists and other segments of the public as well as many policy-makers.[3] We will attempt to find a solution to this puzzle.

2.   Social scientists as technicians

In the late stages of contemporary society the so-called moral sciences (*Geisteswissenschaften*) have but a fluctuating market value; they have to try, as best as they possibly can, to follow the more fortunate natural sciences whose practical value is beyond question. (Max Horkheimer)[4]

The first model we want to discuss claims that the social sciences generate, or should generate, *instrumental knowledge*; the crucial labor as stressed by the model refers, however trivial this may appear, to work social scientists alone must carry out. In the end, science speaks to society, and does so not only with considerable authority but also with significant success – as long as such knowledge lives up to the core principles of the model; as a result, society has little, if any, opportunity to talk back.

Adherents of the model of instrumentality strive to optimize the "scientificity" of social scientific knowledge. The crucial or core indicator of the scientificity of social science knowledge is the ability of such knowledge to capture the full complexity of empirical reality.

Let us call this model not only the model of instrumentality but also the orthodox conception of the uses of *scientific* – and not merely social scientific – knowledge. It goes along with the strong claim that adequate scientific knowledge *as such* is eminently practical knowledge. Moreover, the model is governed by the idea that the transformation of knowledge into action, or what we have elsewhere called the translation of capacities for action into action (Stehr 1992), occurs in a most straightforward manner.[5]

The instrumental or scientific model is part of Auguste Comte's positive philosophy. In Comte's view the social sciences have to progress, like any other science, through three distinct stages of scientific development. In the end, that is, the positive stage, the social sciences will develop into something resembling a "social physics" and

> we shall find that there is no chance of order and agreement but in subjecting social phenomena, like all others, to invariable natural laws […] in other words, introducing into the study of social phenomena the same positive spirit which has regenerated each other branch of human speculation. (Comte 1855, 455)

More importantly, Comte also holds that it is only after social science knowledge has attained these qualities that knowledge produced by social scientists is worth considering by society: Only the advent of social physics would ensure that

> [s]uch a representation may perhaps convince men worthy of the name of statesmen that there is a real and eminent utility in labors of this kind, worthy of the anxious attention of men who profess to devote themselves to the task of resolving the alarming revolutionary constitution of modern societies. (Comte 1855, 400)[6]

In addition, the conventional conception of the power of social scientific knowledge is last but not least based on the conviction that the structure and culture of human groups as producers of knowledge have little relevant influence on such knowledge claims. On the contrary, the development of knowledge is driven and determined by the "logic" of science in conjunction with the nature of the world of objects.[7] Luhmann (1977, 16) suggests calling the sum of these premises the *model of instrumentality*.

Observers who voice their strong suspicion that there is a widespread (ideological) conspiracy between scientists and those in power also tend to rely, if only implicitly, on the model of instrumentality. Following the lead of Mills [1959] 1970, 91–96) who already pointed to the historically much greater *ideological* rather than bureaucratic "use" of the social sciences, Horowitz (1970, 340), for example, emphatically underlines the ideological services rendered by social scientists as the "Great Legitimizers" in an age that had announced the "end of ideology":

> Social scientists engaged in government work are committed to an advocacy model defined by politicians. For the most part, they do not *establish* or even verify policy – only *legitimize* policy. They are, in effect, the great mandarins of the present era.

Thus, if one follows Horowitz' diagnosis from the 1970s, social scientists are merely performing *instrumental* services, albeit at the ideological level. But as John Maynard Keynes is reported to have observed in a much more skeptical vein: "If they only would conspire" (see Luhmann 1977, 17).

That is to say, the model of instrumentality conceives of scientific theory and research as a kind of intellectual *tool* that may be employed in practical situations. Theory, as long as it is "objective", "true" or "adequate", is also reliable and useful. Of course, theoretical knowledge alone does not guarantee the successful execution of a desired social action nor does it ensure the value of the means chosen to reach a specific end. But theoretical knowledge, the model of instrumentality implies, provides a kind of technical relief (*Entlastung*) for actors. In addition, actors are not themselves required to manufacture the knowledge to be utilized, nor is it necessary for them to comprehend the scientific context in which the theoretical knowledge was generated in the first place (also Giddens 1987, 45–46).

As Luhmann (1977, 16) adds, the political hope raised by the instrumental model for a straightforward transition from a theoretical to a practical context is based on a binary logic of true and false propositions. The future simply becomes an extension of the present or past. But we know of course that assertions about a future state of affairs are notoriously unreliable. Yet the model of instrumentality itself is unreflective, incapable of raising this troubling issue about the foundations of the utility of scientific knowledge.

The model of instrumentality or the handmaiden functions performed by the social sciences contains a variety of further assumptions that are of lesser interest because what counts most of all is the core assumption of the model that the knowledge generated – or what constitutes adequate knowledge – is a function of its capturing *the full complexity of social reality*. The organized complexity of economic, social or political relations can only be grasped adequately if one aims to deal "simultaneously with a sizeable number of factors which are interrelated into an organic whole" (Weaver 1948, 539). As long as the social sciences are, for whatever reasons, unable to comply the knowledge they generate is bound to fall short of their ambitious goal to produce what may count as truly powerful applied knowledge. In short, using the instrumental model as a standard, social science and humanities-based knowledge is itself the author of its societal success (or failure).

3. Social scientists as advisors

The social sciences … are establishing themselves as a major constituent of modern outlook on society, and undoubtedly will come to constitute an increasingly significant component of the practical man's image of the world. (Shils 1977, 282)

In addition to being a source of instrumental knowledge, the social sciences and the humanities may attempt to generate enabling knowledge by producing knowledge claims that – in contrast to any more formal, deductive and epistemic knowledge – include up-front references to essential features of existing social conditions such as, for instance, the role of local knowledge and the diversity of natural environments, in their knowledge-generating process (cf. Carolan 2006). The choice of the label of the model is linked, on the one hand, to our conception of knowledge *as a capacity to act* (e.g. Stehr 2001, 31–47) and, on the other hand, to the *capability* approach developed by Sen (1993b).

Social scientists who follow the model of social science expertise as advisory in nature take into account the peculiar empirical circumstances of action in generating such advice. Therefore, the orientation of this model is not to qualities internal to science but to the contingencies of action typical of the target circumstances, for example, a small city, a firm, a hospital or a social movement. More specifically, its attention is on possibilities of action that are open to change as seen from the perspectives of the actors in question. Accordingly, social scientists that follow this model are in general agreement with Max Weber's view of the limits of scientific advice famously expressed in his paper "The Objectivity of Social Science and Social Policy": "An empirical science cannot tell anyone what he *should* do – but rather what he *can* do – and under certain circumstances – what he wishes to do" (Weber 1949, 54).

The capacity model resonates with Amartya Sen's capability approach, and we want to exploit and extend what Sen (1993b, 50) himself suggests, namely that the capability approach has a potentially wide relevance that can even extend to questions concerning the power of knowledge in society. The capability approach was originally introduced by Sen (1980) in the context of evaluating social *inequality* structures. The approach was designed to explore "well-being and advantage in terms of a person's ability to do valuable acts or reach valuable states of being" (Sen 1993b, 30). A corresponding perspective looks at social rather than merely individual advantages. The perspective was subsequently extended to a range of social issues, for example, liberty and freedom (Sen 1993b), living standards and development (1993a) or gender bias and sexual division (Kynch and Sen 1983).

The most elementary notion of the capability approach concerns "functionings". Functionings represent "the various things [a person] manages to do or be in leading a life" (Sen 1993b, 31). Living a life consists of "doings and beings". Functionings, or desirable states of being rather than commodities which one uses, are, for example, being adequately nourished, being in good health, appearing in public without shame, taking part in the life of the community or, more complex, being socially integrated and being happy; differential capabilities represent the ability to achieve intrinsically valuable functionings (capabilities to function). The capability set of a person or group represents their opportunities to realize well-being (cf. Sugden 1993).

A term that might be seen as a meaningful substitute or competitor for the notion of capacity model would be the "enlightenment model". According to Weiss (1977, 544), the enlightenment model "sees its role for research as social criticism. It finds a place for research based on variant theoretical perspectives ... [for] research [that] provides the intellectual background of concepts, orientations, and empirical generalizations that inform policy." We prefer the term capacity model because it is less committed to particular research objectives and likely outcomes. The capacity model actually allows for the possibility that social science knowledge is employed for purposes that are at odds with the enlightenment goal, for example, for the purpose of legitimizing political decisions that have long been ratified and are now embellished with social science conceptions.

The particular importance of the capability approach lies in its potential to clarify the relation between knowledge and action; as a matter of fact, the linkage between the capability approach and the notion that knowledge is a capacity to act is quite straightforward. Capabilities permit an individual or a group to convert capacities of action into action. For example, a firm's capability or resources for action can be deployed to translate knowledge into action. The capabilities held by a corporate actor or an individual allow them to achieve functionings offered by knowledge. The capability of an actor or a group is a function of their power, that is, their ability to influence the conditions of action in question, even against resistance. Such power may derive from legal entitlements such as the ownership of property, from other resources including intellectual abilities but also from other factors such as natural conditions that are beyond the relevant actors' control or choice.

4. Social scientists as meaning producers

The last and most important model of social science knowledge (but not only social science knowledge) refers to the production of meaning (*Sinn*) by the social sciences.[8] That is, the model of the usefulness of the social sciences that stresses meaning production does not focus on practical choices made by the actors but on processes of meaning which may subsequently engender choices (cf. Braun 1999).

The meaning producers model refers to a couple of attributes that make for the practical utility of knowledge claims. As producers of enabling ideas and meanings, the social sciences and the humanities exert practical influence on society and its actors.

The social sciences and the humanities operate as producers of meaning.[9] The social sciences are – to borrow a term from the historian Robinson (1923, 16) – "mindmakers". Robinson (1923, 16–17) refers to a long list of occupations and professions that serve as mind-makers in modern society: "Mind-seekers are the questioners (of the taken-for-granted or the commonplace) and seers. We classify them roughly as poets, religious leaders, moralists, story-tellers, philosophers, theologians, artists, scientists, inventors." But Robinson (1923, 17) also raises the significant follow-up question of "what determines the success of a new idea; what establishes its currency and gives it social significance by securing its victory over ignorance and indifference or older rival and conflicting beliefs?"

In this context, he stresses that the "truth of a new idea proposed for acceptance plays an altogether secondary role" (Robinson 1923, 20). Robinson's question concerning the conditions for a new idea to be successful must of course be extended to the question of why new ideas are incapable of displacing the commonplace and the taken-for-granted; or of what exactly is the "social labor" that established ideas accomplish, and under what circumstances are they able to do so. The power of mind-making rests on the power of the proposed concepts or ideas as capacities to act, which includes suggesting the means of their concrete realization.

The social sciences, even if considered to be a major (if not growing) reservoir of meaning that is disseminated into society via various social "pipelines" (such as the media, teachers, priests, writers), do not have a monopoly on meaning production. But in contrast to the model of instrumentality, the meaning producers model stresses that the agents who "employ" social science knowledge are active agents who transform, re-issue and otherwise re-design social science knowledge. This active attribute of the "mind-seekers" speaks against a straightforward "social scientification" of mundane worldviews by the social science discourse. The meaning model stipulates that social scientific knowledge is an intellectual resource that is contingently open and complex and can, thus, be molded in the course of its "travel" from the social scientific community into society. This model further assumes that neither the production nor the application of this knowledge involves its identical reproduction. The meaning model is therefore associated with the possibility that people may use local knowledge resources to critically engage social science knowledge, and thus make social science accountable to the public.

Hall (1989) and others (e.g. Stehr 1992) who have written about the practical success of Keynesian economic theory have tried to specify the attributes social science knowledge as meaningful knowledge must have in order to be forceful in practice. These perspectives have also pointed to the conditions under which ideas acquire political, economic and social influence. Hall (1989, 369) points out that ideas "did not simply reflect group interests or material conditions"; rather, they "had the power to change the perceptions a group had of its own interests, and they made possible new courses of action that changed the material world itself". Given that meanings influence action in some contexts more than in others (cf. Swidler 1986), congruence between ideas and contingencies of action is crucial.

The normative question whether social scientists *should* be engaged in the production of meaning in the first place has been a contested issue, however. Perhaps the most prominent criticism of social science mind-making may be found in the work of Max Weber. Arguing for a rigid asceticism of sentiment or attitude (*Gesinnungsaskese*) he claimed that

> he who yearns for seeing should go to the cinema, though it will be offered to him copiously to-day in literary form in the present field of investigation also. [...] And, I might add, whoever wants a sermon should go to a conventicle. (Weber 1930, xli)

Always concerned that meaning production by social scientists would imply imprinting the personal beliefs of the researcher on others, Weber categorically states that "neither does the politics [...] belong to the lecture-room on the part of the docent, and when the docent is scientifically concerned with politics, it belongs there the least of all" (Weber 1946b, 139). Weber ultimately adheres to the view expressed by Leo Tolstoy that "science is meaningless, because it gives no answer to our question, the only question important for us: What shall we do and how shall we live our live?" (Weber 1946b, 138). In his view, (social) science should not try to offer meaning but limit itself to help putting "the question correctly" (Weber 1946b, 138).

Whether one should be prepared to describe the meaning model – which conceives of the influence exerted on society by the social sciences and the humanities as a process that is driven by the societal impact of *ideas* – in terms of a "social scientification" of collective and individual patterns of meaning remains, for the time being, an open question. One argument that speaks against the assertion that the capacity model proposes or allows for a social scientification of societal world views would be linked to the cautionary note against overestimating the influence of social science knowledge in modern societies.

The social sciences, even if understood as a major if not growing reservoir of meaning that spreads into society, do not have a monopoly on intellectual resources (cf. Kocka 2005, 21). In contrast to the model of instrumentality, the capacity model also stresses – and this attribute, too, speaks against a straightforward "social scientification" of world views and mundane meaning in modern society by the social science discourse – that agents who "employ" social science knowledge are *active* agents that transform, re-issue and otherwise re-design social science knowledge (cf. Wynne 2005). Nor, finally, does the intellectual development of the social sciences proceed, as it were and as the model of instrumentality proposes, in splendid isolation from all socio-historical realities and dynamics. The "traffic in meaning" is not a one-way street.

5. Conclusions

We started our investigation of the different roles social scientists may play and the different forms of social science knowledge they produce by referring to the difference between the functions scientific knowledge can fulfill in the natural and the social sciences. We argued that the algorithmic model does not apply to the social sciences; becoming a "virtual witness" of social science research is difficult if not impossible.

However, the meaning of the (virtual) witness is consistent with the orthodox role a social scientist may be seen to have, namely the role of the technician. Social knowledge takes the form of instrumental knowledge. Like witnesses in court, stakeholders from the wider society resemble mere recipients of some particular knowledge and cannot engage in a dialogue with the producers of social science knowledge but are limited to testifying about the objectivity or utility of the knowledge "presented to them".

The metaphor of the (passive) witness ceases to be consistent, however, when it comes to the other two social roles and the corresponding forms of social since knowledge. Since knowledge is conceived of as a capacity to act, a more active role of stakeholders must be considered. According to Sen's (1980, 1993b) capability approach or Weiss (1977, 536) enlightenment model social science knowledge provides "orientation" (Weiss) or, more generally, opportunities to realize well-being (Sen 1980, 1993b). Stakeholders from (different groups) within a society actively approach social science knowledge, (seek to) build capacities for action and ultimately use such knowledge to make decisions and act.

The advisory role of the social scientist and the corresponding form of social science knowledge as an element of capacity-building knowledge conforms with another metaphor from the court system: the lawyer or the prosecutor. For both professional roles require an active use of available knowledge, that is, a "calibration" of knowledge or "evidence" to enlarge the argumentative arsenal for winning the case.

This "active" or emergent role of knowledge claims is stressed even more so in the third and final model, that is, social scientists as meaning producers. To take our legal metaphor further, the role of the witness and the role of the attorney now blend with that of the juror in court. For social science knowledge is no longer limited to contributing to a given case but becomes instrumental in making a case. Not unlike an effective lawyer who can re-frame a situation (for instance, presenting a cold-blooded murder as a case of justified self-defense), social science knowledge can be pivotal in (re)framing social situations. For instance, social statistics can be said to be among the most reliable seismographs of social change; social statistics can serve as a kind of call to action. What exactly may growing unemployment rates, increasing social inequality, high rates of illiteracy or an increasing awareness of environmental problems force us to consider?

The meaning of such "irreducible and stubborn facts" (William James, quoted in Whitehead 1925, 2–3) cannot be "read off" the data. Furthermore, since the traffic of meaning is not a one-way street running from science to society, the irreducibility and stubbornness of the "facts" itself may be called into question. Different social scientific conceptions can give different meanings to these facts: From a neo-Marxist perspective, for instance, it appears to be a clear case: rising unemployment and increasing social inequality indicate the persistent exploitation of workers by corporations. Such an account may well convince a jury (corporate actions) and compel specific action (e.g. strikes). This implies that social science, assuming the complicity of a given social group, may not merely represent meaning but be pivotal in creating novel realities. Robert K. Merton's "bank run" (1948) is a textbook example of, in this case, a self-fulfilling prophecy: Economic analysis does not only give a meaning to a situation (by concluding that there are dangerous holes in the balance sheet of a bank) but is creating the crisis in the first place.

However, the self-fulfilling prophecy is not the only contingent issue. Mind-making concepts like the neo-Marxist account referred to above may not only be contested by rival concepts. The selection of a concept, and here the court metaphor ceases to be apposite, affect the very selection, treatment and importance of "facts". For instance, the fields that sociologists in the former GDR could research, the models they could apply and the interpretations they could propose of their findings were heavily constrained by political preferences (Vorstand der Gesellschaft für Soziologie in der DDR 1990, 474ff).

We discussed three ideal-type roles social scientists can play in society and outlined the typical corresponding forms of social science knowledge.

There is but a limited scope for the "pure" social scientist or for instrumental social science knowledge. In contrast, what is often underestimated is the influence social science has on world views and interests, on the realm of policies and on the path of social action in general. This influence stems from the role of social science as a meaning producer, for example, in view of the resolution of ecological problems and the politics of creating an environmentally sustainable society (cf. Stehr 2015).

Notes

1.   The spectacular practical failure of neo-classical economics as a mathematized branch of economic thinking that derives its key concepts from classical physics (cf. Mirowski 2002; Galbraith

2014) indicates that formalizing social science discourse is not necessarily a sure path toward the usefulness of such knowledge.

2. The prevalence of scientific knowledge in society and the extensive respect granted to scientific knowledge to the exclusion of other forms of knowledge provoked Feyerabend ([1975] 2006) in the mid-1970s to ask how society can be defended against science. His answer: with the help of an education system that is intellectually more inclusive. Feyerabend ([1975] 2006, 360) suggests that contemporary science has deteriorated into an ideology with practices of indoctrination and sanctified, oppressive truths that are immune to criticism: "Science has now become as oppressive as the ideologies it had once to fight." The practice of modern science inhibits the freedom of thought and therefore comes into conflict with what is an essential attribute of democracy, namely the peaceful co-existence of sets of ideas. In society, ideological pressures exist that supplant other forms of knowledge, with the exception of those that originate from science. The lesson to be learned from the particular authority that science enjoys in society is, for Feyerabend, a separation of science and the state in the interest of the defense of democracy and liberty, especially in the field of public education.

3. For C. Wright Mills, these problems are to a large extent due to the contrasting self-perception of the social sciences: "The confusion in the social sciences is moral as well as 'scientific', political as well as intellectual" (Mills [1959] 1970, 76). He then goes on to distinguish "types of practicality" (Mills [1959] 1970, 76) to describe the affinity between specific schools within the social sciences and the particular social roles of the respective representatives of these schools (e.g. the willingness of researchers working in the field of "applied sociology" to serve as "research technician[s] available for hire" (Mills [1959] 1970, 76; also Horowitz 1971).

4. Our translation from Max Horkheimer, "Traditionelle und kritische Theorie", *Zeitschrift für Sozialforschung* 6 (1937, 247–248). The translation found in Max Horkheimer, *Critical Theory* (New York: Seabury Press, 1972, 191), is inaccurate.

5. A close relative of the model that stresses the instrumental function of social science knowledge are rational choice theories with their basic assumption that individuals are calculating actors who try to optimize their situation under given restraints (Elster 1986). In such a social context, instrumental knowledge is obviously of considerable utility (cf. Goldstein and Kephane 1993).

6. Adolf and Stehr (2014). Compare also the distinction between *act* and *agency* as two distinctive elements of policy in Joseph Gusfield (1975), who follows Kenneth Burke's (1945) dichotomy of *act* and *agent*. *Agency* refers to widely visible policy statements of a more general and deliberate direction while *act* refers to the often more local outcomes of a multiplicity of acts; in the case of acts, the policy can be inferred from the direction or patterns of action (see Gusfield 1975, 3).

7. In this respect, compare the views of Norbert Elias (1971) or Popper (1972).

8. If, contrary to what its author intended and what its reception among social scientists and the public suggests, one reads Helmut Schelsky's controversial 1975 treatise about the inordinate influence of the social sciences on contemporary German society – The others do the work: Class struggle and the priest-like rule of the intellectuals and scholars – not as a polemic directed against certain intellectual developments within the social sciences of the day but as an attempt to alert us to the ways in which social science knowledge in fact comes to be employed in modern societies, then one reaches a far different conclusion, as compared to the model of instrumentality, about the practical importance of social science knowledge for society as well as the avenues by which such influence is likely to be exercised. The power of social science knowledge then rests on its ability to influence a society's universe of symbolic meaning.

9. Helmut Schelsky's position resonates with Edward Shils' polemic about the state of social science, which also dates from the 1970s. In his essay, Shils stresses, for example, that the "social sciences tend more and more to provide the educated classes with their intellectual response to the world" (Shils 1977, 280). Whether the impact of the social sciences is indeed limited to or primarily felt in the educated classes may be subject to dispute; nonetheless, Shils (1977, 281) is convinced that the influence exerted by the social sciences on the (university) educated classes that results from their *turning to* the social sciences for enlightenment about society is intellectual rather than instrumental in nature. Shils (1977, 282) argues that as a result of this search for orientation by the social sciences the latter enter "as an ingredient into the minds of others through education, through counseling and guidance, through management and advice to managers, through manipulation and propaganda, and through the exercise of legislative and administrative authority". Like Schelsky, Shils (1977, 284) is not at all impressed

by or supportive of the kind of practical "success" the social sciences of the day appear to enjoy, last but not least because "the social science which is being taught in many colleges and universities presents a partial and distorted image of man and of contemporary society". In short, there is an ideological divide between what Shils and Schelsky and their opponents would prefer to transport as social science into society.

References

Adolf, Marian, and Nico Stehr. 2014. *Knowledge*. London: Routledge.

Braun, Dietmar. 1999. "Interests or Ideas? An Overview of Ideational Concepts in Public Policy Research." In *Dietmar Braun and Public Policy and Political Ideas*, edited by Dietmar Braun and Andreas Busch, 11–29. Cheltenham: Edward Elgar.

Burke, Kenneth. 1945. *A Grammar of Motives*. New York: Prentice-Hall.

Carolan, Michael S. 2006. "Science, Expertise, and the Democratization of the Decision-Making Process." *Society and Natural Resources* 19: 661–668.

Collins, H. M. 1992. *Changing Order. Replication and Induction in Scientific Practice*. Chicago: University of Chicago Press.

Comte, Auguste. 1855. *Social Physics: From the Positive Philosophy of Auguste Comte*. New York: Calvin Blanchard.

Elias, Norbert. 1971. "Sociology of Knowledge: New Perspectives." *Sociology* 5: 149–168.

Elias, Norbert. [1970] 1973. "Dynamics of Consciousness Within That of Society." In *Transactions of the 7. World Congress of Sociology*. Varna, September 14–19, 1970. Volume IV, 375–383. Sofia: International Sociological Association.

Elster, John, ed. 1986. *Rational Choice*. New York: New York University Press.

Feyerabend, Paul. [1975] 2006. "How to Defend Society Against Science?" In *The Philosophy of Expertise*, edited by Evan Selinger and Robert P. Crease, 358–369. New York: Columbia University Press.

Galbraith, James K. 2014. *The End of Normal. The Great Crisis and the Future of Growth*. New York: Simon & Schuster.

Giddens, Anthony. 1987. "Nine Theses on the Future of Sociology." In *Social Theory and Modern Sociology*, edited by Anthony Giddens, 22–51. Oxford: Polity Press.

Goldstein, Judith, and Robert Kephane, eds. 1993. *Ideas and Foreign Policy: Beliefs, Institutions and Political Change*. Ithica, New York: Cornell University Press.

Grundmann, Reiner, and Nico Stehr. 2012. *The Power of Scientific Knowledge. From Research to Public Policy*. Cambridge: Cambridge University Press.

Gusfield, Joseph. 1975. *Community: A Critical Response*. New York: Harper & Row.

Hall, Peter. 1989. *The Political Power of Economic Ideas: Keynesianism Across Nations*. Princeton, NJ: Princeton University Press.

Horkheimer, Max. 1937. "Traditionelle und kritische Theorie." *Zeitschrift für Sozialforschung* 6: 245–294.

Horowitz, Irving L. 1970. "Social Science Mandarins: Policymaking as a Poltical Formula." *Policy Sciences* 1: 339–360.

Horowitz, Irving L. 1971. *The Use and Abuse of Social Science*. New Brunswick, NJ: Transaction Books.

Jasanoff, Sheila. 2012. *Science and Public Reason*. London: Routledge.

Keynes, John Maynard. 1936. *General Theory of Employment, Interest and Money*. London: Macmillan.

Kocka, Jürgen. 2005. "Vermittlungsschwierigkeiten der Sozialwissenschaften." *Aus Politik und Zeitgeschehen* 34–35: 17–22.

Kynch, J., and Armatya Sen. 1983. "Indian Women: Survival and Well-Being." *Cambridge Journal of Economics* 7: 363–389.

Luhmann, Niklas. 1977. "Theoretische und praktische Probleme deranwendungsbezogenen Sozialwissenschaften." In *Interaktion von Wissenschaft und Politik. Theoretische und praktische Probleme der anwendungsorientierten Sozialwissenschaften*, edited by Wissensschaftszentrum, 16–39. Frankfurt am Main: Campus.

Merton, Robert K. 1948. "The Self-Fulfilling Prophecy." *The Antioch Review* 8 (2 Summer): 193–210.

Mills, C. Wright. [1959] 1970. *The Sociological Imagination*. Oxford: Oxford University Press.

Mirowski, Philip. 2002. *Machine Dreams. Economics Becomes a Cyborg Science*. Cambridge: Cambridge University Press.

Popper, Karl. 1972. *Objective Knowledge. An Evolutionary Approach*. Oxford: Clarendon Press.

Robinson, James Harvey. 1923. *The Humanizing of Knowledge*. New York: Georg H. Doran.

Sen, Armatya. 1980. "Equality of What?" In *Tanner Lectures on Human Values*, edited by Sterling M. McMurrin, 257–280. Cambridge: Cambridge University Press.

Sen, Armatya. 1993a. "Marktes and Freedoms: Achievements and Limitations of the Market Mechanism in Promoting Individual Freedoms." *Oxford Economic Papers* 45: 519–541.

Sen, Armatya. 1993b. "Capability and Well-Being." In *The Quality of Life*, edited by Martha C. Nussbaum and Armatya Sen, 30–53. Oxford: Basil Blackwell.

Shils, Edward. 1977. "Science as Public Opinion." *Minerva* 4 (3/4): 273–285.

Stehr, Nico. 1992. *Practical Knowledge. Applying the Social Sciences*. London: Sage.

Stehr, Nico. 2001. *The Fragility of Modern Societies: Knowledge and Risk in the Information Age*. London: Sage.

Stehr, Nico. 2015. "Democracy is not An Inconvenience." *Nature* 525: 449–450.

Sugden, Robert. 1993. "Review: Welfare, Resources, and Capabilities: A Review of Inequality Reexamined by Amartya Sen." *Journal of Economic Literature* 31 (4): 1947–1962.

Swidler, Ann. 1986. "Culture in Action: Symbols and Strategies." *American Sociological Review* 51: 273–86.

Tenbruck, Friedrich H. 1984. *Die unbewältigten Sozialwissenschaften oder die Abschaffung des Menschen*. Graz: Styria.

Veblen, Thorstein. [1906] 1919. "The Place of Science in Modern Civilisation." In *The Place of Science in Modern Civilisation and Other Essays*, edited by Thorstein Veblen, 1–31. New York: The Viking Press.

Vorstand der Gesellschaft für Soziologie in der DDR. 1990. "Zur Lage der Soziologie in der DDR und im Prozess der Vereinigung der beiden deutschen Staaten." *Zeitschrift für Soziologie* 19: 474–484.

Weaver, Warren. 1948. "Science and Complexity." *American Scientist* 36: 536–544.

Weber, Max. [1904] 1949. *The Methodology of the Social Sciences*. Translated and edited by Edward A. Shils and Henry A. Finch. With a Foreword by Edward A. Shils. New York: Free Press.

Weber, Max. 1930. *The Protestant Ethic and the Spirit of Capitalism*. Translated by Talcott Parsons. New York: Routledge.

Weber, Max. 1946a. "The Man and His Work." In *From Max Weber: Essays in Sociology*, edited by Hans H. Gerth and C. Wright Mills, 3–76. New York: Oxford University Press.

Weber, Max. 1946b. "Science as Vocation." In *From Max Weber: Essays in Sociology*, edited by Hans H. Gerth and C. Wright Mills, 129–156. New York: Oxford University Press.

Weiss, Carol H. 1977. "Research for Policy's Sake: The Enlightenment Function of Social Research." *Policy Analysis* 3 (4 Fall): 531–545.

Whitehead, Alfred North. 1925. *Science and the Modern World*. New York: Free Press.

Wynne, Brian. 2005. "Reflexing Complexity Post-genomic Knowledge and Reductionist Returns in Public Science." *Theory, Culture & Society* 22 (5): 67–94.

Society as an ethical system[†]

John Crowley

UNESCO Division of Social Transformations and Intercultural Dialogue, Paris, France

The idea of society on which the social sciences are premised is one of a structured pattern of interdependence and interaction that drives participation in a shared communication space and, thereby, a degree of common consciousness. These are also the preconditions for ethics to operate as an internal mode of self-understanding rather than an external imposition. Societies, in other words, are ethical systems. In order to understand in what sense societies, in the context of contemporary transformations, can still be thought of and analysed as ethical systems, the article focuses on inequality as both a practically important and normatively complex challenge – one that the international community, through the 2030 Agenda for Inclusive and Sustainable Development, has recognized to be one of its action priorities. These considerations further bear on the relation between the social sciences and the humanities, which is one important dimension of the future of the social sciences.

Introduction

In its eighteenth-century origins and nineteenth-century early development, social science was closely connected with moral philosophy. Questions about the desirable organization of human affairs were based in part on observations or assumptions about human nature, and conversely considerations about how humans ought to behave were informed by an understanding of how societies function and evolve over time.

Since Durkheim and Weber, this connection has loosened. It would be an exaggeration to say that social science and moral philosophy have entirely parted company, as the work of Jürgen Habermas, to name but one, suffices to show. Nonetheless, it remains true as a generalization that the academic development of the social sciences has been broadly inimical to the kind of fusion of the analytical and the normative that would earlier have been as natural within "social philosophy". On the one hand, the intellectual and institutional requirement to achieve emancipation from the dominion of philosophy has led to a distinction between the social sciences and the humanities that would not previously have been judged meaningful. And on the other hand, the aspiration to constitute a science (or

[†]This article is largely based on an address entitled "Equality, Justice, Inclusion. Ethical Perspectives on Contemporary Social Dynamics", originally delivered to a UNESCO conference on "Rethinking Development: Ethics and Social Inclusion" that took place in Mexico City on 17–18 August 2011.The views expressed in this paper are those of the author and, except where specifically stated otherwise, should not be regarded as official statements of a UNESCO position on the topics addressed.

sciences) of society gave rise to an epistemology in which statements about what "ought" to be were in principle illegitimate.

It has long been recognized that, however historically and conceptually intelligible, such distinctions between the humanities and the social sciences, and between "facts" and "norms", are at best practically convenient simplifications and at worst unhelpful legacies. Furthermore, it is widely acknowledged that the understanding of the physical sciences on which social science premised its foundational epistemology is, and even in the late nineteenth century already was, somewhat misleading. And indeed, there is extensive research in various disciplines that bears on the grey zone in which moral judgement may be understood as social fact, along with ambitious theoretical attempts to make sense of the post-positivistic nexus between facts and norms.

Among the issues that will shape the future of social science, the connection with the humanities, and its epistemological implications, are likely to be of considerable significance, especially as they bear on the social role of social science as it relates not just to understanding but to policies, to social mobilization and to the everyday fabric of social life. The purpose of this article is to consider one fairly circumscribed aspect of this general problem, which reflects in interesting ways some of its characteristic features: the status of ethics as a mode of inquiry into and language of justification within contemporary societies. In order to understand in what sense societies can be thought of and analysed as ethical systems, I will focus on inequality as both a practically important and normatively complex challenge – one that the international community, through the 2030 Agenda for Inclusive and Sustainable Development, has recognized to be one of its action priorities.

The contemporary dynamics of inequality

Statistics show clearly that contemporary social dynamics have led, over the past 20 years, to growing social inequality within most societies. Income distributions have been stretched, with the incomes of the richest rising much faster than the average, while the poorest have been confronted by stagnant real wages and, in many cases, pressure on welfare systems where they exist. In some cases, the impact has been minor, although not trivial; in other cases, including the United States as well as some fast-growing developing countries, the result has been levels of inequality unprecedented since 1945. Inequalities in terms of wealth have sharpened even more strikingly (Piketty 2014). Furthermore, such progress as can be observed in reducing aggregate global levels of inequality is almost entirely attributable to rapid economic growth in certain emerging countries: it is compatible with rising inequalities within nearly all societies (International Social Science Council 2016).

Nor is inequality simply a matter of income and assets. Studies in most countries point to increased inequalities of opportunities, especially with respect to education, and to striking correlations between inequality and ill-health (Pickett and Wilkinson 2015), which are only partly explained by differential insurance or other institutional features. In principle, one could argue that such inequalities are inevitable in periods of rapid economic transition, and will correct themselves over time. While this may turn out to be true, the evidence of the past two decades does not provide any reason to make such a prediction. On the contrary, some studies suggest that, in the most unequal countries, inequalities might be locked in by endogamy, residential and educational segregation, and more sophisticated asset-protection strategies, to the point that they may become, for all practical purposes, self-perpetuating. As readers of nineteenth-century literature know, one could then rely on the heirs to great fortunes to dilapidate them very quickly. Great fortunes today are much less likely to be gambled or drunk away, to the extent that philanthropy has, in the view of some, become the only mechanism of wealth redistribution over time.

Locked-in inequalities have sociological implications that are quite different from transitory inequalities that affect positions open to all in fair conditions of equal opportunity – to paraphrase John Rawls, of whom more later. Once they reach a certain scale, such inequalities negate the very idea of social inclusion – which I understand here are as full participation by all in the characteristic processes of the societies to which they belong. This concern with the "price of inequality" (Stiglitz 2013) has both an objective and a subjective dimension.

In objective terms, a society that is profoundly segmented by entrenched inequalities may simply no longer be a "society", in so far as its members may cease to share any "characteristic processes" at all. If people do not attend the same schools, do not live in the same neighbourhoods, do not consume the same kinds of goods and services, do not visit the same places, are not treated in the same hospitals, do not read the same books or watch the same films and so on, there comes a point when they become literally separate. "Separate development", one might recall, was the polite official rationale for apartheid. Probably no current society quite matches this description. Indeed, one of the features of technological globalization has been to make material culture more uniform than it was traditionally, even though its enjoyment is highly diverse. Furthermore, many societies remain resistant to such centrifugal pressures – populism being perhaps one of the purely ideological ways of managing them. But the tendency is nonetheless very clear. In his classic 1949 essay "Citizenship and Social Class", the British sociologist T.H. Marshall pointed out that the combination of common citizenship and class-based inequalities was a "stew of paradox", but nonetheless a nourishing one provided that a certain uniformity of rights, institutions and material culture was maintained (1950). We are clearly no longer in the world of Marshall.

In subjective terms, even when objective structures of inequality stop well short of "separate development", the idea of society as a common heritage of its members may come to ring very hollow to those who feel excluded from such "characteristic processes" as consumption, production, political participation and social respect. The way in which such perceived exclusion can explode has been seen graphically on the streets of Europe and North America on various occasions in the last 15 years, though the explosions are rare – not least for the good reasons Marx and Engels gave when snootily dismissing the *Lumpenproletariat* in the *Communist Manifesto*. But the seething resentment that makes the explosions possible is ever-present, and is unlikely to go away in current economic and social circumstances. At the same time, the more privileged sections of society are equally – perhaps more – likely to regard themselves as "not belonging" and to seek ways to opt out from the "characteristic processes" by which most of the population defines itself.

Inequality as an ethical notion

Inequalities might in very general terms be compatible with a just society, as Rawls argued they could be, subject to certain demanding conditions, in *A Theory of Justice* (1971). However, the patterns of inequality characteristic of contemporary dynamics do not seem to have the requisite features. They are, *prima facie*, grossly unjust because they reflect not differential modes of social inclusion, but precisely the sharp end of social exclusion. However, this widely shared view, which is by no means radical, is only the starting point of serious ethical analysis. What is necessary is first to identify what is unethical about the kinds of inequality referred to earlier, and secondly to clarify what might constitute an ethical response.

The intrusion of ethics at this point raises a methodological question. While justice is, at some level, an ethical notion, a theory of justice is not necessarily cast in ethical terms. Indeed, the whole point of the Rawlsian approach, and the reason why it has proved so influential, is that it makes it possible to focus on aggregate social outcomes – or even more abstractly, as Rawls himself puts it, on the "basic structure" of society – without needing to identify who is to blame. Within a reasonably cohesive, historically constituted moral community, the question of blame does not arise. A particular basic structure, which produces certain kinds of outcomes, is our shared inheritance and can only be modified and improved by the participation of all – not just the beneficiaries of any particular reform.

On the other hand, the characteristic weakness of this approach is that, in the absence of a pre-existing moral community, its implications might look pretty indeterminate. As is well known, this was Rawls' own view. It led him to the conclusion, in the late work *The Law of Peoples* (Rawls 2001), that it was pointless to seek a theory of justice at the global level. Admirers of Rawls such as Pogge (2008) and Barry (2005) broke sharply with him on this point, though their own arguments for global justice are stronger in establishing what kinds of positions can seriously and cogently be defended than it showing how they might come to be accepted.

An ethical approach to social inequality, on the contrary, presumably needs to argue not simply that certain patterns of outcomes are unjust, but that responsibilities for addressing them can be allocated in some meaningful way. And this, notoriously, constitutes a trap. Critics of Rawls such as Nozick (1974) and Hayek (2012) argued strongly in the 1970s that responsibility can attach only to individual behaviour – to things done intentionally or done unintentionally without due regard to consequences. In other words, in the absence of legal liability or of something analogous to it in areas that the law does not touch, justice has nothing to say. To put it bluntly, an ethical approach to justice negates the very idea of *social* justice, showing it to be, as Hayek put it, a "mirage".

There are two possible strategies to declare unethical contemporary patterns of inequality. One would be to argue that responsibilities can be assigned for aggregate social outcomes, once the notion of responsibility is suitably reinterpreted. The second would be to claim that certain unjust circumstances are unethical, regardless of whether anyone is to blame for them. Their unethical character would, in this case, be a kind of supplement to their injustice, something that adds insult to injury.[1] It should be emphasized that these two strategies, while conceptually distinct, do not necessarily clash. Indeed, they can be articulated quite neatly, as I hope to show in the rest of this section.

The second strategy is very familiar, if one reformulates it slightly. A situation can be regarded as unethical, for instance, if it offends against human dignity or constitutes a gross failure to realize universally recognized human rights. The first of the Sustainable Development Goals (SDGs) as adopted by the United Nations in 2015 – "end poverty in all its forms everywhere" – can, I think, be interpreted in this light. There may of course be specific injustices that contribute to extreme poverty, but even if they cannot be identified, the fact of extreme poverty is in itself an affront to human dignity that demands action, regardless of any kind of specific causal responsibility. The form of the first quantitative target (of seven corresponding to Goal 1) is indicative in this respect, calling as it does on the international community, by 2030, to "eradicate extreme poverty for all people everywhere, currently measured as people living on less than $1.25 a day".[2] At one level, this is a purely rhetorical strategy, but it can in certain circumstances motivate those who have the capacity to act to do so. In addition, other targets related to the same Goal either specify certain preconditions for the main target to be met (establishment of social protection systems, rights to economic resources and enhanced resilience in the face of environmental and other pressures) or point to the need for resources to be mobilized. Furthermore, the SDGs, unlike the MDGs, explicitly relate the eradication of extreme poverty to the reduction of poverty in general,[3] thereby making a further connection between poverty and inequality, which is explicitly addressed in SDG 10 to "reduce inequality within and among countries".

However, making remedial action depend exclusively on the capacity to act is, when pushed to its logical conclusion, a purely charitable approach that actually risks undermining the basis of human rights and human dignity from which the impulse to act proceed in the first place. If the key question is what is *owed* to the very poor, following the title of Pogge's edited volume (2007), then ethics cannot remain divorced from justice without undermining itself. This suggests that, on issues such as extreme poverty, and possibly on all issues of social inequality, extending and reinterpreting the principle of responsibility is essential to the pursuit of social justice.

The nature of ethical responsibility

In order to take this discussion forward, it may be helpful to start from the legal framework that Hayek and Nozick used precisely to counter Rawls.

In civil law, one is liable for breach of duty (deontological malpractice) but also, even in the absence of any specific duty, for tort, meaning harm inflicted on someone else as the foreseeable (though not necessarily foreseen) result of one's actions. Legal frameworks, although they differ widely with respect to the details, share one feature: they typically interpret very narrowly both "foreseeable" and "result" in this context. The self-appointed task of ethics has consistently been to push the legal boundaries by exploring to what extent particular agents should be held morally accountable (though not necessarily legally liable) for outcomes that connect to their actions in ways that are less direct and/or less foreseeable than the law would allow. Clearly, if this cannot be achieved, the pursuit of social justice will be hampered. But this is mere wishful thinking if some cogent grounds for an extension of responsibility beyond the narrow legal framework cannot be established.

With respect to the aggregate outcomes of contemporary social transformations, there appear to be three main grounds of *social* responsibility, each of which has been extensively developed in the literature, particularly perhaps on environmental ethics, though it bears very directly on other areas as well.

First, there is a widely recognized generalized duty of care, which relates the moral agent directly to aggregate outcomes, whether or not there is a direct causal connection between such outcomes and the agent's own actions. In the environmental area, this corresponds to a principle of "awareness", whereby what I should do depends on what others have done. In economic and financial matters, this implies that corporations, policy-makers, financial professionals and others may be reasonably held responsible for actions that contributed to the aggravation of patterns of injustice that had already been created by the reckless or indifferent actions of others. One cannot escape blame simply by pointing out, however correctly, that one is not solely to blame.

In the environmental case, awareness is primarily of complex systemic connections and of their implications, which drive aggregate phenomena such as climate change and biodiversity loss. The same principle can be applied by analogy, say to the financial crisis as it unfolded starting in 2007. It is not unreasonable to argue, even within the fairly narrow terms of causal responsibility, that it was reckless on the part of various operators to ignore, and fail to seek adequate information about, the ways in which their actions related to those of others. It is no accident, in this regard, that the financial crisis was revealed, initially, in the form of a crisis of liquidity. Liquidity is what enables investors to ignore long-term consequences and systemic interactions, since it makes it possible to withdraw from the market at any time. Conversely, the liquidity crisis froze and brought into sharp focus the various forms of asset mispricing that were previously obscured. Metaphorically and systemically, liquidity is to the financial system what the absorption capacities of the atmosphere and the ocean are to the environment.

In a similar manner, it is not absurd to hold corporations morally accountable for the systemic outcomes of their deliberate actions (to depress wages, to relocate production, to avoid taxes, etc.) when the connections were, in principle, capable of being analysed – and indeed were extensively discussed in the public domain. The same reasoning applies to policy-makers, who can justly be held accountable not exactly for the circumstances they were confronted with, but for their failure to take adequate account of those circumstances in choosing their policies. As for demonstrably ungrounded policies that produce predictably disastrous outcomes that disproportionately affect the most vulnerable, one hardly needs even an expanded notion of responsibility to hold their proponents individually accountable.

Secondly, regardless of causal responsibility, there is at least a generic duty to help those in need. In most legal systems, this is institutionalized to some extent, though not usually in a very demanding way. For instance, some criminal codes make it an offence not to help someone in danger, so long as one can do so without endangering oneself. This is obviously a duty that falls on the bystander – the fact that one did nothing to cause the danger to which someone else is exposed is irrelevant to the duty to provide assistance. Only the effective capacity to help matters from an ethical point of view. At one level, as noted earlier, this constitutes a duty of charity that may actually undermine rather than support social inclusion and justice. If, however, the duty to care is explicitly based on human dignity and human rights – which is a logical implication of the United Nations 2030 Agenda, based as it is on the internationally agreed human rights framework – its potentially inegalitarian implications can perhaps be neutralized.

The financial crisis offers a straightforward analogy in this regard. Institutions that have the capacity to provide emergency assistance have a *prima facie* duty to help to stabilize the system, whether or not they contributed to its destabilization in the first place, within the limits of their capacity to do so. Such institutions have, furthermore, a duty on the same grounds to provide relevant assistance to those hurt by the crisis, even apart from systemic instability. These duties need, of course, to be qualified by the moral hazard they imply. If the reckless can count on the help of the prudent, then why be prudent? This is why the legal form of the generic duty to provide assistance is usually quite complex. Nonetheless, the basic moral intuition remains valid.

Thirdly, and most generally, it could be argued, at least within the so-called "virtue ethics" paradigm (see Gardiner 2005, for an overview), that a basic value orientation towards the good of the whole is ethically desirable, and perhaps even mandatory. From this perspective, I should be concerned for the good of others – of my fellow creatures in an ecosystem, of my fellow humans in a shared society – regardless of whether I have played a role in a system that affects them, and regardless of whether they are in any strict sense "endangered". It is rather the combination of their inherent dignity and my own moral identity that places duties upon me. Just as an argument can be made in environmental ethics that "sustainability" is fundamentally an issue of virtue, not prudence, so an ethical approach to development might require that agents judge their actions by their effect on the social system as a whole.

The main reason to be prudent in asserting such a duty is the burden of judgement it entails. Moral agents trying to make the "right" choice with imperfect information might do more harm than good. As the colloquial saying has it, "the road to hell is paved with good intentions". Adam Smith provided a systematic moral theory in this regard, with his idea that the "invisible hand" was more likely to be conducive to the common good than attempts to achieve it directly (Smith 2003). Friedrich Hayek, systematizing the same intuition, went so far as to claim that *any* deliberate attempt to achieve *any* social outcome is necessarily doomed to failure by imperfect information (Hayek 2012). However, the call for prudence in acting on the duty to consider the good of the whole does not negate the duty itself – on the contrary, it precisely the ethical concern that dictates the prudence.

The obsolescence of society?

It is certainly not impossible, therefore, within the global framework as it is, to develop ethical reflections that, by reinterpreting the principle of responsibility, offer normative grounds – more cogent than mere denunciation – for criticism of certain patterns of behaviour and institutional arrangements and for promotion of specific alternatives. The key to this approach, it will have been noted, is a certain kind of connectedness. What makes it possible to combine justice and ethics at the conceptual level – and thereby make applied ethics work for justice in practice – is the premise that inequalities occur within an inchoate moral community.

This premise is undoubtedly awkward, since, observably, social exclusion currently brings with it an erosion of shared recognition of a moral community. Nor, however, is it mere wishful thinking.

The key point is the central plank of sociology since its inception: the idea that a society is not just a grouping of people, but a structured pattern of interdependence and interaction that drives participation in a shared communication space and, thereby, a degree of common consciousness. The point is that the relation between these features is structural: the degree of interaction and interdependence that characterizes modern societies *depends on* a degree of mutual recognition – of trust, of shared institutions, of mutual understanding. In no way does such a hypothesis make consensus or uniformity criteria of social inclusion. On the contrary, complex societies are inherently pluralistic and can function only if they include conflict within themselves.

The central question, therefore, is whether this vision of society is obsolete, and can still offer a framework for ethical thinking about social justice and social inclusion, and more generally about development, which remains an essential reference point for the international community even though its precise implications are increasingly difficult to make sense of. And it will be appreciated, for the specific purposes of this thirtieth-anniversary issue of *Innovation*, that if the idea of "society" is in some sense obsolete, the future of the "social" sciences is necessarily in some sense called into doubt. The stakes are therefore high.

There are two reasons for taking seriously the possibility of obsolescence. The first is ideological: alienation, as analysed in the Marxian tradition, is precisely blindness to connectedness, particularly in the form of the belief that commodities are in themselves autonomous bearers of value. In so far as globalization makes production and consumption even less connected than they were previously, it may indeed foster growing alienation. The second reason is structural. Interdependence relies ultimately on the necessity of employing most people most of the time to ensure an adequate economic state. If a significant part of the population becomes (or is believed to be) durably "surplus to requirements", then the underlying basis for common membership in society is undermined. Clearly this feature does, to some extent, apply in the contemporary world.

On the other hand, a (global) society characterized by large-scale, long-range interdependence risks being unsustainable if it is not normatively defensible, not just because those who are excluded may be tempted to revolt, but because those who benefit may end up lacking the will power as well the capacity to ignore the consequences of their actions. The wave of political instability that began in the Arab region in 2011, with its diverse and often bloody mid-range consequences, has reminded us of the truth of Aristotle's dictum that "men do not become tyrants in order to keep out the cold". Once one ceases to believe in one's right to rule, the magic is gone and flight is the only option.

Therein lies the obvious difficulty for the international community in continuing to refer to its normative horizon as "development" at the same time as the conceptual and analytical framework within which the concept of development was elaborated has been profoundly called into question. To put it very simply, the notion of development is premised upon the same idea of society as the social sciences in general: it sketches a series of possible paths that connect the objective conditions and outcomes of social change – in particular its technical manifestations – with its subjective manifestations – in particular the forms of consciousness characteristic of it and the cultural and political implications that flow from them. In addition, the developmental paradigm does this at two complementary levels: within each society, taking account of its starting point and distinctive national features, and for the world as a whole within a setting of sustainable interdependence.

What, however, if the link between objective and subjective dynamics breaks down? What if the historically attested correlation between structural change, driven mainly by technology, and behavioural, attitudinal and ideational change – what Elias influentially termed the "civilizing process" (2000) – were accidental and reversible? In this case, we may continue to use the term "society" to refer to collections of people who share the same geographical space and are subject to the same structural processes – but this would no longer be the "society" on which the social sciences were originally premised, and it would be a setting within which solidaristic or redistributive approaches to inequality would be very difficult to formulate at all. It would thus also be a profoundly different setting in ethical terms.

Conclusion: reimagining society

The claim that inequality is an ethical notion may thus, on the basis of the arguments presented in previous sections, be understood in two rather different ways, one of which is internal to the idea of society that I have summarized, whereas the other is external to it. To defend the internal approach, as I have been doing and propose to do more assertively in this concluding section, it is necessary to be more explicit about what it is contrasted with.

The alternative social model of ethics, which is of course powerfully supported by many cultural frameworks, might for present purposes be called "preaching". What I mean by this term, which has no specific religious connotation, is a certain kind of social relationship, in which ethical principles are produced by some process and then propounded by a specialized group of people to a broader group of people who are assumed to be prepared to regulate their behaviour by reference to the principles. Two things are socially important here: first, the functional separation between the "preacher" and the "congregation", regardless of the source of the preacher's authority and of the content of what is preached; secondly, the fact that the principles are not a matter for discussion within the relationship itself (although their practical application may be).

There are both general objections to the "preaching" model of ethics and specific problems with its applicability to issues such as inequality.

The most general objection is simply that, in the absence of strong, shared background moral consensus, the principles preached will simply reveal, or even sharpen, divisions within the "congregation". Far from providing a basis for generally accepted ethical regulation of behaviour, preaching may therefore simply ensure fragmentation. Conversely, in a context of moral pluralism – which obtains certainly at the international level and typically also within most social and political settings –, principles are very unlikely to be accepted in practice if they have not actually been discussed.

These pragmatic limitations of the unilateral "preaching" model of ethical exchange deserve further to be supplemented by a more principled objection. Ethics depends on, although it is not reducible to, conscience. An ethical society is, *prima facie*, one each member of which has a conscience that can grasp and make sense of ethical principles and apply them to specific situations. The fostering of conscience is therefore one of the processes by which the ethical texture of a society can be enhanced. It follows that ethics cannot be reduced to preaching without undermining its own social basis.

The objections specific to issues such as inequalities are in many ways more important. The social relationship of preaching may be pragmatically fragile and morally awkward, but it is at least practically sustainable on condition the preacher is endowed with clear epistemic authority. When ethicists preach to ordinary people on matters that are directly and intimately connected to their life experiences, however, the balance of epistemic authority is at the very least uncertain. Undoubtedly, the role of historically attested religions in successfully providing ideological warrant for highly unequal social orders shows that preaching *can* work. It is on the other hand a commonplace of the sociological tradition, explicit in both Durkheim and Weber, that the co-evolution in modernity of religions and societies makes traditional pulpits less accessible. In the age of what Weber famously referred to as "disenchantment" (*Entzäuberung*), the burden of social justification necessarily becomes immanent to the social order itself, leaving external ethics fragile, and unlikely to offer a basis for consensual regulation of conduct.

Overcoming the split enshrined in external models of ethics thus requires the development of an alternative structural model. Rather than separating the development of principles and their social dissemination, the issue is to combine both within a single, reflexive social process of ethical discussion and deliberation. This emphasis on reflexivity is, in social science terms, familiar to the point of cliché. Nonetheless, its implications for ethics are perhaps insufficiently appreciated.

Furthermore, such a model has a significant disciplinary implication. Ethics is often taken to be the distinctive preserve of philosophy. In fact, although philosophers have an important role to play in ethics, the arguments that have just been sketched show the need to connect ethics closely to social science, not to the exclusion of, but rather in close relation to, philosophy. In general terms, the form of this relation derives from the proposed reflexive structure of the ethical process. To say that ethical principles should derive from a social process of discussion and deliberation, involving those to whom the principles are to be applied, is to say, consistently with the traditional emphasis of sociology, that ethical reflection is part of the self-understanding of a society. It is thus a social process that can be studied with the tools of social science – even though the social sciences may have little to say directly about the substantive content of the ethical principles involved. In other words, an understanding of the ethical construction of inequality necessarily blurs the boundaries between the social sciences and the humanities and requires a certain hybridization of concepts, methods and modes of discourse.

In this sense, an ethical approach to the development challenges the international community has agreed to be judged by bears ultimately on the social as well as the environmental sustainability of any possible development project. In demanding that responsibility extend beyond the narrow boundaries of legalistic responsibility, an ethical approach to global justice recognizes and expresses the basic fact that global society is, increasingly, a society, in the strong sense given to the word by the sociological tradition. Furthermore, the more territorially restricted societies that make up the global whole have not ceased to be societies either. Within them, as well as between them, aggregate outcomes are subject to ethical criteria of justice that arise from the social process itself rather than being imposed on it from the outside. What makes inequality something to be cared about, mobilized around, fought against – and not simply measured or theorized – is precisely this imaginary construction of social facts.

To specify the actual content of the ethical principles that might apply to key development issues such as inequality, as well as the procedures by which they might be elaborated and justified, is therefore a work of imagination. However, the imaginative or fictional character of justice does not mean that it is imaginary or fictitious, subtle though those lexical differences may appear to be. In complex societies, solidarity is a (contentious) fact, embedded in but not reducible to structures of objective interdependency. It is not simply a state of mind or an aspiration or even, in the usual sense of the word, a discourse. It is one dimension of a process of making sense, and it expresses the powerful egalitarian current that Tocqueville pointed to as central to the very idea of democracy. Indeed, an indirect indication of the power of this current is the intensity of the ideological investment in damming it, by producing arguments – which are equally works of imagination – to justify inequalities as naturally or divinely ordained.

The ultimate question, therefore, which goes to the heart of how an egalitarian society can be imagined in contemporary circumstances, is how to understand the conditions in which competing discourses, competing social imaginaries, coexist and compete. An argument could be made that discourses interact with reference to what they claim to account for, and that discourses become hegemonic because of their formal properties, or because of the resources that back them. If so, *any* social configuration is in principle compatible with *any* discursive configuration.

The whole point of this article is to suggest, without fully establishing, that this perspective is wrong in important respects. The conditions for discourses to flourish are connected to the objective conditions in which they circulate, as long argued by the proponents of ideology as a structural understanding of ideas. And conversely, structures are sensitive to the sense made of them. The question is, therefore, whether there is compatibility between the desire to reduce inequalities and the conditions within which the desire emerges. For society is not a competition run for the benefit of those who happen to win it. It is a structure of interdependence of which reciprocity is the very lifeblood. It is, in a word, an *ethical* system, but one the ethical features of which require considerable further exploration.

Notes

1. I leave aside here the question whether certain situations might be unethical without being unjust. It is clear enough that behaviour can in principle be unethical without being unjust, in particular when no one would possibly be harmed by it. Whether this can apply to social patterns is less clear. However, more importantly for present purposes, the debate is not really about the injustice of the patterns of inequality referred to, which is widely recognized. It is rather whether anything can be done about them and, in particular, whether anyone is to blame.
2. The target adopted in 2015 represents a significant change compared to the target connected to the first of the Millennium Development Goals (MDGs) adopted in 2000, which committed the international community to halve by 2015 the proportion of the world's population living in extreme poverty. As is well known, this was criticized both as too modest, given what extreme poverty actually entails for the people who suffer it and in light of a goal, in principle, of *eliminating* extreme poverty, for which halving it would be a very poor substitute; and as normatively weak. The latter criticism would claim that extreme poverty is not merely an affront to human dignity but a violation of human rights, which demands therefore not just quantitative amelioration, but actionable justice, for the very poor. (For a detailed discussion of these ideas, see Pogge 2007.) These, however, were debates within an ethical approach, not alternatives to it, and the validity of the criticisms has been recognized, at least rhetorically, in the 2030 Agenda.
3. SDG target 1.2 reads: "By 2030, reduce at least by half the proportion of men, women and children of all ages living in poverty in all its dimensions according to national definitions."

References

Barry, B. 2005. *Why Social Justice Matters*. Cambridge: Polity.

Elias, N. 2000. *The Civilizing Process: Sociogenetic and Psychogenetic Investigations*. Oxford: Wiley-Blackwell (originally published in German in two volumes in 1969 as *Über den Prozess des Zivilisation*).

Gardiner, Stephen, ed. 2005. *Virtue Ethics, Old and New*. Ithaca, NY: Cornell University Press.

Hayek, F. A. 2012. *Law, Legislation and Liberty. A New Statement of the Liberal Principles of Justice and Political Economy*. One-volume ed. London: Routledge Classics (originally published in three volumes in 1973, 1976 and 1979).

International Social Science Council. 2016. *Challenging Inequalities: Pathways to a Just World. World Social Science Report 2016*. Paris: UNESCO/ISSC.

Marshall, T. H. 1950. "Citizenship and Social Class." In *Citizenship and Social Class and Other Essays*, 1–85. Cambridge: Cambridge University Press. http://www.jura.uni-bielefeld.de/lehrstuehle/davy/wustldata/1950_Marshall_Citzenship_and_Social_Class_OCR.pdf.

Nozick, R. 1974. *Anarchy, State and Utopia*. New York: Basic Books.

Pickett, K. E., and R. G. Wilkinson. 2015. "Income Inequality and Health: A Causal Review". *Social Science & Medicine* 128: 316–326.

Piketty, T. 2014. *Capital in the Twenty-First Century*. Cambridge, MA: Harvard University Press (originally published in French in 2013 as *Le capital au XXIe siècle*).

Pogge, T., ed. 2007. *Freedom from Poverty as a Human Right: Who Owes What to the Very Poor?* Oxford: Oxford University Press/UNESCO.

Pogge, T. 2008. *World Poverty and Human Rights*. 2nd ed. Cambridge: Polity.

Rawls, J. 1971. *A Theory of Justice*. Cambridge, MA: Harvard University Press.

Rawls, J. 2001. *The Law of Peoples*. Cambridge, MA: Harvard University Press.

Smith, A. 2003. *An Inquiry into the Nature and Causes of the Wealth of Nations*. New York: Bantam Classics (first published in 1776).

Stiglitz, J. 2013. *The Price of Inequality*. New York: W.W. Norton.

Travelling concepts and crossing paths: a conceptual history of identity

Liana Giorgi

Independent Scholar

The concept of identity is ubiquitous in public discourse even though its meaning is often imprecise or nebulous – it is maybe because of this that its contents can be taken for granted. One speaks of individual, personal, group, social, collective and political identity; of identity formation, crisis, diffusion, conflict and politics; a multiple identity may be pathological or a component of an integrated identity; culture and ideology but also knowledge and experience supposedly enrich identity; identity may be rigid or open to development and growth – and so on. Against this background the present paper explores the argumentative uses of the concept of identity in psychoanalysis and in social psychology and sociology.

There are two aspects to most uses of identity. The first is that of sameness under different conditions; the second is that of difference under same conditions. We typically use identity to refer to that part of ourselves or a group we associate with, which is the same or remains the same over time and under different circumstances. Or, we use identity to distinguish ourselves and our groups from others, who are presumably different from us. It is not unlikely, however not proven, that our capacity to distinguish ourselves from others – or the fact itself that we do – is dependent on our own sense of sameness or identity: alternatively, we could argue that the manner in which we identify or differentiate ourselves from others and the outcome of these identifications and distinctions is what moulds our sense of identity as individuals – and similar processes could be said to apply to groups and society more generally.

Bilgrami (2006) explains this conundrum while demonstrating its strong affective components. In a discussion of political identity along the lines of culture, ethnicity or religion, he notes that such identities are usually intensely held self-conceptions that are upheld for intrinsic reasons, "in a way that approximates the Ulysses-Siren model" (10). Ulysses, it will be recalled, was afraid of being seduced by the sirens. He nonetheless wanted to hear their song. Following the advice of Circe, he put wax in the ears of his men and had them tie him on the mast till they had passed through the dangerous territory. In other words, identities tend to be activated in the context of confrontation with something new and mysterious (which is assumed to be both seducing and dangerous); yet ultimately, so Bilgrami, what is essential about them is the *wish* that the values and desires that originally formed them are permanent. This wish and the actions (or reactions) they give rise to can function as a protection but equally frequently they operate as defence. This conveys in a nutshell both what is useful and what is detrimental about (political) identities.

Identity is a concept linked to psychological and cognitive development, socialization and social interaction. Against this background, this paper is an attempt to explore the conceptual history of identity within psychoanalysis and in social psychology and sociology. I understand conceptual history in line with Quentin Skinner as a review of the argumentative uses made of specific concepts over time in different contexts. This is to be distinguished from the history of concepts proper, which pays more attention to the precise documentation of direct transmissions of concepts over time.

A conceptual history of identity is interesting for a number of reasons. Besides its value for the theory and sociology of knowledge it is also a good starting point for exploring the linkages between the way we think about the human mind, on the one hand, and social relations within communities and society, on the other hand.

The choice for psychoanalysis from among psychological theories has been motivated by two reasons. First, one of the main proponents of identity theory in the twentieth century with a strong impact on both psychology and sociology, especially in the United States, was Erik Erikson, a psychoanalyst. Secondly, psychoanalysis is the first psychological science to offer a comprehensive non-behaviourist theory of mental life. For the social sciences, I will consider theories on social (and group) identity relevant for the study of so-called identity politics in the context of community conflicts or multiculturalism. This is the most evident field in the social sciences for exploring the concept of identity.

Psychoanalytic perspectives on identity

Freud's thinking on identity by way of the ego ideal

Freud's dynamic approach to psychical phenomena and mental representations – first by way of his instinct theory, later in terms of the structural agency model of the mind, throughout with a focus on the interplay between conscious and unconscious processes – did not necessitate the explicit definition of the concept of identity. Identity as *self-regard* is secondarily considered with reference to the discussion of the development and function of the ego, super-ego and the ego ideal as well as the role of internal and external object relations. Two essays, in particular, provide insight into Freud's thoughts on the subject, namely "On Narcissism: An Introduction" (1914) and "Group Psychology and the Analysis of the Ego" (1921).

In the third part of his essay on narcissism, Freud links the feeling of self-regard to the ego ideal, the origins of which are to be found in infantile, primary, narcissism. The ego ideal, and with it the feeling of self-regard, grows, already during childhood, by way of the gratification derived from various accomplishments as well as the satisfaction that comes from object-libido. Persons that are loved are idealized and their views internalized. This is a formative process with respect to conscience and self-observation – functions, which in later works, beginning with "The Ego and the Id" (1923) would be attributed to the super-ego. This highlights the social dimension of the ego ideal and, by default, the super-ego. Freud writes:

> For what prompted the subject to form an ego ideal, on whose behalf his conscience acts as a watchman, arose from the critical influence from his parents (conveyed to him by the medium of the voice), to whom were added, as time went on, those who trained and taught him and the innumerable and indefinable host of all the other people in his environment – his fellow-men and public opinion. (SE, XIV, 96)

In "Group Psychology and the Analysis of the Ego", Freud assigns this ego ideal a key role with regard to the impulsive affectionate organization of groups. The twin processes of identification and internalization that can be observed with small children are similar to those occurring in primary groups that are formed around a leader or a leading idea:

> A primary group of this kind is a number of individuals that have put one and the same object in the place of their ego ideal and have consequently identified themselves with another in their ego. (1921, SE, XVIII, 116)

This identification by way of the ego ideal is as important for group formation as the so-called herd instinct. Freud sees in the herd instinct a reaction-formation to envy, of the type already felt by small children when they realize that they are not the only ones to benefit from their mother's love. Thus social feeling emerges out of the reversal of an originally hostile affect "under the influence of a common affectionate tie with a person outside the group" (1921, SE, XVIII, 121).

Freud's thoughts on self-regard point to the inherent ambiguity of the process of identification and, consequently, identity. Individuals strive for the approval of those they identify with; yet this process, which has also a key function with respect to thinking and emotional experience more generally, is impossible without the repression of aggressive feelings towards significant others, albeit rivals. The destiny, so-to-speak, of these repressed feelings delineates a good part of what psychoanalysis is about and explains the essentially neurotic character of individuals and human civilization.

Erik Erikson and ego-psychology

Erikson (1950) took up Freud's ideas about self-regard and transformed them into a model of psychological development. Erikson thought that the conflict between libidinal and aggressive impulses could be settled during adolescence thus achieving integration in the form of ego identity. He writes:

> In their search for a new sense of continuity and sameness, adolescents have to re-fight many of the battles of earlier years, even though to do so they must artificially appoint perfectly well-meaning people to play the role of adversaries; and they are ever ready to install lasting idols and ideals as guardians of a final identity. The integration now taking place in the form of ego identity is, as pointed out, more than the sum of childhood identifications. It is the accrued experience of the ego's ability to integrate all identifications with the vicissitudes of the libido with the aptitudes developed out of endowment and with the opportunities offered in social roles. The sense of ego identity then is the accrued confidence that the inner sameness and continuity of one's meaning for others. (1950, 235).

Erikson's model of psychological development comprises eight stages extending over a person's lifetime. These are defined in terms of critical steps in relation to basic orientations. Thus in childhood, the oral childhood stage is said to be about basic trust versus mistrust, the anal stage about autonomy versus shame and doubt, the genital stage about initiative versus guilt and the latent phase about industry versus inferiority. When in adolescence ego integrity fails the result is role confusion. Subsequent adult stages are about intimacy versus isolation, generativity versus stagnation and finally about ego integrity versus despair. Modern models of psychological development within and outside psychoanalysis follow a similar approach.

From the conceptual historical viewpoint it is nonetheless important to understand that Erikson's adaptation of Freud's views was particular insofar as it relied on specific assumptions that were not necessarily those of Freud. Erikson's two underlying assumptions, in his own words:

> (1) that the human personality in principle develops according to steps predetermined in the growing person's readiness to be driven towards, to be aware of, and to interact with, a widening social radius; and (2) that society, in principle, tends to be constituted as to meet and invite this succession of potentialities for interaction and attempts to safeguard and to encourage the proper rate and the proper sequence of their unfolding. This is the "maintenance of the human world". (1950, 243)

These two assumptions are a reformulation of Freud's thoughts about hereditary dispositions and environmental influences, respectively, whereby, unlike Freud, Erikson frames these in normative terms. Indeed Erikson's book *Childhood and Society* – including the "case-studies" of "the" American adolescent or Hitler's childhood – often reads like a handbook of dos and don'ts for raising children. At societal level, the objective is to promote "social health", "cultural solidarity" (370) and "the reduction of economic and political prejudice which denies a sense of identity to youth" (375).

This shift away from Freud's scientific discourse to a more normative discourse is a characteristic more generally of ego-psychology, that is, the school of psychoanalysis that is most widespread in the United States. American psychoanalysis tried to "make psychoanalysis both into a general psychology … and into a general science" (Wallerstein 2002, 140). This led to a focus on the ego as the main agency of the reality principle, the seat of anxiety and, therefore, for defence against (or adaptation to) infantile and instinctual forces. Consequently the concepts of autonomy and adaptation gained in significance at the expense of questions of dependency and conflict.

In the therapeutic context this theoretical approach in conjunction with an emphasis on abstinence in terms of technique (Wallerstein 2002, 141) worked well with those patients whose ego was well-formed and functioning, even if sub-optimally, but it worked less well with those who displayed a borderline or narcissistic pathology. Addressing the problems of these patients, who appear unable to hold on to a composite view of self and other besides displaying excess negativity, led Otto Kernberg (2006) to re-emphasize both the object relations and affective components of Freud's writings. Kernberg adopted Erikson's term of identity diffusion to refer to this mental state.

Erikson's and Kernberg's integrated ego identity corresponds to Kohut's (1977) integrated sense of self. The self, according to Kohut, is established early in a person's lifetime by way of bonding with significant others. Thus so-called self-objects are created that are important in terms of identification and, through this, the integration of the self. Narcissistic patients, according to Kohut, will have often failed to develop a functioning or integrated self in the sense of "a psychological sector in which ambitions, skills and ideals form an unbroken continuum that permits joyful creative activity" (1977, 63). Kohut's self psychology differs from Kernberg's identity approach in two ways. Whereas Kernberg emphasizes conflict and the need to work through negative affect, in particular aggression and destructiveness, Kohut highlights structural deficits and prioritizes the treatment of anxiety. A middle position is provided by Volkan and Ast (1994).

Melanie Klein, object relations and the mechanisms of projection and introjection

In Europe, and especially in the UK, psychoanalysis followed a different course of theoretical development in accordance with Melanie Klein's meta-psychology. This was largely developed on the basis of her observations of young children engaged in play therapy. This work sensitized her to the omnipresence of unconscious phantasy[1] and its significance for the development of symbolization and thinking. Unconscious phantasy is "in the first instance, the mental corollary, the psychic representative, of instinct" (Isaaks 1948, 81), and is most likely some form of imagery or visual representation. According to Klein, such phantasies are very concrete because they are at first activated in the context of the earliest awareness of bodily experiences – for instance, by way of the infant's mouth sucking on the mother's breast.[2]

The second major discovery of Melanie Klein concerned the emergence of the super-ego during the pre-Oedipal phase. In this, its primal form, the super-ego encapsulates the dread experienced by a child when in the course of weaning, or even earlier, it gradually becomes aware of the non-continuous availability of its mother. This feeling of frustration, which following Freud is pivotal for the consolidation of the reality principle, assuming it can be tolerated, is originally experienced as aggression. What this implies is that the aggressive feelings that during later development stages will be directed against rivals are originally experienced towards one and the same person. In other words, the first identification figure, which by being the first probably assumes a formative function for all later identifications, is experienced ambivalently. This is an important extension of Freud's thinking about identification processes.

Klein's later ([1935] 1998, [1946] 1998, [1955] 1998) description of these processes in terms of the transition from the paranoid-schizoid to the depressive position helped expand the clinical scope of psychoanalysis to the treatment of psychotic conditions but also provided an alternative model of psychological development as compared to the one established by ego-psychology. In Klein's own words:

> Super-ego development can be traced back to introjections in the earliest stages of infancy; the primal internalized objects form the basis of complex processes of identification; persecutory anxiety, arising from the experience of birth, is the first form of anxiety, very soon followed by depressive anxiety; introjection and projection operate from the beginnings of post-natal life and constantly interact. This interaction both builds up the internal world and shapes the picture of external reality. The inner world consists of objects, first of all the mother, internalized in various aspects and emotional situations. The relationships between these internalized figures, and between them and the ego, tend to be experienced – when persecutory anxiety is dominant – as mainly hostile and dangerous; they are felt to be loving and good when the infant is gratified and happy feelings prevail. This inner world, which can be described in terms of internal relations and happenings, is the product of the infant's own impulses, emotions and phantasies. It is of course profoundly influenced by his good and bad experiences from external sources. But at the same time the inner world influences his perception of the external world in a way that is no less decisive for this development. ([1955] 1998, 142)

Compared to the ego-identity model of psychological development associated with Erikson, Klein's model is less concerned with stages and more interested in the mechanisms of dealing with primal affects such as excitement, aggression and anxiety, and how these mould our mental representations (and our capacity as such for representation, symbolization and thinking). According to Klein, the ego exists already at birth, albeit in primitive form, and begins to take shape, by way of projective identification, during the first six months of life. Projective identification combines the mechanisms of projection and introjection and provides the basis for linking the internal and external world and for learning from experience.[3] From the perspective of identity theory, Klein's model of psychological development shifts attention to the emotional bearings of identity, its dynamic character as well as its representational, hence, interpretative function.

Even though the ego-psychology and object relations schools of psychoanalysis are often thought of as opposed, their approaches are to a great extent complementary, assuming that their theories are accepted as relating to different levels of analysis. Whereas ego-psychology is concerned with the macro-level of repressed pre-conscious conflicts, object relations emphasizes the impact of unconscious phantasy on consciousness. When theoretical disagreements do arise, these have more often to do with the extent to which the assumption of unconscious phantasy as such is accepted and, in turn, with the weight assigned to internal psychic reality as a driver for development as compared to external environmental circumstances.

Psychoanalytic work on group identity

This overview of psychoanalytic perspectives on identity would be incomplete without consideration of the work of Vamik Volkan and Wilfred Bion on group identity.

Volkan's work on large-group psychology has explicated the processes of distinction that are critical for the formation of group identity, often by way of discrimination whereby good attributes are assigned to one's own group, and bad ones to the other. This splitting process is a repetition of the much earlier process of differentiation of the child from its mother. According to Volkan, such mechanisms are never entirely given up by either individuals or groups. Instead they are frequently used to establish so-called "shared reservoirs for permanent externalizations" (Volkan 2013, 215), which are the origin of prejudices. We all carry and reproduce such cliché representations of others, often without consequence. Yet in the context of conflict, these will often turn out to be serious obstacles towards reconciliation and conflict resolution. They help sustain what Volkan calls "psychological borders" between us and them. Charismatic leaders and specific glorified or traumatic historical events act as additional "identity markers" that stand in the way of cooperation. Thus is formed a repertoire of symbolic representations and a reservoir of negative affect that is transmitted from one generation to the next.

While Volkan's work throws light on the significance of inter-group behaviour and out-group representations, Bion's ([1961] 1989) explorations of experiences in groups help understand in-group behaviour. His findings confirm Freud's earlier insights with regard to the way social feeling is formed via reaction-formation, that is to say by reversing hostile feelings towards peers. Large-group psychology tends to treat groups as homogeneous collectives. By contrast, small-group psychology pays more attention to internal processes of bonding and differentiation. Basic mechanisms include pairing, flight/fight and dependence. The basic assumption behind "pairing" is preservation. Basic groups characterized by flight/fight also want to preserve themselves but can only do this by fighting or taking flight. Finally, dependency groups seek security from a leader. Bion considers that basic groups behave in psychotic manner, complain excessively and avoid intellectual work. Furthermore, according to Bion, these tendencies are present in all groups at one time or another.

Using these assumptions, it is possible to explore how groups collaborate and grow or, more often, how they disintegrate. Identification figures, social institutions or, in the ideal situation, the learned experience of verbal exchange as "a method of thought" (Bion [1961] 1989, 186) and a means of communication are the ways through which basic groups can be transformed into benign work groups. Social institutions such as the church, the army and aristocracy represent ways of transforming basic groups into work groups, thus structuring them and stabilizing them in terms of identity. Freud (1921) had already described how the church and the army function in terms of identification. Bion added aristocracy to this list, which, I contend, could be expanded to refer to the political system more generally.

The social science perspective on identity

Contemporary applied research on community conflicts

Let me start by considering contemporary research on community conflicts. As exemplified by Vamik Volkan's work, this is a field that addresses questions that fall within the scope of psychoanalytic inquiry. Yet there is little direct evidence for the consideration of psychoanalytic insights by contemporary social scientists.

One central concern of contemporary social sciences is throwing light on the phenomenon of nationalism, racism, ethnic and religious violence. At issue: how to explain the historical emergence of nationalism and, within modern societies, the persistence of right-wing extremism, religious fundamentalism and the associated phenomena of xenophobia, racism, terrorism and anti-Semitism? What facilitates or hinders the emergence of a post-national democracy that is not centred on primordial identifications of ancestry, origin, homeland, language and history? Is it possible to ferment a European cosmopolitan identity that is comparable to national identity in terms of affective ties, but without the latter's negative traits, for example, a "fortress Europe"? These are some of the questions that researchers have been looking at either in relation to specific community conflicts or in comparative perspective. Practically all these research questions centre on the issue of "identity" and the extent to which it may be possible to preserve the latter's positive aspects without falling into its traps.[4]

Early ethnicity research and debate tended to "pit[s] an understanding of ethnicity as rooted in deep-seated or primordial attachments and sentiments against an understanding of it as an instrumental adaptation to shifting economic and political circumstances" (Brubaker, Loveman, and Stamatov 2004, 49).[5] By contrast, contemporary ethnicity research and research on community conflicts pays equal attention to so-called objective and subjective factors and perspectives. Objective dimensions tap on materialist issues such as socio-economic inequalities or geo-political aspects; subjective dimensions relate to factors such as the existence of ancient hatreds and the latter's reproduction through the discourse of memory and symbolic representations. And yet, despite extensive empirical research it has not been possible to arrive at definite conclusions entailing predictive power regarding what causes ethnic violence to erupt in the first place or repeatedly at various points in time. This is taken to indicate the strength of interaction effects for eliciting specific behaviours, whereby the persistence of large unexplained residuals suggests that accidental factors have also a role to play (cf. Pinker 2012).

The complex interplay of factors in the analysis of ethnic conflicts is beginning to raise interest in unconscious processes. Interestingly, this literature does not refer to psychoanalysis as a possible source of knowledge but to the cognitive sciences. For instance, Brubaker, Loveman, and Stamatov (2004) write:

> … cognitive research indicates that much cognition … is unselfconscious and quasi-automatic rather than deliberate and controlled. This suggests that the explicit, deliberate and calculated deployment of an ethnic frame of reference in pursuit of instrumental advantage may be less important in explaining the situational variability of ethnicity than the ways in which ethnic – and non-ethnic – ways of seeing, interpreting and experiencing social relations are unselfconsciously "triggered" or activated by proximate situational cues (51)

The use of the term "unselfconscious" to refer to the unconscious is quite telling with regard to the cautious attitude of present-day social science vis-à-vis psychoanalysis. Further insight into this difficult relationship is provided by sociological research on terrorism. For instance, in a review of the relevant literature, Victoroff (2005) acknowledges the usefulness of psychoanalysis for understanding the formation of the terrorist personality, yet rejects its tenets on the grounds of its presumed unscientific method. Victoroff writes:

> The great strengths of psychoanalytic interpretations [of terrorism] are their acknowledgement that individual developmental factors beginning in early childhood probably influence adult behavioural proclivities, their recognition of the enormous power of the unconscious to influence conscious thought, and their observation that covert psychodynamic forces of groups may subsume individuality. The great weakness is their lack of falsifiability. Psychoanalysis has been largely abandoned among modern psychiatrists precisely because it rejects the scientific method, asking that adherents accept its propositions as received wisdom. (2005, 26)

Both of the above quotations testify to the misconceptions about psychoanalysis within modern social sciences as reproduced through secondary literature.

On social identity theory

Despite this partial or cautious attitude of mainstream social sciences towards psychoanalysis, the latter has in fact already had a considerable impact on social theory by way of the study of identity.

It was Erik Erikson, who introduced this concept in American sociology and social psychology. According to Weigert (1983), Erikson's identity concept found echo both among symbolic interactionists like Blumer (1969) as well as among social constructionists like Berger and Luckmann (1967). Both symbolic interactionism and social constructionism emerged in reaction to behaviourism, which views individual and group behaviour in mechanistic stimulus–response terms or action–reaction processes that are guided by utilitarian interests. While it is not the case that ideas have no place within behaviourist theories, their role as adaptable intermediaries facilitating or obstructing learning or communication is basically functional. By contrast, symbolic interactionists assign ideas, and the identities formed around them, a more central position with respect to group affiliations and motivations, while social constructionists consider meaning per se as the basic driver of social interaction and change.

One other central figure for both theories of symbolic interactionism and social constructionism was George Herbert Mead, an American philosopher in the tradition of pragmatism and a contemporary of Freud, who studied psychology with William James (at Harvard) and Wilhelm Wundt (in Leipzig). George Herbert Mead developed a theory of the self that emphasized object relations. According to Mead, social interaction, beginning with gestures and acoustic stimulation in childhood, enables the formation of a sense of self by providing stimuli that activate specific responses in the individual. In a paper entitled "The mechanism of social consciousness" written in 1912, Mead describes the emergence of consciousness in terms matching Freud's (1911) principles of mental functioning and suggestive of Bion's (1962) later formulations on the so-called alpha function:

> … we may define the social object in terms of social conduct as we defined the physical object in terms of our reactions to physical objects. … The social object will then be the gestures, i.e. the early indications of an ongoing social act in another, *plus* the imagery of our own response to that stimulation. *To the young child the frowns and smiles of those about him, the attitude of body, the outstretched arms, are at first simply stimulations that call out instinctive responses*

of his own appropriate to these gestures. He cries or laughs, he moves towards his mother, or stretches out his arms. When these gestures in others bring back the images of his own responses and their results, the child has the material out of which he builds up the social objects that form the most important part of his environment. ... If we assume that an object arises in consciousness though the merging of the imagery of experience of the response with that of the sensuous experience of the stimulation, it is evident that the child must merge the imagery of his past responses into the sensuous stimulation of what comes to him through distance senses. (Mead, *A Reader*, 2011, 55, own italics)

In accordance with his philosophical and psychological training and consistent with the *Zeitgeist* of his time, which saw in physics the model of scientific explanation, Mead in the above excerpt is using a descriptive language that can easily be misunderstood as behaviourist, hence also his depiction by some of his students as a social behaviourist.[6] However, a second closer reading shows that the process Mead is describing, while involving attention and imitation, is more significantly, about alternating sets of introjections and projections. In this regard, Mead explicitly refers to psychoanalysis. In the essay "The Objective Reality of Perspectives" (1926) he writes:

It [human intelligence] arises in those early stages of communication in which the organism arouses in itself the attitude of the other and so addresses itself and thus *becomes an object to itself, becomes in other words a self*, while the same sort of content in the act constitutes the other that constitutes the self. *Out of this process thought arises, i.e. conversation with one's self, in the role of the specific other and then in the role of the generalized other*, in the fashion I indicated above. It is important to recognize that the self does not project itself into the other. The others and the self arise in the social act together. The content of the act may be said to lie within the organism but it is projected into the other only in the sense in which it is projected into the self, a fact upon which the whole of psychoanalysis rests (199, own italics).

Thus the individual ends up internalizing a sense of identity, on the one hand, and an agency for self-observation, on the other hand. Mead refers to the former sense of self as "me" and to the latter as "I". According to Mead, there can be no self-observing agency, and by default no consciousness, without internalized social interaction.

Blumer (1969), who was instrumental in disseminating the work of Mead within social psychology in the United States,[7] assumed a more negative view of psychoanalysis, dismissing it along with mainstream psychology and sociology as a deterministic science that ignores the significance of interpretative frameworks and meaning in general:

Common to both of these fields [psychological and social science] is the tendency to treat human behaviour as the product of various factors that play upon human beings; concern is with the behaviour and with the factors regarded as producing them. Thus, psychologists turn to such factors as stimuli, attitudes, conscious or unconscious motives, various kinds of psychological inputs, perception and cognition, and various features of personal organization to account for given forms or instances of human conduct. In a similar fashion, sociologists rely on such factors as social position, status demands, social roles, cultural prescriptions, norms and values, social pressures and group affiliation to provide such explanations. In both such typical and sociological explanations the meanings of things for the human beings who are acting are either bypassed or swallowed up in the factors used to account for their behaviour. (Blumer 1969, 3)

It is quite ironic that a science like psychoanalysis that works mainly with interpretation should be rejected on deterministic grounds, yet this is one of those social facts that demonstrates quite succinctly the operation of social representations as studied by Moscovici

([1961] 2008) and later used by some of his students for explaining how social identities are constituted. A similar approach, albeit from the perspective of the sociology of knowledge, was followed by the social constructionists Berger and Luckmann (1967).

Moscovici was interested in how ideologies, myths and scientific theories are incorporated into our mental reference framework and how, in turn, they are used for guiding action by individuals and groups. His work was equally influenced by Emile Durkheim and Sigmund Freud. A seminal study by Moscovici ([1961] 2008) entitled *Psychoanalysis: Its Image and its Public* was concerned with the reception and representation of psychoanalysis in the French media and among French intellectuals and lay persons in the 1960s. Among else this study showed how psychoanalytic theories have been appropriated by different audiences and adapted to their needs – a process which in many contexts has contributed to the misinterpretation and/or vulgarization of psychoanalysis.

Moscovici's fastidious exploration of social representations[8] has provided some very interesting insights into the way consciousness "naturally" operates, or what he calls "natural thought". The latter deals rather economically with information, focuses on social relations and relies extensively on associations and inferences within a hierarchical system, which explains the diffusion of stereotypical thinking. This first-order cognitive system is to be distinguished from the second-order reflective meta-system, except that the latter is not always "switched-on". More than 50 years later Daniel Kahneman, a psychologist and winner of the Nobel Prize in Economics, published a book entitled *Thinking, Fast and Slow* (2011), summarizing experimental research that confirms the existence of this dual mode of thinking. This also explains why "argument is essentially constructive and rarely corrective" (Moscovici [1961] 2008, 170). Indeed, or so Moscovici, many social representations are determined by their conclusions, and it is this "primacy of the conclusion" that explains the strength of normative and ideological frameworks. The result is a form of concrete and at times infantile intelligence that is partial yet makes it possible for "a plurality of modes of thought [to] coexist within the same individual" (Moscovici [1961] 2008, 185). A couple of examples:

> "Complex", "unconscious" and "psychoanalysis" are terms that convey specific images and contexts, but they can also become part of everyday conversation, provided that they are relocated in a familiar world. In the course of one interview, we asked a worker if psychoanalysis had anything to do with politics. He found the question difficult. The dialogue seemed to have broken down. All at once, the interlocutor found a vital lead: psychoanalysis is a particular kind of conversation that induces behaviours. Politicians address citizens in speeches that are intended to influence their opinions. Our informant began to outline an answer: "In politics, you use every possible means. Speech means influence, so it's a form of psychoanalysis." The dialogue picked up again. (Moscovici [1961] 2008, 176)
>
> [Another interviewee reports]: "Communists are against psychoanalysis because it is an individualist and mystifying method that does not take social realities into account. It is also decadent: it decomposes individuals. The Pope condemned psychoanalysis, but I don't know much about that. It really cannot be applied to social problems. Social problems are group problems. Psychoanalysis is therapy for individuals. Applying individual discoveries to groups is a swindle. You can apply it in order to destroy the personality of people who get in the way. Imperialists rule over consciousness. You can compare it with the Nazis' methods. Is there a lot of talk about it? There is in France, in bourgeois and petty bourgeois circles. Not amongst the workers. It is being systematically popularized by the press and the papers, with the backing of the United States. In a word, psychoanalysis has made real discoveries about human behaviour: complexes for example. But when it comes to treatment, its whole approach has to change. You can't cure people by getting them to tell their dirty little secrets. That's charlatanism. We would be better off giving the unhinged good living conditions rather than psychoanalyzing them". (Moscovici [1961] 2008, 182)

Both these examples demonstrate yet another characteristic of concrete intelligence, namely its schizoid-paranoid character – and thus we are back to Melanie Klein's hypotheses about the development of infantile thought. Moscovici's conclusion:

> Is the cognitive system of social representations as we have described it because our reason conceals intellectual organizations belonging to a younger age? Or is it because it corresponds to a situation and a collective interaction to which it is adapted? At bottom one could show that there is no contradiction here.

Even though Moscovici tends to finds these findings disturbing he is intent on keeping up his scientific neutrality and on avoiding either pessimism or optimism. Individuals are not driven to apply their concrete intelligence "to any and every content". Rather, "the change of environment and its complexity – as well as the complexity of the subject – can reverse the order of these mechanisms" (189). What is nonetheless important to acknowledge, is that we are here confronted with a coexistence of cognitive systems or "a state of cognitive polyphasia" (190) even within one individual and definitely at societal level.

Using Moscovici's work and especially his emphasis on the mechanism of distortion that characterizes social representations, Tajfel and Turner (Tajfel and Turner [1979] 1986) defined social identity as linked to social categorizations used as self-references in and through comparisons:

> [Social categorizations] do not merely systematize the social world; they also provide a system of orientation for self-reference; they create and define the individual's place in society. Social groups, understood in this sense, provide their members with an identification of themselves in social terms. These identifications are to a very large extent relational and comparative: they define themselves as similar to or different from, as "better" or as "worse" than members of other groups. (16)

The key point about Tajfel's and Turner's social identity theory is the close link between identity and comparison. In other words, there is no social identity without comparisons – a conclusion that echoes, in my view, Freud's early thoughts about self-esteem in relation to group identity. Indeed, that social identity should be so dependent on comparisons also explains why in specific situations individuals may sacrifice individual or even group gains in order to maintain group distinctiveness, since this ultimately is what grants them self-esteem (Tajfel and Turner 1986, 19).

Tajfel's and Turner's social identity approach also relativizes the sociological understanding of status hierarchies and social change based on objective conditions: "Status is not considered here as a scarce resource or commodity; it is the outcome of intergroup comparison" (1986 [1979], 19). Taking social identity processes seriously into account allows a better understanding, or so Tafjel and Turner, of the emergence or not of social competition, the relative significance of individuation processes under different socio-political conditions, and the scope (and pitfalls) of identity politics.

Tajfel and Turner do not use the term identity politics since this was not common back in the 1970s when their work was first published. They instead talk about "social creativity" processes whereby groups "seek positive distinctiveness for the in-group by redefining or altering the elements of the comparative situation" (19–20). For instance, they may compare the in- and out-group on a different dimension; change the values assigned to specific attributes (e.g. "black is beautiful", "the new normal") or change the out-group with which comparisons are made. Evidently such "social creativity" in conjunction with real-life changes in terms of political rights or socio-economic position may result in the emergence of new, more inclusive, narratives, as when, say, black or homosexual identity is positively rather than negatively endowed. However, such shifts in values are no guarantee that the mechanisms underlying social identity and comparison no longer operate. More often than not, they are accompanied by less benevolent social creativity processes whereby a new out-group is found to serve as point of reference for aggressive comparisons or, even worse, as scapegoat. A good case in point is that of contemporary European identity, which is triumphant about its enlightened attitudes and liberal accomplishments while, at the same time, assuming an illiberal attitude towards refugees from the Middle East and Africa.

Conclusion

To conclude: The concept of identity has a long history across different scientific fields, notably psychoanalysis, social psychology and sociology. Overall, these discourses share a number of similarities despite their different areas of application and distinct terminologies. Indeed it could be shown that these disciplines have more often crossed paths than is usually assumed.

Both in individual and in group psychology identities are revealed as conglomerates of identifications that are used self-referentially in social relations. The mechanisms that bring about identities as revealed by the psychoanalytic method are projection and introjection. Those that that help sustain them as studied by the social psychological research on social representations are associational thinking within a hierarchical system of thought that is both concrete and normative, and rarely reflective. All these mechanisms are part of normal development and habitual thinking per se, however they may also display pathological offshoots leading to either individual psychopathology or social conflicts and disintegration.

That individual and social identity should be so close in terms of their underlying mechanisms also underscores the affinity and constant intermingling between conscious and unconscious processes as well as between infantile and adult emotional experiences and modes of thought.

Insofar as individual theories are concerned, it is not surprising that these should often be specialized, covering only particular aspects of the problem. Yet even at this level of abstract thinking it is possible to identify interesting omissions or mis-understandings of previous work, both within and outside one's own discipline – a fact that suggests that identity theory is itself "creative" in the social representational manner. It is to be hoped, that it nonetheless remains reflective.

Notes

1. On the use of "ph" to write "phantasy" cf. explanation of Isaaks (1948, 80):

    > The English translators of Freud adopted a special spelling of the word "phantasy", with the *ph*, in order to differentiate the psycho-analytic significance of the term, i.e. predominantly or entirely unconscious phantasies, from the popular word "fantasy" meaning conscious day-dreams, fictions and so on. The psycho-analytical term "phantasy" essentially connotes unconscious mental content, which may or may not become conscious.

2. Freud also talked about the ego as emerging out of the body-ego. If such unconscious phantasies are taken to be mental representations of instincts then this implies that they are innate. This remains a point of contestation within psychoanalysis. The debate here exhibits similarities

with that within the philosophy of the mind about the origin and nature of mental representations.

3. Learning from Experience is also the title of Wilfred Bion's book from 1962 on the subject of projective identification and how this helps builds our apparatus for thinking.

4. With regard to the positive aspects of identity, it is worth here recalling, the historical context that led to the latter's recognition. As Weigert (1983) notes,

> with the spread of social conflict attending the rise of civil rights and counter-cultural movements, the language of identity was generalized from clinical, socialization or radical contexts, and used positively by groups to legitimize their own claims to recognition, socially and legally. (202)

5. Brubaker et al. add that the representatives of either side of the debate are often not as one-sided as presented in the secondary literature. For instance, Geertz's primordialism was misunderstood:

> In the oft-cited but seldom closely analyzed formulation of Geertz, primordial attachments stem "from the givens" – or more precisely, as culture is inevitably involved in such matters, the assumed "givens" of social existence, including blood ties, religion, shared language and customs. In most discussions, this crucial distinction between perceived "givens" and actual "givens" is lost. Primordialists are depicted as analytical naturalizers rather than "analysts of naturalizers". (Weigert 1983, 49)

6. In his introduction to the 2011 collection of Mead's essays, his editor, Filipe Careira da Silva writes that Morris' "creative edition" of Mead's most known book *Mind, Self and Society*, which was first published posthumously, "goes as far as preventing the reader from knowing what were Mead's words and what were Morris's additions – 'social behaviorism', the label that later generations came to associate with Mead's social psychology, is actually Morris's term" (Mead, *A Reader*, 2011, Introduction, x).

7. In Europe, the work of Mead was disseminated through Jürgen Habermas, who relied on his theories to develop his theory of communicative action.

8. The 1961 study on psychoanalysis was based on interviews with 2265 subjects using both quantitative and qualitative questionnaires. Six groups were formed: (a) a representative population, (b) a middle-class population made up of people in industry artisans, office workers and housewives, (c) a professional population including teachers, doctors, lawyers, technicians and priests, (d) a working-class population that covered both skilled and unskilled workers, (e) a student population and (f) a population of pupils at technical schools. Moscovici was interested not only on how social class impacts on the perception and knowledge of psychoanalysis but also how the views of psychoanalysis are mediated by political ideologies and religion.

References

Berger, P. L., and T. Luckmann. 1967. *The Social Construction of Reality: A Treatise in the Sociology of Knowledge*. New York: Anchor Books.

Bilgrami, A. 2006. "Notes toward the Definition of 'Identity'." *Daedalus* 135 (4): 5–14.

Bion, W. R. (1961) 1989. *Experiences in Groups*. London: Karnac Books.

Bion, W. R. 1962. *Learning from Experience*. London: Karnac Books.

Blumer, H. 1969. *Symbolic Interactionism*. Berkeley: University of California Press.

Brubaker, R., M. Loveman, and P. Stamatov. 2004. "Ethnicity as Cognition." *Theory and Society* 33: 31–64. doi:10.1023/B:RYSO.0000021405.18890.63.

Erikson, E. H. 1950. *Childhood and Society*. New York: W. W. Norton & Company.

Freud, S. 1911. "Formulierungen über die zwei Prinzipien des psychischen Geschehens." *GW* VIII: 230–238.

Freud, S. 1914. "On Narcissism: An Introduction." The Standard Edition of the Complete Psychological Works of Sigmund Freud XIV: 67–102.

Freud, S. 1921. "Group Psychology and the Analysis of the Ego." *SE* XVIII: 65–143.

Freud, S. 1923. "The Ego and the id." *SE* XIX: 13–66.

Isaaks, S. 1948. "The Nature and Function of Phantasy." *International Journal of Psychoanalysis* 29: 73–97.

Kahneman, D. 2011. *Thinking, Fast and Slow*. New York: Farrar, Straus and Giroux.

Kernberg, O. F. 2006. "Identity: Recent Findings and Clinical Implications." *Psychoanalytic Quarterly,* 75: 969–1004. doi:10.1002/j.2167-4086.2006.tb00065.x.

Klein, M. (1935) 1998. "A Contribution to the Psychogenesis of Manic Depressive States." In *Love, Guilt and Reparation and Other Works 1921–1945*, edited by H. Segal, 262–289. London: Vintage.

Klein, M. (1946) 1998. "Notes on Some Schizoid Mechanisms." In *Envy and Gratitude and Other Works 1946–1963*, edited by H. Segal, 1–24. London: Vintage.

Klein, M. (1955) 1998. "On Identification." In *Envy and Gratitude and Other Works 1946–1963*, edited by H. Segal, 141–175. London: Vintage.

Kohut, H. 1977. *The Restoration of the Self*. New York: International Universities Press.

Mead, G. H. 1926. *The Objective Reality of Perspectives*. Edited by F. C. da Silva. London: Routledge.

Mead, G. H. 2011. *G.H. Mead: A Reader*. Edited by F. C. da Silva. London: Routledge.

Moscovici, S. (1961) 2008. *Psychoanalysis: Its Image and its Public*. Translated from the French by David Macey. Cambridge: Polity.

Pinker, S. 2012. *The Better Angels of Our Nature: Why Violence Has Declined*. New York: Penguin Books.

Tajfel, H., and J. C. Turner. 1986. "The Social Identity Theory of Inter-group Behavior." In *Psychology of Intergroup Relations*, edited by S. Worchel and L. W. Austin, 33–48. Chicago: Nelson Hall.

Victoroff, J. 2005. "The Mind of the Terrorist: A Review and Critique of Psychological Approaches." *The Journal of Conflict Resolution* 49 (1): 3–42.

Volkan, V. 2013. "Large-group-psychology in its Own Right: Large-group Identity and Peace-making." *International Journal of Psychoanalytic Studies* 10: 210–246.

Volkan, V., and G. Ast. 1994. *Spektrum des Narzißmus*. Göttingen: Vandenhoeck & Ruprecht.

Wallerstein, R. S. 2002. "The Growth and Transformation of American Ego Psychology." *Journal of the American Psychoanalytic Association* 50: 135–168.

Weigert, A. 1983. "Identity: Its Emergence within Sociological Psychology." *Symbolic Interaction* 6 (2): 183–206.

Knowledge, International Relations and the structure–agency debate: towards the concept of "epistemic selectivities"[†]

Alice B.M. Vadrot

CSaP Centre for Science and Policy, University of Cambridge, Cambridge, UK

The aim of this article is to develop a framework within which the role and social construction of knowledge in International Relations can be understood and theoretically underpinned. In order to do so, the article discusses post-structuralist and neo-Gramscian answers to the structure–agency debate and argues that the role of knowledge remains rather implicit in both understandings on how structure and agency are mutually constituted. The main argument of the article is that the social construction of knowledge can only be understood, if International Relations are analysed in terms of a dialectically constituted relationship between structure and agency visible in and through processes whereby science and expert knowledge are referred to as true and policy relevant. On this basis, the article develops the concept of "epistemic selectivities", which describes how the use of science and expert knowledge to underpin strategic action leads to hegemonic patterns in the way in which (scientific) expert knowledge is related to particular claims of policies and facts.

Introduction

Since early Greek thinking, knowledge has been the object of analysis and logic. In Plato's dialogue *Theatetus* Socrates asks Theatetus "What is knowledge? Can we answer that question?" (Plato 360 B.C.E., 143d–145e). Their dialogue first centres on the question whether knowledge is equitable with perception (151d–e). However, *inter alia* the difficulty in justifying that the subjective perception of an object could be generalized leads Socrates to reject this definition. Thereafter, Theatetus presents the definition of knowledge as "true belief" and finally both conclude that knowledge is a "true belief with an account" (201c–d), that is, a justified true belief, a definition commonly used to define knowledge today. Interestingly, this definition is put into perspective towards the end of the dialogue, where Socrates points to his observation that the attribution of knowledge or knowledge-ability is a social act that relates to power struggles and asymmetries between the rulers and the ruled in a particular social order. Those that (seem to) possess knowledge are seen as legitimate holders of power (Vadrot 2011).[1] Or, as Foucault has argued, knowing is controlling and controlling enables knowledge (1975).

[†]This article includes parts of my unpublished Ph.D. thesis "Understanding the establishment of the Intergovernmental Platform for Biodiversity and Ecosystem Services (IPBES): Epistemic Selectivities in International Biodiversity Politics", University of Vienna, 2013.

The way in which knowledge is or can be controlled or ordered is at the heart of ongoing debates on international science–policy interfaces such as the Intergovernmental Panel on Climate Change (IPCC) or the Intergovernmental Science-Policy Platform on Biodiversity and Ecosystem Services (IPBES). Both institutions produce regular policy-relevant assessments by combining the principles of scientific credibility and political consensus among their members, which are nation states. Understanding the role of these "hybrid" institutions in International Relations is a challenging task, not least because of inherent difficulties in separating knowledge production from politics and power.

One way to tackle the role of knowledge in International Relations is to look at the way in which "epistemic communities" emerge and enable the political recognition of a problem previously defined by the scientific communities. Epistemic Communities are defined as "a network of professionals with recognized expertize and competence in a particular domain and an authoritative claim to policy-relevant knowledge within that domain or issue area" (Haas 1992, 3). In this respect, the concept of "epistemic communities" tries to make sense of the observation that a group of scientists succeeds in transforming knowledge claims into a political agenda. However, and as Mai'a K. Davis Cross argues, "[t]he epistemic community literature thus far has focused too narrowly on scientists because of the misguided notion that scientific knowledge is somehow superior to other forms of knowledge". She suggests that "[…] the recognition and legitimation of expert knowledge is socially constructed […] in part [depending] on the integrity of the experts themselves, and also on whether or not they have reached consensus among themselves" (Cross 2013, 159). But, if knowledge is socially constructed, what are the mechanism underlying these processes and how can they be studied? Foucault would have argued that we have to look at "strategies of relations of forces supporting, and supported by, types of knowledge", a strategic apparatus, which

> permits of separating out from among all the statements which are possible those that will be acceptable within, I won't say a scientific theory, but a field of scientificity, and, which it is possible to say are true or false. (1980, 196 ff)

In other words, knowing is controlling and controlling knowing insofar as knowledge depends on discursive (and, as Foucault says, non-discursive) strategies delimiting the modes of justifying and legitimizing true beliefs within a particular field of scientificity.

What does this mean for our understanding of the international institutions interfacing science and policy and how can we analyse the role of actors in such institutional settings in relation to the discursive and non-discursive patterns, within which they act? Ultimately, and this is my main argument, the relation between knowledge and power depends on our understanding of how structure and agency interrelate.

This is particularly true if we want to understand how "new" phenomena such as the IPCC or the IPBES can be conceptualized and analysed in terms of the relation between power and knowledge. It has much to do with the ontological and epistemological conditions of studying International Relations. Understanding if and under what conditions knowledge can be related to the structure-and-agency debate provides a starting point for conceptualizing the role of knowledge in International Relations.

Before elaborating on this I will first retrace the structure-and-agency debate in International Relations studies and take a closer look at post-structuralist and neo-Gramscian approaches. I will argue that the role of knowledge remains rather implicit in both understandings on how structure and agency are mutually constituted and propose the concept of "epistemic selectivities" to overcome this gap. "Epistemic selectivities" describe how, in pursuing their interests, actors employ strategies that reflect both the politics knowledge and the policy knowledge they hold and the insight they have on the likeliness of particular forms and accounts of knowledge to be legitimized throughout the decision-making process. I will conclude by showing how clarifying the structure–agency problem can be used as an entry point to study the role of knowledge in International Relations, which ultimately leads to the theory of epistemic selectivity.

The structure–agency debate in and beyond International Relations[2]

Traditionally, political phenomena have been explained in two ways: Firstly, through the analysis of structural factors and secondly, in terms of agency factors. Structure "refers to the setting within which social, political and economic events occur and acquire meaning" (Hay 2002, 94). Agency is a form of political conduct implying a specific sense of choice, free will and autonomy. Whilst the concept of structure implies the assumption "that political behaviour tends to be ordered" in one way or another, the concept of agency implies the ability of actors to reflect upon their actions and the context within which they operate (Hay 2002, 94). The challenge, however, is to address the duality of structure and agency, that is, the relationship be-tween "the political actors we identify [...] and the environment in which they find themselves [...]" (Hay 2002, 89).

The structure-and-agency debate raises questions and provides answers to many aspects of politics in general and International Relations in particular. The most fundamental one is how activities of a nation state or of a network of actors, for example, a network of scientific experts, are defined by the structure of International Relations. Making an argument about the social construction of knowledge in this context and in terms of recognition and legitimisation processes taking place somewhere between the unit of analysis of the nation state and the structure of International Relations, is not trivial and significantly benefits from an ontological and epistemological underpinning. The reason for this is simple: What do I actually look at when I study the role of knowledge in International Relations? Is knowledge inherent in the "system" or is it located at the level of the units? As Waltz argues,

> [t]he problem [...] is to contrive a definition of structure free of the attributes and the inter-actions of units. Definitions of structure must leave aside, or abstract from, the characteristics of units, their behavior, and their interactions. Why must those obviously important matters be omitted? (1979, 79)

The logic of differentiating between unit and level is the same like the consequence of separating structure from agency. The state can be a structure as well as an actor in International Relations, depending on the level of analysis and the definition of its units. Waltz argues that related questions "must be omitted so that we can distinguish between variables at the level of the units and variables at the level of the system" (1979, 79). He, in a very pragmatic and simplistic way, reduces ontological and epistemological questions to the feasibility of studying these. Waltz assumes that the underlying structure, which may be framed better as "system", is constituted by the interaction of its units – that is, states – , a neorealist assumption that rests upon an overly simplified ontology of the state (e.g. Wendt 1987, 342). Whilst Waltz's attempts to connect patterns of state behaviour to the system-wide distribution of power were rejected by many scholars, his structural theory of International Relations was nonetheless used by many scholars of International Relations as a starting point for theorizing the relationship between structure and agency in International Relations (Wight 2006, 91). Even though the interpretations of Waltz's structural theory differ significantly, they all share the same conclusion, namely that Waltz, who derives his theory from microeconomics, conceptualizes system structure as emerging from the interaction of units, that is, of states (see note 1) (e.g. Dressler 1989; Wendt 1999; Hollis and Smith 1994). The reduction of agents to states,[3] perceived as a priori objects of the studies of International Relations, constitutes a major problem in this type of theory and has led to a more sophisticated understanding of the relationship between structure and agency in International Relations. Bieler and Morton (2001) give a good overview of the history of the debate in general. They describe the development of the debate as a two-phase process.

The early phase is characterized by the work of scholars such as Wendt, Dresser, Carlsnaes, and Hollis and Smith, who initiated the debate on structure and agency in International Relations (Carlsnaes 1992; Wendt 1987; Hollis and Smith 1994; Dessler 1989). Alexander Wendt is often referred to as the initiator of the structure–agency debate in International Relations theory. He has entrenched his approach of "structuration" in structural idealism. In his article: "The Agent-Structure Problem" (1987) he understands structure and agency as mutually constitutive. Hence, structure just exists in the present moment. This moment is in Wendt's view the moment of the appearance of social activity. In this respect Wendt's approach takes up the theory of structuration of Anthony Giddens. According to Giddens, these moments are defined as "structural moments", in which the duality of structure and the structural principles are mediated and become hence objects to be studied. "Structural moments" are those moments of social practice that visibly produce and reproduce structural principles. It constitutes the basis of the analysis of structures as through social activity and practice the structures are renewed and can be observed. In this respect, Wendt's approach draws on Gidden's theory of structuration – both Giddens and Wendt claim that structure and agency are two sides of the same coin.

The second phase is characterized by the assimilation of post-structuralist approaches, and general analyses concerning social theory and the structure–agency debate beyond International Relations (e.g. Doty 1997, 1999; Suganami 1999; Wight 1999).

Towards a post-structural understanding of the structure–agency problem[4]

According to Doty, earlier understandings of the structure–agency problem either prioritized structure in the sense of structural determinism or agency with regard to pre-given autonomous individual actors (Doty 1997, 366). She argues that the structure–agency problem is actually deeply entrenched in the philosophical foundations of post-structuralism and argues that structure and agency are the result of practices through which both are activated and reproduced (Doty 1997, 379). Practices are viewed as indeterminate and determined. They are indeterminate insofar as they have the potential to at least slightly modify structures and they are determinate insofar as practices rest upon the structures within which they appear and which make them effective (Doty 1997, 377). Effective insofar as practices that do not address structures do not have an impact on them and are thus not defined as practices.

This, at least, would be the reading of Judith Butler that, rather than talking about "practices", would refer to speech acts and performative utterances (Butler 1997). The idea, expressed differently, is that words have the ability to do things in the sense that they have the potential to activate and modify the structural or, as Butler would say, the embodied conditions within which they are used (1997, 237). This reference is important since it illustrates the notion of structure and agency in place in its post-structural interpretation that ultimately rests upon the role of signs and meaning in the production of the social (and the body, i.e. the physical). Similarly, Laclau and Mouffe (1985)[5] also conceptualize the way in which signs constitute meaning as reference points for addressing the structure-and-agency problem in post-structuralist terms (Scherrer 1995).

Whilst Doty succeeds in explaining "indeterminate determinism" (Wight 1999, 121) with regard to the argument that meaning constituted out of signs referring to other signs is always both indeterminate and determinate, she does not succeed in linking this argument back to the idea of practices (Doty 1997, 377). Indeed, and as Wight argues, Doty does not provide a definition of practices even though these are the anchor point of her argument that structure and agency are the effects of practices. She argues that "Practices, because of their inextricable link with meaning have an autonomy which cannot be reduced either to intentions, will, motivations, or interpretations of choice-making subjects or to constraints and enabling mechanisms of objective but socially constructed structures" (Doty 1997, 377). This is convincing, but again meaningless if practices as such are not defined, neither as speech acts not as face-to-face or day-to-day practices in the tradition of Anthony Giddens. For Giddens, these moments of social practices are conceptualized as the moments where either structure or agency becomes assessable from an outside perspective and where the reproduction of these takes place.

Another post-structuralist approach to structure and agency is developed by Hidemi Suganami, who argues that narratives need to be seen as factors that are constitutive of both agents and structures. She states "that an agent is that category of being concerning which a society constructs a narrative, presenting it to be capable of deliberate acts" (Suganami 1999, 379). In this sense, she argues, "'the agent' is narratively constituted". She concludes that "if agents are narratively constituted, so also is society" and hence, structures, agents and narratives shape one another in a complex relationship "where narratives, in turn, will encompass 'the remarkable trinity' of mechanistic processes, chance factors and deliberate actions" (Suganami 1999, 379). By contrast to Doty, Suganami does not refer to the role of meaning, but to the constitutive role of narratives in, mediating between structure and agency.

The post-structuralist "solution" to the structure-and-agency problem was profoundly criticized by Wight, who argued that in the end related approaches are based on a misunderstanding of the work of the authors of the first phase (Wight 1999, 121). Beyond the critique that Doty does not provide a convincing definition of practices, Wight challenges Doty's conclusion that scholars investigating the structure–agency problem finally have to decide whether structure or agency figures as point of departure for explaining and understanding society.

Towards a neo-Gramscian understanding

The third wave of scholars, as I would call it, is characterized by its attempt to tackle the structure–agency problem by questioning the problem as such, namely how can one demonstrate that structure and agency are mutually constitutive. In their critique of second wave approaches, Bieler and Morton follow the arguments provided by Wight (2006), but argue that "the intersubjective realm, indicated by Doty and Suganami, is important for the identity and interests of agents" and that this proposition is essential in the neo-Gramscian perspective of the structure–agency debate. Indeed, the "third wave" combines the structure–agency debate with the intersubjective realm and a neo-Gramscian theory of hegemonic dominance (e.g. Bieler and Morton 2001; Joseph 2008). Arguably, Bieler and Morton can be understood in this perspective: by emphasising the role of historical structures in combining agency and structure, Bieler and Morton's (2001) approach the issue in a different way than the authors mentioned above. They depart from a Gramscian understanding of the state as "the entire complex of practical and theoretical activities with which the ruling class not only justifies and maintains its dominance, but manages to win the active consent of those over them they rule" (Gramsci 1971, 244).

Hence, the state is a specific form of social relations through which capitalism and hegemony express themselves (Bieler and Morton 2003, 347). Hegemony operates on two levels, namely as construction process of the "historic block"[6] ensuring social cohesion within the state, and through the international expansion of a specific mode of production and the projection of hegemony at the international level (Bieler and Morton 2003, 350). With regard to the application of such an approach to the agency–structure problem they conclude that in such a perspective the problem cannot be solved. The input of the neo-Gramscian reading of the transformation model of society introduced by Bhaskar is to combine "a compatible understanding of structure resulting at least partly from actions in the past whilst acknowledging the possibility that social forces can choose among several available strategies" (Bieler and Morton 2001, 27).

The authors argue that a "historicist epistemology focuses on the unity of the subjective and the objective by understanding how structures confront people as part of objective social reality" (Bieler and Morton 2001, 17). For them the "objective" is equal to "the very deep level" where macro-structures such as the capitalist mode of production or feudalism are located. Bieler and Morton aim to bridge the gap between the "objective", that is, the macro-structures and the "subjective", that is, people's perceptions of the world. This is done through the introduction of the micro-level and the meso-level of structures. The meso-level introduced by Cox and Sinclair (1996) is defined as "the successive state of world order"; the micro-level is defined as "those structures instantiated through day-to-day interaction" (Bieler and Morton 2001, 26). This differentiation is a means of explaining the resilience and relative stability of structures and the inherent contingency anticipating transformation and change.

Whilst Bieler and Morton (2001) argue that the problem of agency–structure cannot be solved but only enrich(ed) (by) neo-Gramscian perspectives on International Relations, Joseph (2008) argues that a structural approach to hegemony coupled with the epistemological and ontological accounts of scientific realism makes it possible to define the intermediate stage between structure and agency in International Relations (Joseph 2008).

The constitutive idea of scientific realism goes back to the transcendental approach of Kant, picked up by Roy Bhaskar, based on the question: "What must be the case for knowledge to be possible?" (Wight 2006, 23). This question lies at the heart of a realist theory of science that constitutes the basis for critical realism and a critical realist understanding of structure and agency (Bhaskar 1975). Bhaskar's transformational model of social activities is based on this assumption; it posits that social structures are both a precondition for social activities and a product of these activities. Bhaskar also argues that social structures depend on concept, activity, and temporal and spatial elements. Whilst agents potentially act intentionally in one way or the other, they always – and this unintentionally – reproduce social structures and contribute to their manifestation, by which they in turn constitute actors (Bhaskar 1975). In this respect, structure is a precondition for social activity and, at the same time, its reproduced outcome. In other words, since human knowledge, social practices, and events are intelligible, the social world is ordered and structured in a way that is both open to investigation and relatively enduring over time (Joseph 2008, 115).

According to Joseph, hegemony is "located within structural conditions that define its possibilities and the possibilities of the relevant agents and their projects" (2008, 115). His approach is informed by the groundings of scientific realism and the transformational

model of society introduced by Roy Bhaskar. The reason for introducing the transformational model of society is the attempt to conceptualize the possibility of transformative
action, that is, of social activities that do not just reproduce, but also transform the
context and structures within and through which they act.

Joseph argues that such transformations relate to actions in the struggle for hegemony
that take place in the context of structural crisis "when the unconscious process of social
reproduction is thrown into question and agents become more conscious of the situation
confronting them and the possibilities open to them" (2008, 119). In turn, this awareness
of some of these social actors leads to the resistance of other actors who wish to maintain
those existing structures that potentially favour the realization of their own strategies over
the strategies of the other actors. For Joseph, this process designates hegemonic struggles,
as these are struggles for either the conservation or transformation of structures. He
deduces that "[h]egemony here represents the political moment in the process of structural
reproduction" and concludes that "hegemony becomes a mediating factor between the
reproduction of structures and conscious efforts to transform or prevent the transformation
of structures" (Joseph 2008, 120). Hence, Joseph both conceptualizes hegemony as an
intermediate between structure and agency and as a level of analysis to assess the interrelation between them, and consequently considers that hegemony provides the key for
resolving the structure–agency problem – interpreting the manifestation of hegemony as
a "concrete contingent outcome of these different causal powers" (Joseph 2008, 120).

From my point of view, hegemony, as described by Joseph, is congruent with what
Foucault described in terms of "strategic apparatus", which "permits of separating out
from among all the statements which are possible those that will be acceptable within,
[…] a field of scientificity, and, which it is possible to say are true or false" (Foucault
1980, 197). Hegemony is the result of and the condition under which knowledge
emerges. However, such an understanding tends to favour structure over agency. Instead
of focusing on hegemony or on practices, as Doty suggest, I propose to look at the strategic
and selective elements involved in both, structure and agency. In the following, I will refer
to the work of Jessop and Hay and their strategic-relational approach to set the basis for my
concept of "epistemic selectivities".

Towards the concept of epistemic selectivities

Jessop develops the concept of "strategic selectivities" to address the problem of structure
and agency (1990). His approach provides a tool for the analysis of the strategic contexts
within which action takes place. Strategic contexts anticipate various options for acting and
define the framework within which specific actors opt for specific actions that in turn
impact on the strategic selectivities of specific social structures (Jessop 2010, 11). On
the basis of his previous work, Jessop and others develop an approach that combines critical political economy and critical semiotic analysis, that is, the cultural political economy
that takes into account critical discourse analysis in the tradition of Fairclough (Jessop
2004a, 2004b, 2004c, 2007; Jessop and Sum 2001). By developing the constructivist insti-
tutionalist approach in his earlier work Hay proposed the concept of discursive selectivity
by bringing together structure, agency and discourse (2002). Whilst Jessop underlines that
the contexts and structures are strategically selective, Hay argues that "access to the context
itself is discursively mediated" and institutionally reflected (2002, 382). Hence, as individual knowledge and understanding of the context, the context within which actors form their
interests and their strategy is discursively mediated (Hay 2002, 282). The specific understanding of a context determines the set of alternatives out of which actors choose their

strategy and can amount to a "systematic misinterpretation of the context in question" (Hay 2002, 382). In this respect, discursive selectivity is conceptualized as a mechanism determining the information and knowledge that actors have at a given point about the context within which they act and about the possibilities of realizing their intentions. This knowledge is partial, but potentially increasing. Hay shares the idea of Jessop that actors are likely to adapt their strategies in a reflexive process including the context and their position within this context:

> Thus for instance, policy makers typically conceptualise the policy-making environment through the lens of a particular policy paradigm – such as Keynesian or monetarist economics. Once again, access to the context itself is discursively mediated. How actors behave – the strategies they consider in the first place, the strategies they deploy in the final instance and the policies they formulate – reflect their understanding of the context within which they act. Moreover, that understanding may eliminate a whole range of realistic alternatives and may, in fact, prove over time to be a systematic misinterpretation of the context in question. (Hay 2002, 382)

In order to relate the ideational to the material, or in other words, to integrate the notion of discourse somewhere in between structure and agency, Hay argues that the continuance of narratives, ideas, and paradigms rests upon the resonance with the direct and mediated experiences of actors, along with the underlying and resulting relatively stable cognitive templates through which actors understand and interpret the world. Whilst the strategic selectivity of the context favours some strategies over others, the discursive selectivity of the context selects, but never determines, those discourses and narratives through which the context might be appropriated by actors. For Hay and for Jessop the context is both strategically and discursively selective. According to Jessop, the ideas presented by Hay anticipate "the significance of the discursive turn in the strategic-relational approach [that] lies in its ontological, epistemological and methodological implications for the development of the strategic-relational approach as a whole" (Jessop, Fairclough, and Wodak 2008, 50). For Jessop, this turn highlights the ontological importance of semiosis in the analysis of selectivity and selective action, and the challenge of combining discursive and material concerns.

Hence, the concepts of strategic and discursive selectivities are an important step to clarify the way in which different actors act in a particular discursively and non-discursively mediated context that is defined by a dialectical interrelation between structure and the agency. They explain how specific actors choose specific strategies, namely in light of the knowledge they hold on the context within which they act. Such knowledge is knowledge about both the political context, within which actors act, and about the likeliness of success of certain strategies in light of the material and non-material resources actors have or are expected to have. In this respect, structure and agency relate to each other in strategic and epistemic terms, re-producing patterns of hegemony in the way in which knowledge about politics and policy is influencing strategic political action. This is why it is not enough to look at practices and narratives. Knowledge is not always embodied; it is dialectically mediated, situated between structure and agency as a constituting part of strategic selectivity.

In other words, knowledge emerges from the expectations about the suitability of particular strategies. The suitability is not only depending on the actors' knowledge about the political context, but rests as well on the insight on the hegemonic patterns that constitute the policy field. This, in turn, includes the science and expert knowledge, which is used to justify certain factual information and political claims. However, the insight on hegemonic patterns is always partial, and the reference to science and expert knowledge used to underpin political strategies and political decision-making is not just strategic, but selective as well. This is the reason for introducing the concept of "epistemic selectivities".

Epistemic selectivities leads to hegemonic patterns of defining a specific political problem in terms of content and importance by strategies based on the use of science and expert knowledge. Knowledge is used to justify particular problem solutions, to delegitimize alternative pathways, and to enforce arguments for future directions of scientific research, research funding, and science advice.

To summarize "*epistemic selectivities* are those mechanisms in political institutions that favour specific forms of knowledge, problem perceptions, and narratives over others" (emphasis in the original) (Brand and Vadrot 2013, 207; Vadrot 2014a, 2014b, 76). The idea of epistemic selectivities assumes that specific patterns of selectivity lead to the domination of specific forms of knowledge and the related contents, problem perceptions, and narratives over other knowledge and contents. This power of definition then stabilizes the governance of the understanding and the assessment of the object to be governed. An important step towards stabilization is the manifestation of such knowledge, perceptions and narratives in the form of institutions, and in the shape of what actors expect from the establishment of specific institutions (Brand and Vadrot 2013; Vadrot 2013a; 2014a, 2014b).

Conclusion

The aim of this article was to conceptualize the role of knowledge in International Relations. I was starting my argumentation with reference to Plato, who showed that knowledge is more than just perception and that in the end knowledge cannot be seen as independent from social order and political power. Then, I was referring to the recent debates on intergovernmental institutions aligning science to policy. I was arguing that such phenomena necessitate a new conceptualization of knowledge in International Relations that goes beyond the concept of "epistemic communities". I do agree with current attempts to enlarge the "epistemic communities" concept with the assumption that knowledge is socially constructed, but I am not convinced of the way in which social construction is understood and how this understanding can be used as a starting point to understand the role of knowledge in International Relations. This is why I propose to go back to the structure-and-agency debate for a better understanding of the relationship between the states and the international system on an abstract level.

I was looking at the way in which the structure-and-agency problem was addressed in International Relations theory in the 1980s and 1990s in a more systematic way. By discussing post-structuralist and neo-Gramscian approaches, I shed light on the necessity for paying attention to the concepts of power and hegemony. The struggle for hegemony, which is mediating between structure and agency, is, however, related to the conditions for successful strategic action. In order to better understand the role of knowledge in this process, I argue that knowledge emerges from expectations of actors related to the strategies they use to pursue certain political interests. The development of expectations and the selection of related strategies depend on two types of knowledge. Firstly, the type of knowledge actors dispose on the political context within which they act, and, secondly, the knowledge they dispose on the policies constituting a particular policy field. This kind of knowledge can be defined in terms of the selective insight actors have on the hegemonic patterns constituting a policy field, which includes science and expert knowledge. The reference to and the use of science and expert knowledge in the development and implementation of strategic action is always partial and selective. In this regard social constructions of knowledge result from acts of justification and legitimisation at the intersection between scientific knowledge, policies and politics, which is particularly true and visible in institutions interfacing science and policy at the international scale. This leads to epistemological consequences: The analysis of International Relations requires a focus on the dialectically constituted relationship between structure and agency. This relation becomes manifest in and through processes that distinguish between science and expert knowledge considered as true and policy relevant and exclude other forms and contents of knowledge as wrong and/or irrelevant. In other words, knowledge depends on strategies delimiting the modes of justifying and legitimizing true beliefs within a particular policy field.

In this regard, we can talk about "epistemic selectivities", when the use of science and expert knowledge to underpin strategic action leads to hegemonic patterns in the way in which (scientific) expert knowledge is related to particular claims of policies and facts. Hegemony occurs in the understanding and the communication of a political problem, and, furthermore, in the justification of particular problem solutions. This, in turn, delegitimizes alternative pathways, and defines the future directions of scientific research, research funding and science advice. If such processes take place in institutional science–policy interfaces, this creates subsequently selectivities that delimit the success of certain strategies in the context of both policy-making and the development of science and research.

Funding

This work was supported by the Austrian Science Fund.

Notes

1. In the hour of danger, when they are in perils of war, or of the sea, or of sickness, do they not look up to their commanders as if they were gods, and expect salvation from them, only because they excel them in knowledge? Is not the world full of men in their several employments, who are looking for teachers and rulers of themselves and of the animals? And there are plenty who think that they are able to teach and able to rule. Now, in all this is implied that ignorance and wisdom exist among them, least in their own opinion. (Plato 360 B.C.E.)
2. The following section is composed of unpublished parts of my Ph.D. thesis at the University of Vienna "Understanding the establishment of the Intergovernmental Platform for Biodiversity and Ecosystem Services (IPBES): Epistemic Selectivities in International Biodiversity Politics" (Vadrot 2013b). Earlier ideas related to the concept of "epistemic selectivities" were published in 2010, 2013, and 2014. See bibliography.
3. Agents in Waltz's logic may better be defined as units.
4. A very condensed version of this issue was published in my book *The Politics of Knowledge and Global Biodiversity* (2014) as part of chapter 2.2.
5. Laclau and Mouffe start from the assumption that meaning is never fixed and that thus it is important to study the means by which ideas and social practices acquire meaning. For them, all practices and objects are discursive as they acquire meaning if, and only if, they are articulated in particular discourses and with reference to momentously fixed meanings and understanding of the object in a particular configuration within time and space (Laclau and Mouffe 1985).
6. The historic bloc in the tradition of Gramsci is conceived as assemblage of social forces that builds the basis of consent to the way in which society is ordered by means of providing the ideological superstructure that creates and maintenance social relations (of production).

References

Bhaskar, R. 1975. *A Realist Theory of Science [RTS]*. Leeds: Leeds Books.

Bieler, A., and A. D. Morton. 2001. "The Gordian Knot of Agency-Structure in International Relations: A Neo-Gramscian Perspective." *European Journal of International Relations* 7 (1): 5–35.

Bieler, A. and A. D. Morton. 2003. "Globalisation, the State and Class Struggle: a 'Critical Economy' Engagement with Open Marxism." *The British Journal of Politics & International Relations* 5: 467–499.

Brand, U., and A. B. M. Vadrot. 2013. "Epistemic Selectivities Towards the Valorization of Nature in the Nagoya Protocol and the Making of the Intergovernmental Science-Policy Platform on Biodiversity and Ecosystem Services (IPBES)." *LEAD – Law, Environment and Development Journal* 9 (2): 202–222.

Butler, J. P. 1997. *Excitable Speech: a Politics of the Performative*. London: Routledge.

Carlsnaes, W. 1992. "The Agency-Structure Problem in Foreign Policy Analysis." *International Studies Quarterly* 36: 245–270.

Cox, R., and T. J. Sinclair. 1996. *Approaches to World Order*. Cambridge: Cambridge University Press.

Cross, M. K. D. 2013. "Rethinking Epistemic Communities Twenty Years Later." *Review of International Studies* 39: 137–160.

Dessler, D. 1989. "What's at Stake in the Structure-agency Debate." *International Organization* 3: 441–473.

Doty, R. L. 1997. "Aporia: A Critical Exploration of the Agent-Structure Problematique in International Relations Theory." *European Journal of International Relations* 3 (3): 365–392.

Doty, R. L. 1999. "A Reply to Colin Wight." *European Journal of International Relations* 5 (3): 387–390.

Foucault, M. 1975. *Surveiller et Punir*. Paris: Gallimard.

Foucault, M. 1980. *Power/Knowledge: Selected Interviews and Other Writings 1972–1977*. London: Harvester.

Gramsci, A. 1971. *Selection from the Prison Notebooks*. Edited and translated by Quintin Hoare and Geoffrey-Nowell Smith. London: Lawrence and Wishart.

Haas, P. M. 1992. "Introduction. Epistemic Communities and International Policy Coordination." *International Organization* 46 (1): 1–35.

Hay, C. 2002. *Political Analysis: Contemporary Controversies: A Critical Introduction*. New York: Palgrave Macmillan.

Hollis, M., and S. Smith. 1994. "Two Stories About Structure and Agency." *International Studies* 20 (3): 241–251.

Jessop, B. 1990. *State Theory. Putting the Capitalist State in its Place*. Cambridge: Polity Press.

Jessop, B. 2004a. "Beyond Developmental States: A Regulationist and State-Theoretical Analysis." In *Asian States: Beyond the Developmental Perspective*, edited by R. Boyd, and W. Ngo, 19–42. London: Routledge.

Jessop, B. 2004b. "Critical Semiotic Analysis and Cultural Political Economy." *Critical Discourse Studies* 1 (2): 159–174.

Jessop, B. 2004c. "Institutional (Re) turns and the Strategic-Relational Approach." In *Governing Local and Regional Economies: Institutions, Politics and Economic Development*, edited by A. Wood, and D. Valler, 23–56. Aldershot: Ashgate.

Jessop, B. 2007. *State Power: A Strategic-Relational Approach*. Cambridge: Polity.

Jessop, B. 2010. "Cultural Political Economy and Critical Policy Studies." *Critical Policy Studies* 3 (3–4): 336–356.

Jessop, B., N. Fairclough, and R. Wodak. 2008. *The Knowledge-based Economy and Higher Education in Europe*. London: Sense.

Jessop, B., and N. L. Sum. 2001. "Pre-Disciplinary and Post-Disciplinary Perspectives in Political Economy." *New Political Economy* 6 (1): 89–101.

Joseph, J. 2008. "Hegemony and the Structure-Agency Problem." *Review of International Studies* 34 (1): 109–128.

Laclau, E., and C. Mouffe. 1985. *Hegemony and Socialist Strategy. Towards a Radical Democratic Politics*. London: Verso.

Scherrer, C. 1995. "Eine diskursanalytische Kritik der Regulationstheorie." *Prokla* 25 (3): 457–482.

Suganami, H. 1999. "Agents, Structures, Narratives." *European Journal of International Relations* 5 (3): 365–386.

Vadrot, A. B. M. 2011. "Reflections on MODE 3, the Coevolution of Knowledge and Innovation Systems and How It Relates to Sustainable Development. Conceptual Framework for "Epistemic Governance." *International Journal for Social Ecology and Sustainable Development* 2 (2): 44–52.

Vadrot, A. B. M. 2013a. "Epistemische Selektivitäten im Institutionalisierungsprozess der Inter-governmental Platform for Biodiversity and Ecosystem Services: Die Rolle von Wissen und Wissenschaft." In *Conference Proceedings of Biodiversity and Society. Societal Dimensions of the Conservation and Utilization of Biological Diversity*, edited by J. Friedrich, A. Halsband, and L. Minkmar, 99–119. Goettingen: Goettingen University Press.

Vadrot, A. B. M. 2013b. "Understanding the Establishment of the Intergovernmental Platform for Biodiversity and Ecosystem Services (IPBES): Epistemic Selectivities in International Biodiversity Politics." Unpublished PhD thesis, Vienna, University of Vienna.

Vadrot, A. B. M. 2014a. "The Epistemic and Strategic Dimension of the Establishment of the IPBES: Epistemic Selectivities at Work." *Innovation-The European Journal for Social Science Research* 27 (4): 361–378.

Vadrot, A. B. M. 2014b. *The Politics of Knowledge and Global Biodiversity.* London: Routledge.

Waltz, K. N. 1979. *Theory of International Politics.* Reading, MA: Addison-Wessley.

Wendt, A. E. 1987. "The Agent-Structure Problem in International Relations Theory." *International Organization* 41 (3): 335–370.

Wendt, A. 1999. *Social Theory of International Relations.* Cambridge: Cambridge University Press.

Wight, C. 1999. "They Shoot Dead Horses, don't they? Locating Agency in the Agent-Structure Problematique." *European Jounral of International Relations* 5: 109–142.

Wight, C. 2006. *Agents, Structures and International Relations.* Cambridge: Cambridge University Press.

The creative economy: invention of a global orthodoxy

Philip Schlesinger

Centre for Cultural Policy Research, University of Glasgow, Glasgow, UK

This essay considers how policy thinking about culture has been steadily transformed into an overwhelmingly economic subject matter whose central trope is the "creative economy". The development of current ideas and their background are discussed. Policy ideas first fully developed in the UK have had a global resonance: the illustrative examples of the European Union and the United Nations are discussed. The embedding of creative economy thinking in British cultural institutions such as the BBC and cultural support bodies is illustrated. The impact of current orthodoxy on academic institutions and research is also considered. Countervailing trends are weak. New thinking is now required.

Introduction

In reflections on different forms of academic writing, the philosopher Vilém Flusser (2002, 194) remarked that the "essay is not merely the articulation of a thought, but of a thought as a point of departure for a committed existence". The virtues of this particular style of expression greatly appeal to me for present purposes, which involve the somewhat dogged pursuit of an argument because it matters greatly. Flusser counter-posed this style of argument to what he called the "academicism" of the treatise, which claimed the qualities of rigour and detachment. Were he one of our contemporaries writing about the creative economy, he would probably inveigh against the fetishism of "evidence-led policy", which has been key to the discourse I shall describe here.

This piece is less essayistic than I would wish. It pays obeisance to the need to document the case in ways that befit this 30th anniversary contribution to *Innovation* and naturally, it must be referenced, as the detail will be unfamiliar to many readers. The slightly polemical tone is a necessary antidote to scholasticism and mealy-mouthed approval. I have been increasingly struck by how difficult it is *not* to talk approvingly and largely uncritically about the "creative industries" and the "creative economy". These tropes presently dominate policy debate and media discussion about culture. This discursive dominance has become both a conceptual and practical obstacle to thinking afresh and in the round about culture and the complexity of cultural work in the digital age. In short, I would contend that the idea of the creative economy has increasingly obscured and crowded out conceptions of culture that are not in some way subordinate to economic considerations. Intelligent policy-makers and smart government advisers know that this is so and that their evidence rests on uncertain ground – at least, that is what they tell me privately. What figures in such conversations does not, on the whole, enter the public domain because the expedient argument that turns culture into economic value is seen as the only really comprehensible and sellable formula in our times. That is one of my conclusions from empirical research on and engagement in this topic.

The cultural analyst, George Yúdice, has described how a particular version of what he terms the "expediency of culture" has come to dominate public discourse and key institutions, both global and national. The state's interest in culture, he argues, is presently legitimized by instrumental and utilitarian arguments. First, he contends, this is due to the scale of migration in a globalized world: this has rendered problematic "the use of culture as a national expedient" through which a common value system for a citizenry might be built. Second, he suggests that in the USA the end of Cold War ideological competition led to the withdrawal of much public subvention for the arts. A rapid shift ensued to "an expanded conception of culture that can solve problems, including job creation. … Because almost all actors in the cultural sphere have latched onto this strategy, culture is no longer experienced, valued, or understood as transcendent". This means that "artists are being channeled to manage the social" and have become the focus of a specialized couche of "managerial professionals" (Yúdice 2003, 11–12).[1]

That expert grouping includes not only cultural bureaucrats but also academics, as I can testify. Over the past couple of decades, I have been deeply involved, over considerable periods of time, as a board member or adviser in the work of several bodies in the UK concerned with culture and media.[2] That experience has reinforced my view that in the field of cultural policy the pragmatic adaptation to ruling ideas – conformity often without conviction, if you like – is a functional and highly serviceable equivalent to committed belief.

Because this article is anatomizing a resilient ideology, in all probability it will be cited by similar-minded critics but ignored where it really counts – namely, by those with the greatest power to frame strategies and practices in cultural policy. That is an observation and certainly not a complaint, as we can and do make choices about the spaces we occupy in an "intellectual field" – to use Pierre Bourdieu's phrase – and these decisions duly shape the strategies that we then pursue. As with earlier pieces that I have written on this theme (Schlesinger 2007, 2009, 2013), I know that the central argument will bounce off the resilient carapace of creative economy adherents' belief system. The same may be said for the related work of like-minded critical colleagues internationally (Bustamante 2011). There is indeed a "counter-discourse" (Vötsch and Weiskopf 2009) that critiques the assumptions and blind spots of creative economy thinking but although of analytical importance, this has not influenced the juggernaut's seemingly inexorable progress. To be ignored in these matters, then, perhaps confers a perverse badge of honour. It is not that interested and contending parties cannot quite politely and even amicably discuss their different perspectives. It is, rather, that when it comes to the public projection of argument and analysis, there is no great meeting of minds. Rather, there is an increasing tendency for contending views to become self-sustaining and self-contained.

This is not the place for a detailed deconstruction of the different forms of discourse that substantiate these contentions. In an imperfectly realized essay such as this, one may let the contention stand and offer passing illustration rather than seek to provide exhaustive demonstration. If we take recent academic compilations of work in the field as an indication of the existence of different camps gathered under distinct conceptual banners, these offer a useful marker of, for instance, the divergence between advocates of the *"creative* economy" and proponents of the *"cultural* economy" (Jones, Lorenzen, and Sapsed 2015; Oakley and O'Connor 2015). For the latter, rallying round this term may offer an alternative starting point for those opposed to the economization of culture.

The politics of recent discourse

The origins of the discourse of the creative economy are indeed political, *sensu stricto*, because it is positions taken by governments that have most often have been the prime movers of this kind of perspective. Given its reproductive character, much of the discourse itself falls into another specific, subordinate, category, namely the expert domain of policy-making and practical implementation (Maasen and Weingart 2005).

Both official and expert discourses that find their way into reports, parliamentary debate and academic works in the cultural field are commonly recycled rather uncritically by media reports, taken seriously by not a few academics seeking funding, and most consequentially, become embedded in the practice of intermediary bodies acting in, and on, the cultural field. This incorporation into thought and practice takes place at various, interconnected, levels of the global system: in world bodies such as the United Nations (notably, UNESCO); inside regional entities such as the European Union (EU); and, of course, within states.

To understand how a particular form of political discourse is fashioned and disseminated, we need to explain its conditions of existence – in particular, the agency of the producers, the material and symbolic means at their disposal and the interests that they pursue. We may think of such discourses as situated within intellectual fields that are constituted as spaces of contestation: loci in which strategies are pursued by given groups and individuals by way of contention in argument, the provision of evidence and the fashioning of symbolic representations, and also in respect of fierce competition for public attention and the quest to secure positions of influence in government and public bodies.

What Bourdieu (1993) calls the "cycle of consecration" – the development of reputation, if you like – is quite distinctive when it comes to selling policy. It is different, for instance, from creating demand for an artwork or artist. Rather, it is a matter of flooding the market with an ideology so as to crowd out or marginalize alternatives. To establish and defend such symbolic capital requires continual effort in securing the dominance of a given set of definitions. It is the need for such continuous action to secure definitional advantage that explains the repetitive (if continually modified) discursive production in the field.

If the struggle to command attention and, with it, the desire to occupy the commanding heights of credibility, is central to the pursuit of argument in the politics of policy, the distribution of resources to prepare discursive strategies is of key importance in how well it equips antagonists to perform in the public domain.

The structural advantage in framing policies often (but not invariably) lies with official and expert sources, which tend to peddle a rather simple storyline when it comes to presenting accounts prefabricated for media reporting. Typically, the UK Government's *Creative industries economic estimates 2015* told us that one in 12 UK jobs was in the creative economy and that the creative industries accounted for 5.6% of total employment and also 5% of the UK economy's turnover (DCMS 2015, 4). This became headline news – and more importantly, common sense.

If we restrict ourselves to considering only policy outputs that appear in the public domain, we end up failing to recognise that *sub rosa* there has already been considerable lobbying and manoeuvring within a policy community to favour given options. Seemingly authoritative pronouncements are commonly the outcome of a hidden process of selection and elaboration inside government and related policy elites. Hidden, because it is largely conducted behind the scenes. But that does not mean it is secret. Such dealings can sometimes be reconstructed by way of research (Schlesinger 2009).

The creative turn

How did the so-called creative turn become so pervasive? And what *is* the "creative economy" supposed to be?

The tale could be told in several ways. One illustrative account goes as follows. It was the marketing of the term the "creative industries" in 1997–1998 by the first British New Labour government, led by Prime Minister Tony Blair, which firmly put this trope on the national agenda. Then, as the ideas caught on beyond the UK, they shifted by stages onto the global plane. Creative industries discourse was developed as a political-economic project in the Department for Culture, Media, and Sport (DCMS) by the team around Chris Smith, New Labour Secretary of State for that ministry. Expertise provided by think tanks, policy advisers and industry figures contributed significantly to shaping the policy process (Hesmondhalgh et al. 2015).

The socio-linguist Norman Fairclough (2000, 22–23) has shown how "assumptions about the global economy' led to an emphasis on competition between Britain and other countries", a "project of renewal designed to improve Britain's competitive position". In the UK, this framework has remained in place, irrespective of the government in power.

Thus, contrary to the view that the intellectuals are at best a marginal force in our society – that they have become mere "interpreters", rather than "legislators" in the terms espoused by Bauman (1992) – there is plainly a public policy intelligentsia eager to shape the world of cultural policy through discourse and action. The production of discourse and related policy proposals has now continued for some two decades in the UK and not only there, because ideas have circulated globally through policy spaces and institutions, and moreover, become increasingly embedded in academic research and teaching internationally.

Reflecting in retrospect, former UK Culture Secretary Chris Smith (2013) – himself part of the policy intelligentsia – has remarked:

> In 1998 – as secretary of state for culture, media and sport in the newly-elected Labour government – I published a book, *Creative Britain*. In it, I argued that the arts were for everyone, not just the privileged few; and that the creative industries – dependent for their success on individual artistic creativity – had moved from the fringes to the centre of the UK economy, with huge benefits for the social and economic health of the nation. I called for the nurturing and celebration of creative talent to be at the heart of the political agenda.

This quotation – reflecting afterthoughts some 15 years on – encapsulates the essentials of the creative economy belief system.

It was not Smith's book, however, that became the original keystone of the discourse. Looking back, it is striking just how much an expediently written policy paper came to exert an exceptional influence in generating an initial framework for discussion. The UK DCMS' definition of the creative industries in the very first *Creative Industries Mapping Document* has been cited copiously not only in the Anglosphere but everywhere:

> Those activities which have their origin in individual creativity, skill and talent and which have a potential for wealth and job creation through the generation and exploitation of intellectual property. (1998, 3)

The key move was to *aggregate* 13 distinct fields of cultural practice, to *designate* these as "industries", and so to *constitute* a new policy object whose central purpose was – and remains – to "maximise economic impact … at home and abroad". Moreover, by making the exploitation of intellectual property so crucial, the complexity of cultural value was subordinated to economic value.

Some have denounced this approach as the acme of neo-liberalism – understood in this instance as the celebration of individualistic entrepreneurship in a free market. As a corrective, in their definitive new book on New Labour cultural policy, Hesmondhalgh et al. (2015) have rightly pointed to wider objectives pursued by the British *creativistas* – the boost to arts spending, the attempts at social inclusion, the educational aspirations. The question, perhaps, is how much these other goals have truly acted as counterweights to the centrality of economics.

Naturally, the "creative turn" had antecedents. One influential interpretation of the history of pertinent ideas suggests that the conceptual journey started with the "*culture* industry" of mass communication critiqued by Horkheimer and Adorno (1997 [1944]). Subsequently, this approach was reformulated by figures such as Garnham (1990 [1984]) in Britain and Miège (2004 [1984]) in France, who developed a Marxist political economy of the "cultural *industries*" (to which media were central). The political economization of culture became the intellectual basis for cultural industries policies pursued by left-wing policy-makers as one response to urban decline and de-industrialization, and also in some instances (notably in France) as part of the struggle to secure necessary material conditions for combatting cultural imperialism (Mattelart, Delcourt, and Mattelart 1983). Later, New Labour recoded these concerns in their "*creative* industries" trope. Ever since, that particular formulation has been used incessantly and widely, irrespective of the political colour of its protagonists or indeed, the nature of their political regime.

Creative industries thinking became a kind of blueprint to be applied or modified. Read the official and academic literature and you will find that the number and type of "industries" may – and do – vary from one country to another. And then, at times, the "cultural industries" may be carefully distinguished from "creative industries", with culture often depicted as more fundamental or at the core of a society's symbolic production (The Work Foundation 2007). What, however, remains common and largely undisturbed is the overall strategy pursued by many states: namely, to construct the creative industries and latterly, the "creative economy", as a policy object that can be managed to secure primarily economic and sometimes social outcomes so as to increase competitiveness.

The economization of national culture is a globally attractive proposition. Any nation can adopt it and policy transfer has proven relatively easy. The creative industries idea is protean and can be readily indigenized to fit local circumstances. It can become the official policy of the Chinese Communist Party or a development ideology espoused by the United Nations (Keane 2007; United Nations 2013). It can be used supra-nationally, at nation-state or sub-state levels, and in the region or city. Consequently, creative nations, regions and cities, are now so much part of the competitive landscape that everyone takes them for granted. First, the curatorial institutions invent new spaces, and then they seek to employ themselves to mow the lawns and trim the hedges that they have themselves designed.

Thus, for instance, what is called "creative place-making" (Markusen 2014) is an inherently restless, unfinished process, because new icons of brand differentiation have continually to be found and new policies to be devised the better to compete, for instance, in film, TV, games, mega-events or performances. Or new incentives have to be found to stimulate the earth-scouring quest for location and relocation. This means that the marketplace for cultural gabfests for the like-minded and the demand for advice by creative consultants is never exhausted. Neither is the continuous flow of academic commentary nor the litany of instruction to up-and-coming generations on how best to prepare themselves for pursuing the chimera of creative entrepreneurship.

If the UK made the initial policy moves, it was in the USA that the best-known academic interventions were initially fashioned. The economist, Richard Caves (2000), was first to offer a serious book-length analysis of the creative industries. His work avoided the now commonplace fetishization of the term. He wrote of diverse "creative goods" that had something in common – contending rightly that the production of films, recorded music, the visual arts, and cultural events and performances are all highly risky in terms of any calculation of success or failure. Caves focused on the specifics of contracts and the industrial organization of relevant sectors. He did not create a unitary policy object. That was left to others.

Hot on his heels, another US economist, Richard Florida (2002), writing in a very different, more popular, style took centre stage, to conjure up and hail the rise of the "creative class". In essence, he sold the attractive notion to policy-makers that almost one-third of Americans could be classified as "creative" and that by making sure that local conditions were right for those engaged in cultural work, a wide range of places could be transformed into creative cities or regions. In this funky re-versioning of Gouldner's (1979) New Class theory, erstwhile symbol-manipulating intellectuals were restyled as productive creatives. Of course, even earlier, post-industrial theorists such as Daniel Bell had presaged such thinking (1973) but not with such resounding policy éclat.

Enter the creative economy

It was a short step from increasingly pervasive talk about creative industries to the follow-on coinage of the creative economy that now dominates the scene. We may interpret this locution as an invitation to think of designated industries as systemically interconnected, as constituting a whole. The British business consultant, John Howkins (2001), first effectively marketed this notion. Like the UK's DCMS, he laid emphasis on the value of intellectual property and the consequent "global battle for comparative advantage". From this perspective, creativity becomes interesting because it is identified with "human capital" – a terminology that by analogy first and foremost defines human beings as the objects of various kinds of investment – education to the fore – that might enhance the qualities of labour (Becker 2008).

For the most part, the "creative economy" has been a mobilizing slogan. It has been deployed alongside a range of cognate ideas – and associated practical interventions. The incessant conceptual parade includes "creative cities", "creative innovation", "creative skills", "creative education" and "creative ecology". Moreover, as during the past decade the digital revolution has reshaped policy thinking everywhere, the "creative turn" has spawned compound neologisms that try to capture current transformations in production, circulation and consumption: the "digital creative economy" is a case in point.

The EU provides an illuminating case study of diffusion. While not all member states have taken up the creative economy cause with equal enthusiasm, by degrees the European Commission (EC) has been won over to treating it as something to be taken into account. The creative and cultural industries (CCIs) are at the heart of the European Agenda for Culture, part of the framework of the EU's Lisbon Strategy for Jobs and Growth, originally set out in March 2000.[3] In May 2007, the European Council endorsed the role that the CCIs might play in supporting the Lisbon Strategy and in April 2008, the European Parliament

(EP) welcomed the Council and Commission's recognition of the importance of culture and creativity for the European project.

The EP singled out the contribution of *The Economy of Culture in Europe*, a report commissioned by the EC in 2006 from KEA, a Brussels-based consultancy. This was an undoubted scene-setter for the EU's "creative turn". It has been followed by a plethora of other reports. We might note another major contemporary reference point as, in fact, the creative turn has been global. The *Creative Economy Report 2013* (United Nations 2013) and, in 2008 and 2010, its predecessor versions, have set the frame for much subsequent global debate and policy work.

The EU uses the CCI formulation as a diplomatic balancing act between states that stress cultural industries and those that emphasize creative industries but overall it is presently inflected towards the economization of culture.

In the second of its major reports for the EC, *The Impact of Culture on Creativity*, KEA (2009, 3; emphasis added) further reworked the conceptual landscape and posed the problem in this way:

> The objective of the study is to have a better understanding of *the influence of culture on creativity, a motor of economic and social innovation.*

As "productivity gains at manufacturing level are no longer sufficient to establish a competitive advantage", what is needed is "culture-based creativity – the kind of thinking beyond production that has made Apple such a global force in design, or Virgin's adding to the 'experience' of long-haul aviation". From a policy point of view, the argument was intended to insert creativity into innovation policy, among whose objectives was to "[b]rand Europe as the place to create" along with establishing new programmes, institutions and regulatory frameworks to support "creative and cultural collaboration". The key ambition, though – still a work in progress involving several different collaborators – was "to establish a Creativity Index (with a set of 32 indicators) whose aim is to assess the creative environment in EU Member States and to enable the development of a creative ecology in Europe through art and culture" (KEA 2009, 9). The creative economy policy agenda from the very beginning has been a pitch to governments everywhere to change the emphasis of policy-making.

A clear turning point was reached inside the EU by 2010, by which time the creative economy had become part of the EC's *doxa*. Its *Green Paper* (European Commission 2010) was an *omnium gatherum* of things that CCIs might do for economic development anywhere, and a rehearsal of what by now had become the conventional wisdom about their nature and role.[4] The EC was seeking a strategy in the context of global competition, embodied in Europe2020 as well as steps taken to develop a European Agenda for Culture. The *Green Paper* pointed forward to what has since become a strategic concern with the "digital economy": the creation of "a true single market for online content and services"; an Innovation Union that would "strengthen the role of CCIs as a catalyst for innovation and structural change"; and the Strategy on Intellectual Property, especially "the use and management of rights" (European Commission 2010, 6, 8).

The uneven diffusion of creative industries discourse

While the creative policy turn has not by any means produced uniformity of thinking inside the EU, there is no doubt that it has impacted on the terms in which culture is thought about in policy-making circles. Two responses illustrate the point. Others could be cited.

In Italy, the European Year of Creativity and Innovation 2009 was launched with the local aim of "growing the awareness of creativity and innovation, key competences for personal, social and economic development" (Rolando 2009, 1). It involved collaboration between various government departments in the wake of publication of the *Libro bianco sulla creatività* (*White Paper on creativity*) in 2007. Chaired by an economist, the late Walter Santagata, the White Paper concentrated on industrial sectors rather than categories of creative work. Distinctions were drawn between material culture, content industries, and artistic and historical heritage. In Stefano Rolando's words, the point was to bring together *"il valore del 'bello e utile'"* ("the value of 'the beautiful and the useful'"). The creative turn taken in London a decade earlier, and by then endorsed in Brussels, provoked an attempt to measure the total value of the creative sectors in Italy, in particular, the percentage of GDP and the workforce for which these accounted.

Santagata's report aimed to delineate an Italian "model of creativity" to assist national development and establish a statistical basis for international comparison. The 14 designated fields of activity were analogous to, but significantly different from, the well-worn nostrums of the UK's DCMS. They were creative cities, design and material culture, fashion, architecture, the knowledge economy, advertising, cinema, TV, radio, publishing, the food industry, contemporary art, music and cultural heritage (Santagata 2007, XI).

National differences persist about which creative industries include or exclude, in keeping with the diverse institutional development of each state. In Germany, the term *Kulturwirtschaft* was the starting point for discussing the "creative industries". In 2007, on the basis of its report, *Kultur in Deutschland*, the Bundestag agreed upon an official federal definition, intended to bring statistical consistency to research and analysis.

> The term [...] Creative Industries, is generally and broadly applied to [...] those cultural or creative enterprises [...] that predominantly operate commercially and are concerned with the creation, production, distribution and/or medial [*sic*] circulation of cultural/creative goods and services.
>
> Included under the definition of "Cultural Industries" are the following core sectors: the music industry, the literary market, the art market, the film industry, radio, the performing arts, the design industry, architecture and the press. The term "Creative Industries" incorporates additional sub-segments that include the advertising industry, the software/gaming industry as well as a category denoted as "miscellaneous". (As originally translated from German in Projektzukunft 2008, 5; cf. Reich 2013, 16)

This is another variation on the theme of classification, with creative industries on this occasion clearly subordinate to cultural industries. Both the German and Italian examples link the need for categorization to the desire for measurement, a matter of growing importance for the global governance of the creative economy, and a policy question in its own right for bodies such as the World Intellectual Property Organization (WIPO).

By 2012, the question of how to measure the CCIs was firmly on the EU agenda. In parallel with wider arguments rehearsed elsewhere (Cooke and De Propris 2011; Cunningham 2014) innovation policy had also been adjusted to include "smart specialization strategies" sensitive to the creative economy and KEA (2012, 30) had been commissioned "to create a benchmarking raster ... or set of indicators, to measure policies focusing on local economic development through CCIs". The new framework was intended to aid European regional and urban centres in accessing EU structural funds, with the central focus of the new toolkit on "policy instruments which impact on local economic and business development" (KEA 2012, 3). However unevenly, a dominant way of seeing was being established in the EU.

The approach outlined above extended to the EP. In a report for its Committee on Culture and Education on how culture could be used in the interests of cohesion, an appeal was made to European solidarity beyond the economy, with a clear recognition of the strains and stresses provoked by the present economic crisis. The report, speaking of a "paradigm shift" in recognition of the connections between "different dimensions of culture", noted key moves in European policies but also bluntly underlined the inadequacy of that acknowledgement, given that culture was not merely "a sector but a resource" that – conceived more broadly – might enhance EU social and economic development in multifold ways and "keep the European utopia alive" (European Parliament 2012, 10, 15).

While, the term "culture" was deployed in line with the EP's broad preference, the overwhelming focus was on its economic and social uses, underlining the present emphasis on an instrumental approach, inflected by the incorporation of creative economy thinking. It is not surprising then, that in Brussels as in London, the economic value of European culture is routinely summarized in a familiar kind of headline statement: that the creative sectors represent more than 3% of European GDP and employ some 3% of the EU's workforce (EC 2016).

Alongside such regional shifts, as have taken place in Europe, the globalization of these ideas has been best illustrated by UNESCO's series of three *Creative economy reports*, the first of which, published in in 2008, called the creative economy a "new development paradigm" covering all forms of cultural work. Diverse political regimes and distinct levels of economic development have shaped the specific take-up of ideas originally minted in London. These have been indigenized in East Asia, China and Australasia (Flew 2012).

Some now argue that the 2013 version of the trio of United Nations reports has represented a challenge to the dominant discourse and, in effect, is subverting it from within. Great hopes are placed on rehabilitating of the idea of a "cultural economy" – with the emphasis on culture rather than economy, on the social rather than the individual (Isar 2015). Although such views do not occupy the mainstream, they are part of an international counter-discourse to that of the creative economy.

The practical embodiment of ideas

Cultural policy is by no means exclusively concerned with economic outcomes. But its dominant focus on accountability through quantitative measures has set the parameters for bodies intervening in the cultural sphere – whether these be arts councils, museums and galleries, public service broadcasters, operas and orchestras or theatres and libraries. This takes us into the realm of "cultural intermediaries", a term influentially deployed by Bourdieu (1984). A little-studied area until recently, this is now of growing academic interest (Smith Maguire and Matthews 2014).

One telling instance of the impact of creative economy orthodoxy in the UK may be illustrated by the case of the BBC, still the UK's premier mainstream cultural and journalistic body and a brand of huge importance in the serious global game of exercising "soft power".

The future orientation of the BBC will be decided after the conclusion of a process known as the Charter Review. The new Charter will run until 2027. The Review is meant to be a period of reflection that occurs every decade to revisit the BBC's purposes, scope and scale, and to result in a new deal for the British public (and by extension for the global audiences that increasingly access the BBC's output).

Under political pressure, the BBC has sought to redefine its legitimacy. Positioning itself for the Charter Review its submission to the UK Government's consultation was tellingly titled *British Bold Creative*. It was not just the title, though, that proclaimed membership of the creative club. The corporation professed its ambition to become "Britain's creative partner and a platform for this country's incredible talent and the work done by its great public institutions" (BBC 2015, 6). The UK government responded in kind. It enjoined the BBC to make "supporting the creative industries [...] the heart of its operations, taking care to minimize any undue market impacts" (DCMS 2016b, 10).

The case of the BBC reflects the increased normalization of creative industries thinking. The discursive mélange of constant gardener and patriotic marketer captures perfectly the reflex, modal way of talking about the role of culture in the public sphere, across arts bodies, support agencies, government and indeed higher education. Ever-ready creative partners proclaim their virtue and relevance by being useful to the national or global economy.

The *extent* of this thinking can readily be judged from the publications routinely produced by the major British arts and cultural organizations. Its *depth* of penetration may be illustrated by some of my most recent research into British cultural agencies where, together with colleagues, I have illustrated the ideological force of policy intervention by government in shaping the work of bodies officially designated part of the creative economy.[5]

In what follows, I wish to use the term "cultural intermediaries" in a particular sense: to describe public bodies whose mission is to make the creative economy work more effectively in line with the overarching national goals pursued by states. In that regard, although the examples presented here concern British agencies, the organizational rationales pursued are typical of many bodies worldwide that have been set up to intervene purposefully in culture.

First, we should note the importance of the distinct institutional landscapes within which such support agencies work. They are shaped by a distinct history of policy ideas as well as fashionable thought about what at any moment constitutes relevant knowhow for intervening in, and building, a competitive creative economy. Each agency connects with its political masters and funders, its clientele, and a range of businesses of diverse scales. Most typically, the latter are small- to medium-sized enterprises or microbusinesses.

One of our studies, which took the form of both contemporary history and cultural sociology, concerned the creation, life and death of the UK Film Council (UKFC) (Doyle et al. 2015). The UKFC was the strategic body set up in 2000 to bring an elusive "sustainability" to the film industry and culture in Britain. Based in London, its institutional life lasted for just over a decade. Film policy, constantly oscillating between cultural and economic goals, was the Ur-model for the wider creative industries policies now in place in the UK. Yet, even in the digital age film policy has retained a certain distinctiveness – which underlines the continuing importance of the distinct sectors that persist within the creative industries framework.

After a decade's intervention, on the agency's demise nothing really fundamental had changed: crucially, the British film industry was still fragmented – "unsustainable". There were some positive outcomes: the key form of support for the British film industry, inward investment in UK film production by the USA, grew; British box office receipts increased somewhat; the digitization of exhibition was accelerated; regional film funding rose. Ironically, the Oscar-winning movie, *The King's Speech*, was an outstanding post-mortem success for a defunct agency, which had part-funded this production.

The political architects of creative industries policy – the first New Labour government – had created the Film Council for *industrial* reasons. The British Film Institute (BFI), until then the premier film body, tasked with a primarily *cultural* role, became a subordinate institution. This was a strong signal of the pre-eminence of industrial purposes over cultural policy. A decade later, the UKFC was summarily closed down on supposed efficiency grounds by Conservative ministers at the start of the Conservative-Liberal Democrat coalition government of 2010–2015. More money was spent than saved by shifting its functions – ironically – into the BFI. Now this body itself has been repurposed – defined as a creative industries body that straddles, and must negotiate, industrial and cultural priorities that often diverge (BFI 2012). Viewed historically, film policy in the UK has produced a scrapheap of defunct agencies – each originally set up to make things more efficient. What has not changed, though, is the state's interest in managing a prime cultural industry.

Our second case concerns an ethnographic, sociological study of a Scottish business support agency, Cultural Enterprise Office (CEO), set up in Glasgow by a coalition of public sector bodies in 2001 (Schlesinger, Selfe, and Munro 2015a). A true embodiment of the creative turn, the formation of CEO was typical of moves taking place all over the UK at the time.

We found that, over its lifespan, whichever political party was in power, intervention in the Scottish creative economy was modelled on the received wisdom produced by policy-makers, think tanks and academics working in London – *the* pre-eminent centre of such thinking in Europe. In this inherited policy framework, CEO assisted microbusinesses in Scotland to become more "businesslike", providing "soft" business support – advice and training. This type of intervention is one of the instruments that policy-makers use when trying to increase the scale and robustness of creative enterprises, although it can be really difficult for support bodies of this kind to demonstrate the impact of their intervention to funders.

The two studies discussed above focused on the mediation of policy – the day-to-day implementation of policy-influenced practice in the cultural field that occurs in response to the formulation of grand ideas, such as that of building a globally competitive creative economy. Completed only recently, they have demonstrated the tenacity of dominant ideas and the extent to which intervention by cultural intermediaries is deeply influenced by policy frameworks and the supporting discourses that both justify and amplify them. Of course, on the ground, public policy initiatives may be cherry-picked by those in creative work, and what are seen as irrelevant ideas simply ignored. Such stratagems, however, do not change the overall picture. Variants of creative economy thinking have set the terms of reference for any sort of entry to the conversation.

Shaping the academic agenda

Cultural intermediation of an analogous kind also occurs in higher education. At least 30 universities around the UK – my own included – presently offer undergraduate and masters courses in the creative and/or cultural industries, or the creative economy, with or without some explicit admixture of the digital dimension – and this kind of provision is emulated elsewhere. What holds for teaching also applies to research. Like their counterparts in other countries, the UK Research Councils have invested heavily in research into the creative and digital economies. This agenda has developed hand in glove with that of government policy, to which the Research Councils are extremely responsive. Although their priorities do not determine the precise scope of what research can be done, like all agenda setting, the themes laid down by such influential funding bodies and the terms in which they are presented do tell us what to think about, even if disaffectedly.

In parallel with public cultural bodies, the institutionalization of the creative economy agenda in British universities has developed apace. The bevy of degree courses already mentioned supplies talent for a saturated and largely under-paying marketplace, where personal connections count hugely, unpaid internships are common, and in which precarious "portfolio" work is the norm – although these tough conditions do not diminish its attractiveness, as McRobbie (2016) has shown in her illuminating studies. Aware of the fragility of such forms of cultural work, she contends that a reflexive pedagogy "permits ... 'shards of light' to emerge as prefigurative forms of social understanding and political consciousness" (McRobbie 2016, 9–10). On her evidence, though, this progressive take appears to be more a consolatory belief than an unambiguously demonstrable conclusion. In many respects, the exigent conditions of work in the creative sectors sum up the state of play for generations entering the wider job market right now as members of the "precariat" (Standing 2011).

Along with the growth of university courses, in the past few years the UK Research Councils have been committed to research on the creative economy and the overlapping "digital economy" and to effecting brokerage between the higher education and creative sectors. Similar kinds of investment have been made in other countries.

A key illustrative initiative in the UK was the establishment of five major university consortia, four of which were designated "knowledge exchange hubs for the creative economy".[6] The fifth grouping was set up as a research centre, with a remit to research copyright and new business models in the creative economy.[7] At the end of 2016, all of these centres came to the end of their funded four-year lifespan, although it seems highly likely that the research focus on the creative economy will continue.[8]

Such initiatives mobilize significant numbers of academic researchers and organize their connections with a range of enterprises, artists and performers, public bodies and governments, and therefore understandably become a focus of public accountability for money spent (AHRC 2015). Engagement of this kind can undoubtedly be valuable because academics are also citizens and may benefit society by their knowledgeable involvement outside the academy. Arguably, we *should* use our expertise to play into policy debate and advice. That said, *how* we do this, and on what terms, is surely a major matter for discussion. My own participation in the work of several bodies concerned with the creative economy has certainly given me insights into the pressures these encounter, not least from government and major business interests determined to pursue their own goals. It has also added considerably to my professional academic knowledge of how things really work.

In essence, then, the terms of trade for academic researchers of the creative economy are ambiguous, not least in the much-vaunted pursuit of "knowledge exchange" with the worlds of practice, which is extremely complicated (Schlesinger, Selfe, and Munro 2015b). Although the programmatic approach currently taken by the UK Research Councils does not necessarily exclude any particular project nor preclude the possibility of critique, the framework has been shaped by the continuous demand to demonstrate the relevance of the research or engagement in question to the overarching aim of building up specific sectors of the national economy so that these will operate more effectively under conditions of global competitiveness.

Countervailing trends?

Of course, the creative turn has not been an exclusive goal but rather a dominant one. In this section, I shall retain the focus on currents at play in the British case which, given its wider influence, may portend wider shifts. Let us consider two recent interventions that have begun to sound a different note, repositioning the creative economy in relation to wider conceptions of first, cultural policy, and second, cultural value.

In the first instance, the UK Government published *The Culture White Paper* in March 2016. This was proudly proclaimed to be the first such document since 1965, and underlined the broad value of culture to British society, noting the importance of three types of cultural value:

- the **intrinsic** value: the enriching value of culture in and of itself;
- the **social** value: improving educational attainment and helping people to be healthier; and
- the **economic** value: the contribution culture makes to economic growth and job-creation. (DCMS 2016a, 15)

It has been rare for "intrinsic value" to be taken seriously by governments in recent years. "Social value", which fits a broadly utilitarian calculus, has certainly figured in the thinking of all governments, but has not been accorded the weight of "economic value", as will be clear from the argument so far.

Perhaps the new, expressly cultural turn is not too surprising, as the UK has been convulsed of late by a number of crises that take a cultural form. These include anxieties in major sections of the public about the extent of migration from the EU and immigration more generally; the UK's ambivalent relationship to the EU, evidenced by the "Brexit" Referendum of 23 June 2016; the existence of home-grown jihadism and both official and public concern about the social integration of some elements of the British Muslim community; and the continuing challenge to Great Britishness of the quest for Scottish independence. Appeals to the creative economy really cannot offer a new roadmap for how to address such shortcomings in the workings of UKanian culture. It is no accident, surely, that the official cultural policy agenda has broadened precisely to take in concern about social inclusion, building employment opportunities for ethnic minorities and economically disadvantaged young people, and how to address and capitalize on the UK's growing diversity. As the present cultural crisis is also a crisis of the British state, is it surprising that how the UK projects itself internationally – the question of its "soft power" and "brand" – and how it attracts visitors and tourists, also figure large?

All of this, however, plays in the White Paper against the Conservative government's enthusiastic advocacy of reductions in public support for the cultural sectors and its encouragement to those working in these fields to make good the shortfall by raising more private funds. In the end, one must conclude, it is not so easy to abolish the continuing salience of the creative economy under the nominal cover of cultural policy. When providing figures about the economic value of culture, recourse was made in the White Paper to the government's creative economy statistics (DCMS 2016a, 16). Moreover, when discussing the uses of a "measurement framework" that "seeks to consolidate evidence on the value of culture", the White Paper not surprisingly noted that assessing the impact of cultural policy was "strongest for economic development. For personal wellbeing, educational attainment, life chances and soft power, more work is needed to refine how we measure the specific impact that culture makes" (DCMS 2016a, 58). It remains to be seen, therefore, whether this is a first step on a new road or – more likely – simply the setting up of a diversion on an old one.

The second example concerns a report published by the AHRC in April 2016. This summed up the results of the Research Council's "cultural value project", an initiative taking up "the imperative to reposition first-hand, individual experience of arts and culture at the heart of enquiry into cultural value" (Crossick and Kaszynska 2016). This intervention intended, *inter alia*, to question the primacy of economic value and was also an attempt to reframe the purposes and character of evaluation in the prevalent discourse and policy framework.[9] Although this initiative sought to extend the Research Council's agenda in the field of cultural research, it was recognized that the very concept of cultural value "may be seen as a construct of policy" and that, consequently, research has "tended to be driven by the case for public funding, and this has led to a focus on the publicly-funded arts" (Crossick and Kaszynska 2016, 24). In short, the project itself was unavoidably framed by the creative economy agenda to which it has been a riposte and therefore constrained to broaden debate without, however, surmounting the original epistemological obstacle.

This effort to enlarge the scope of what is relevant to academic research has made use of the concept of an "ecology of culture", stressing the interconnections of distinct publicly funded, commercial, third-sector, amateur and participatory practices. While it is important to note this existing complexity, the concept of a cultural ecology is itself freighted with unexplored meaning. Unnoticed by the authors, in the context of the UK, where the multinational character of the state is under deep strain, the use of ecological metaphors may be interpreted not only as a way of virtuously conjoining diverse cultural funding regimes and practices but also – much more significantly – as one of carelessly erecting enclosures around the component national cultures of the state. In the context of arguments for Scottish independence, consider the potential political uses to be made of an English or a Scottish cultural ecology.[10] Cultural ecologies can easily be reformulated as "national ecologies", with profound consequences for identities.[11]

Conclusion

Since the creative economy became a policy object, this has gradually given rise to a supporting "creative economy industry", which is not only national but also international. Academic research and publishing have become an important part of this, alongside the incessant flow of reports from policy advisers, creative consultants and conferences organized by profit-driven ideas brokers and interest groups.

The espousal of creative economy thinking means that culture is seen primarily as embodying tradable economic value. A self-sustaining, self-referential framework of ideas has developed that has become largely impervious to critique. The omnipresence of creative economy thinking raises questions about how the research agenda is being formulated and the consequent positioning of academics in debate.

To note the prevalence of the economic dimension does not at all mean that other valuations of culture have been eclipsed. There are counter-discourses and, as has been shown, the expediency of policy means that compromises can be effected and different registers adopted, according to circumstances. Mostly beyond the imaginings of the policy world, people continue to engage in cultural practices for their inherent satisfaction, the pursuit of aesthetic goals, their own and others' fulfilment and self-development. Craft sensibilities – such as those that shape the patient achievement of high-level skills or the fastidious making of objects, described so well by Sennett (2008) – have not disappeared.[12]

If we stopped talking about the creative economy would anything be lost? Hardly. We still have ways of discussing human inventiveness and originality. Nothing stops us speaking comprehensibly about the diversity of cultural practices that continue to exist but which have long been overshadowed by a compelling label of convenience that has put the economy in the driving seat and shaped the public discourse so insistently. Surely, that is enough of an invitation to think afresh.

Acknowledgements

This article began as a Public Lecture at the London School of Economics and Political Science, delivered on 25 November 2015, with Angela McRobbie and Jonothan Neelands as my much appreciated respondents. Subsequently, it was revised for delivery on 3 February 2016 as a Major Lecture for the Network for Oratory and Politics held at the University of Glasgow. I offer my thanks to Nick Couldry at the LSE and to Ernest Schonfield and Henriette Van Der Blom at Glasgow for inviting me to speak. This is the third iteration of the argument.

Funding

This essay draws on reflections provoked by recently completed and continuing research projects. I gratefully acknowledge the support of the UK Arts and Humanities Research Council for "The UK Film Council: a study of film policy in transition" [AH/J000457X/1] and "Supporting creative business: Cultural Enterprise Office and its clients" [AH/K002570/1] as well as that of the European Commission for my present work on cultural creativity, conducted under the Horizon2020 project "CulturalBase" [EC649454].

Notes

1. This point is considered later when discussing the role of "cultural intermediaries".
2. I was a member of the boards of Scottish Screen (the erstwhile national audiovisual agency) from 1997 to 2004, and of TRCMedia (a not-for-profit media training body) from 1998 to 2008. I have also been a member of the Advisory Committee for Scotland of Ofcom (the UK communications regulator) from 2004 to date, and since 2014 of that body's Content Board. In respect of the latter, this article has been written in a purely professional academic capacity and any views expressed here are entirely my own.
3. In the six lines above, I have drawn directly on Schlesinger, Selfe, and Munro (2015a, 15).
4. The *Green Paper* (EC 2010, 5) aimed "at capturing the various connotations ascribed to the terms 'cultural' and 'creative' throughout the EU, reflecting Europe's cultural diversity". It defined "cultural industries" as

   > producing and distributing goods or services which at the time they are developed are considered to have a specific attribute, use or purpose which embodies or conveys cultural expressions, irrespective of the commercial value they may have. Besides the traditional arts sectors (performing arts, visual arts, cultural heritage – including the public sector), they include film, DVD and video, television and radio, video games, new media, music, books and press.

   For their part, "creative industries"

   > use culture as an input and have a cultural dimension, although their outputs are mainly functional. They include architecture and design, which integrate creative elements into wider processes, as well as subsectors such as graphic design, fashion design or advertising.

5. Although that work draws out some features of current practice in the UK it has much wider, comparative implications.
6. Funded until April 2016, these were: The Creative Exchange; Design in Action; Creative Works London; and REACT.
7. CREATe. I must declare an interest. I have been Deputy Director of this centre from its inception; its funding ends in December 2016.
8. In June 2016, the AHRC issued a call for candidates competing to become Creative Economy Champion to consolidate existing work and shape future strategy and partnerships in the field.

9. The category of "experience" is treated as conceptually unproblematic in this project, being characterized as "fundamental and irreducible" (Crossick and Kaszynska 2016, 21) – itself a highly questionable assumption.

10. In an as yet unpublished paper on "Cultural Policy and Ecology", I have argued that the underlying holism underplays culture's agonistic qualities and that the concept of the cultural ecosystem biologises culture, thereby turning the analyst into a "doctor" concerned with its health and ailments. For instances of such curative thinking, see Holden (2015) and The Warwick Commission (2015).

11. An analogous point about constructing English history in ways that ignore the UK's other nations has been made by Thomas (2016, 73).

12. McRobbie (2016, 13–14 and Ch. 6) has reservations about Sennett's idealization of craft, not least because of his treatment of gender. But his work, nonetheless, offers an important normative counter-narrative to that of the *creativistas*.

References

AHRC. 2015. *The Impact of AHRC Research, April 2014-March 2015*. Swindon: Arts and Humanities Research Council.

Bauman, Z. 1992. *Intimations of Postmodernity*. London: Routledge.

BBC. 2015. "British Bold Creative." The BBC's submission to the Department for Culture, Media and Sport's Charter Review Public Consultation, October. London: BBC.

Becker, G. S. 2008. "Human Capital." Accessed May 2, 2015. http://www.econlib.org/library/Enc/HumanCapital.html.

Bell, D. 1973. *The Coming of Post-industrial Society*. Harmondsworth: Penguin Books.

BFI. 2012. *Film Forever: Supporting UK Film. BFI Plan 2012–2017*. London: BFI.

Bourdieu, P. 1984. *Distinction: A Social Critique of the Judgement of Taste*. Cambridge, MA: Harvard University Press.

Bourdieu, P. 1993. "The Market of Symbolic Goods." In *The Field of Cultural Production*, edited by R. Johnson, 112–141. Cambridge: Polity.

Bustamante, E. ed. 2011. *Industrias Creativas: Amenazas Sobre la Cultural Digital*. Barcelona: Editorial Gedisa.

Caves, R. E. 2000. *Creative Industries: Contracts between Art and Commerce*. Cambridge, MA: Harvard University Press.

Cooke, P., and L. De Propris. 2011. "A Policy Agenda for EU Smart Growth: The Role of Creative and Cultural Industries." *Policy Studies* 32 (4): 365–375.

Crossick, G., and P. Kaszynska. 2016. *Understanding the Value of Arts & Culture. The AHRC Cultural Value Project*. Swindon: Arts and Humanities Research Council.

Cunningham, S. 2014. *Hidden Innovation: Policy, Industry and the Creative Sector*. Lanham, MN: Lexington Books.

DCMS. 1998. *Creative Industries Mapping Document*. London: Department for Culture, Media and Sport.

DCMS. 2015. *Creative Industries Economic Estimates*. London: The Stationery Office.

DCMS. 2016a. *The Culture White Paper*. London: Department for Culture, Media & Sport.

DCMS. 2016b. "A BBC for the Future: A Broadcaster of Distinction." Presented to Parliament by the Secretary of State for Culture, Media and Sport by Command of Her Majesty, May 2016. Cm 9242.

Doyle, G., P. Schlesinger, R. Boyle, and L. W. Kelly. 2015. *The Rise and Fall of the UK Film Council*. Edinburgh: Edinburgh University Press.

European Commission. 2010. "Green Paper: Unlocking the Potential of Cultural and Creative Industries." Brussels, 27.4.2010 COM(2010) 183 final. Accessed May 31, 2016. http://eur-lex.europa.eu/legal-content/EN/TXT/PDF/?uri=CELEX:52010DC0183&from=EN.

European Commission. 2016. "Culture: Supporting Europe's Cultural and Creative Sectors." Accessed May, 31 2016. http://ec.europa.eu/culture/index_en.htm.

European Parliament. 2012. "Use of Structural Funds for Cultural Projects." Study: A Document Requested by the European Parliament's Committee on Culture and Education. Directorate General for Internal Policies. Policy Department B: Structural and Cohesion Policies, Culture and Education, July 2012. IP/B/CULT/FWC/2010–001/LO14/C2/SC/PE.474.563. Accessed May 31, 2016. www.europarl.europa.eu/studies/.

Fairclough, N. 2000. *New Labour, New Language?* London: Psychology Press.

Flew, Terry. 2012. *The Creative Industries: Culture and Policy.* London: Sage.

Florida, R. 2002. *The Rise of the Creative Class and How it's Transforming Work, Leisure, Community and Everyday Life.* New York: Basic Books.

Flusser, V. 2002. "Essays." In *Writings*, edited by A. Ströhl, 192–196. Minneapolis, MN: University of Minnesota Press.

Garnham, N. 1990 [1984]. "Public Policy and the Cultural Industries." In *Capitalism and Communication: Global Culture and the Economics of Information*, edited by F. Inglis, 154–168. London: Sage.

Gouldner, A. 1979. *The Future of Intellectuals and the Rise of the New Class.* London: Macmillan.

Hesmondhalgh, D., K. Oakley, D. Lee, and M. Nisbett. 2015. *Culture, Economy and Politics: The Case of New Labour.* Basingstoke: Palgrave Macmillan.

Holden, J. 2015. *The Ecology of Culture. A Report Commissioned by the Arts and Humanities Research Council's Cultural Value Project.* Swindon: Arts and Humanities Research Council.

Horkheimer, M., and T. W. Adorno. 1977[1944]. "Culture Industry: Enlightenment as Mass Deception." In *Dialectic of Enlightenment*, edited by G.S. Noerr, 94–136. London: Verso/NLB.

Howkins, J. 2001. *The Creative Economy: How People Make Money From Ideas.* London: Penguin.

Isar, Y. R. 2015. "Widening Local Development Pathways: Transformative Visions of Cultural Economy." In *The Routledge Companion to the Cultural Industries*, edited by K. Oakley and J. O'Connor, 477–487. Abingdon: Routledge.

Jones, C., M. Lorenzen, and J. Sapsed, eds. 2015. *The Oxford Handbook of Creative Industries.* Oxford: Oxford University Press.

KEA European Affairs. 2006. "The Economy of Culture in Europe." Study Prepared for the European Commission (Directorate-General for Education and Culture), October. Accessed August 20, 2015. ec.europa.eu/culture/library/studies/cultural-economy_en.pdf.

KEA European Affairs. 2009. "The Impact of Culture on Creativity." A Study Prepared for the European Commission (Directorate-General for Education and Culture), June. Accessed August 20, 2015. ec.europa.eu/culture/library/studies/cultural-economy_en.pdf.

KEA European Affairs. 2012. "Measuring Economic Impact of CCIs Policies: How to Justify Investment in Cultural and Creative Assets." Accessed August 14, 2015. http://www.keanet.eu/docs/measuring-economic-impact-of-ccis-policies_final_creare.pdf.

Keane, M. 2007. *Created in China: The Great New Leap Forward.* London: Routledge.

Maasen, S., and P. Weingart, eds. 2005. *Democratization of Expertise? Exploring Novel Forms of Scientific Advice in Political Decision-making.* Dordrecht: Springer.

Markusen, A. 2014. "Creative Cities: A Ten-year Research Agenda." *Journal of Urban Affairs* 36 (S2): 1–23.

Mattelart, A., X. Delcourt, and M. Mattelart. 1983. *La culture contre la démocratie: l'audiovisuelle à l'heure transnationale.* Paris: la Découverte.

McRobbie, A. 2016. *Be Creative!.* Cambridge: Polity.

Miège, B. 2004[1984]. "Postface à la 2è edition de *Capitalisme et industries culturelles.*" In *L'information – communication, objet de connaissance*, edited by B. Miege 71–84. Bruxelles: Éditions de Boeck Université.

Oakley, K., and J. O'Connor, eds. 2015. *The Routledge Companion to the Cultural Industries.* Abingdon: Routledge.

Projektzukunft. 2008. *Creative Industries in Berlin: Development and Potential.* Berlin: Senatsverwaltung für Wirtschaft, Technologie und Frauen.

Reich, M. P. 2013. *Kultur- und Kreativwirtschaft in Deutschland: Hype oder Zukunftschance der Stadtentwicklung?* Wiesbaden: Springer.

Rolando, S. 2009. "Creatività in Italia in Europa." Sintesi del rapporto introduttivo SR a Eurovisioni 2009. 'Dall'utilità alla bellezza'. Accessed September 2, 2015. http://www.stefanorolando.it/index.php?option=com_content&view=article&id=214:creativita-in-italia-e-in-europa-sintesi-rapporto-introduttivo-sr-a-eurovisioni-2009&catid=39:testi&Itemid=63.

Santagata, W. (Chairman). 2007. *Libro Bianco sulla Creatività in Italia, Commissione sulla Creatività e Produzione di Cultura in Italia*. Rome: Edizione per il Ministero per i Beni e le Attività Culturali. Accessed September 2, 2015. http://www.beniculturali.it/mibac/export/ UfficioStudi/sito-UfficioStudi/Contenuti/Pubblicazioni/Volumi/Volumi-pubblicati/visualizza_ asset.html_1410871104.html.

Schlesinger, P. 2007. "Creativity: From Discourse to Doctrine." *Screen* 48 (3): 377–387.

Schlesinger, P. 2009. "Creativity and the Experts. New Labour, Think Tanks, and the Policy Process." *The International Journal of Press/Politics* 14 (3): 3–20.

Schlesinger, P. 2013. "Expertise, the Academy and the Governance of Cultural Policy." *Media, Culture & Society* 35 (1): 27–35.

Schlesinger, P., M. Selfe, and E. Munro. 2015a. *Curators of Cultural Enterprise: A Critical Analysis of a Creative Business Intermediary*. Basingstoke: Palgrave Macmillan.

Schlesinger, P., M. Selfe, and E. Munro. 2015b. "Inside a Cultural Agency: Team Ethnography and Knowledge Exchange." *The Journal of Arts Management, Law, and Society* 45 (2): 66–83.

Sennett, R. 2008. *The Craftsman*. London: Penguin Books.

Smith, C. 2013. "Creative Britain: Where Have We Got To?" *The Guardian*, November 18. Accessed May 4, 2016. http://www.theguardian.com/culture-professionals-network/culture-professionals-blog/2013/nov/18/creative-britain-chris-smith-2013.

Smith Maguire, J., and J. Matthews, eds. 2014. *The Cultural Intermediaries Reader*. London: Sage.

Standing, G. 2011. *The Precariat: The New Dangerous Class*. London: Bloomsbury Academic.

The Warwick Commission. 2015. *Enriching Britain: Culture, Creativity and Growth. The 2015 Report by the Warwick Commission on the Future of Cultural Value*. Coventry: University of Warwick.

The Work Foundation. 2007. *Staying Ahead: The Economic Performance of the UK's Creative Industries*. London: The Work Foundation.

Thomas, K. 2016. "Was There Always an England?" *The New York Review of Books* 63 (8): 71–73.

United Nations/UNCTAD/UNESCO. 2013. *Creative economy report 2013: Special Edition. Widening Local Development Pathways*. New York: United Nations.

Vötsch, M., and R. Weiskopf. 2009. "'Thank you for your creativity': 'Arbeit' und 'Kreativität' im Diskurs der creative industries." In *Diskursanalytische Perspektiven auf Märkte und Organisationen*, edited by R. Diaz-Bone and G. Krell, 293–316. Wiesbaden: VS Verlag für Sozialwissenschaften.

Yúdice, G. 2003. *The Expediency of Culture*. London: Duke University Press.

In search of experiential knowledge

Stuart Blume

Department of Anthropology, University of Amsterdam, Amsterdam, Netherlands

In recent years, the concept of "experiential knowledge" has increasingly been used to characterize the distinctive contribution patients make to decision-making in the health field. Even though it seems well-nigh impossible to characterize it precisely, there is no doubting its significance for decision-making contexts ranging from the individual to the political. Since individual experiences of any condition or treatment differ widely, whose experiences come to constitute "knowledge"? In this paper, I argue that, rhetoric notwithstanding, numerous constraints "filter" the experiences which come to function as "experiential knowledge". Looking to the future of health care, likely to be marked by growing inequalities, I suggest that a reflection on the notion of experiential knowledge leads to two challenges for social scientists.

What do sick people know?

Twenty-five years ago, psychiatrist and anthropologist Arthur Kleinman published his recording of part of a clinical encounter between a physician and "Mrs Flowers", a black 39-year-old single parent of five children (two of them pregnant teenagers, one in prison) whose man friend had recently been killed in a fight and whose partially paralysed mother lived with her. Mrs Flowers feels unwell, the physical symptoms she tries to describe – sleeplessness, headaches – are fused with dreams of her friend's death, feelings of inability to cope, the general state of her life. She tries to present them as a single whole, which is how she experiences them. Her physician is willing only to hear "hypertension", to change her medication and to recommend a low-salt diet. This patient is struggling to provide an account of her illness which her physician is unwilling to hear (Kleinman 1988).

Kleinman's text points to two issues, both of which have intrigued social scientists (of different persuasions) for many years. One relates to Mrs Flowers' attempt to express herself: to articulate her subjective knowledge of her own body's (mal)functioning. Such expressions of embodied subjectivity, whether in words or actions, are the stuff of phenomenologically inspired sociology and anthropology (e.g. Csordas 1994). The other relates to the distinction between the perspective of people who are sick or disabled and that of the people who treat or care for them. As far as the latter is concerned, for half a century, anthropologists have used the term "emic" perspective to categorize attempts at looking at the world from within a distinctive community, life world or culture. Introductions to the field of medical anthropology are replete with references to emic and etic perspectives, referring to those who suffer and those who treat, respectively. So if we focus on

91

the "emic" perspective, specifically on the perspective of people coping with ill health or disability, what do we find? Or perhaps better put, how have social scientists characterized what they found?

A decade ago, Lindsay Prior argued that through the 1980s and 1990s, a shift had taken place in the status sociologists accorded this "patient perspective" (Prior 2003). Prior claims that in attempting to articulate and interpret the perspective of the patient, sociologists had modified the terms they used. What had previously been referred to as "lay health beliefs" had gradually evolved into "lay knowledge and expertise". Prior thought this that had been a mistake. Patients might have knowledge of their own lives and circumstances, and they might sometimes pick up enough knowledge to challenge medical professionals on one or two issues. However, he argued that "for the most part, lay people are not experts", since they typically know nothing about which facts merit particular attention, important or how to distinguish one disease from another. "What is more they can often be plain wrong about the causes, course and management of common forms of disease and illness". But if he was correct in his assessment of the changing sociological landscape, even though unwilling to accompany his colleagues down that particular path, then a question that follows is "why?" What had inspired this change in the way sociologists viewed the patient perspective?

Perhaps, it was changes taking place in society more generally that had led sociologists to look with greater attention, greater respect even, at how sick people described their lives and their conditions. One aspect of this was the declining status of professional expertise, which had been theorized by Habermas and by others. Another, related, aspect, was a growing sense that patients – or "health care consumers" – had rights that should be respected. From the 1970s onwards, there had been a growing acknowledgement in many countries of patients' right to be consulted regarding their own treatment. In a report written 15 years ago for an interesting (though now defunct) Dutch patient movement think-tank, Geerke Catshoek and I suggested that there were a number of reasons for this. It had something to do with changing perceptions of minority rights and of ethics, but it also reflected the rise of consumerism.

> Consumer organisations have often supported patient groups in demanding greater responsiveness to their needs from health service providers. The "consumer of a service" seems a more "empowered" individual than a patient ... The patient – anxious, naked and in pain – has become the consumer, critically assessing the availability and quality of care available from competing institutions. This has long been the case at the edges of health care: in the private nursing home sector, for example, or health resorts and clinics whose customers are happy to pay to have their bodies look good. But now it has wider application. (Blume and Catshoek 2001, 7)

The concept of the "health care consumer" has the benefit of being more inclusive. Someone visiting the doctor briefly for a 'flu vaccination for example would not necessarily regard him or herself as a "patient". But this term can also be questioned. After all, there are people who are sick but who, for financial reasons, or legal status, are excluded from health service "consumption". Not everyone was happy with the transformation of the "patient" into the "health care consumer".

> It seems to legitimate the encroachment of market forces into a domain once hallowed by a morality of care, rights, and obligations: the domain of citizenship. Is access to health care to reflect the morality of the community or that of the market? (Blume and Catshoek 2001, 7–8)

Another question also follows from what Prior suggests was a change in sociologists' perspective. What is the "lay knowledge and expertise" that patients are now said to possess? In our 2001 report, we added a definition of the patient perspective. It refers, we proposed, to

> accounts of sickness and disability which take for granted the patient's right to autonomy and citizenship: to full participation in society. It seeks to articulate the experience of living with a (chronic) illness or disability, of which encounters with the health care system form one part. (9)

What kinds of accounts could these be? Some of them are texts in which patients themselves have written of their own experiences of illness or disability. These autobiographical accounts – which some writers have referred to as "pathographies" (Hunsaker Hawkins 1993) though others have explicitly rejected the term – often display the evolution of the disease or handicapping condition through the course of the individual life. They show how life goals may have had to be redefined in terms of changes in the possible and the to-be-expected, and in terms of the limitations imposed by social arrangements (e.g. Murphy 1990). The importance of these accounts, or at least the importance of the best of them, cannot be overestimated. This literature obviously has a privileged place in any exposition of the patient perspective. But why do people write them? Or perhaps the question is better formulated as "why did people write them long before public exposure of personal experiences in TV shows like Dr Phil or on social media became unremarkable?"

Arthur Frank, ex-cancer patient and sociologist, has argued that an important motivation for writing personal accounts of illness experiences is to show others how it is possible to live a rewarding and worthwhile life with – and not just "despite" – a chronic or even terminal illness (Frank 1995). The accounts of fellow sufferers can be an important source of inspiration and advice for people who are sick, or who are coping with the sickness or the disability of a relative. Indeed, an important function of the self-help groups that were growing in number in the 1980s was to provide the opportunity for the telling, and the witnessing, of accounts of personal experience. But as far as these groups and associations were concerned, members' stories also had a different kind of value for the group or association as such. More was – and is – involved than the provision of a forum in which stories could be told.

The UK-based non-profit organization called DIPEx (database of individual patient experience) took shape at the beginning of the present millennium (Herxheimer et al. 2000).[1] The website that it now publishes (*Healthtalkonline*)[2] feature clips of people talking about their experiences of living with a range of health conditions and has proved a valuable resource for patients, their carers, family and friends, doctors, nurses and other health professionals. When DIPEx began, its originators surveyed associations representing a wide variety of conditions in the UK regarding their use of patients' stories (Yaphe et al. 2000). Sixty-five per cent of the 309 associations which responded said that they use patients' stories in some or other ways. They did so for a whole range of reasons, ranging from attracting media attention to encouraging others to help change professional behaviour or structures. Personal experiences are clearly an important political resource.

But what exactly is the patient perspective? How does it relate to the personal experiences of individuals? Is it some kind of a "distillation" from individual experiences (which will obviously not all be the same)? In what ways a distillation? If so, how and where does the distilling take place? The question becomes all the more intriguing in the light of the claim that the patient perspective can be seen not of a set of idiosyncratic beliefs but of "knowledge": the knowledge that is now widely referred to as "experiential knowledge". The question then is: what sort of knowledge is this? Is it like knowing how to swim, for example, or to blow glass? (O'Connor 2007) Is it akin to the kind of deep conviction that Michael Polanyi called "personal knowledge": for example, knowing what constitutes moral behaviour in a given situation? (Polanyi 1962) Is it more like scientific knowledge that has passed tests of veracity or replicability, and can be codified and transmitted? Or different from all of these?

Social scientists' analyses of experiential knowledge

The term "experiential knowledge" seems to have been introduced by Borkman in a 1976 article in the *Social Service Review*. It did not achieve any immediate currency, and when writing our report in 2001, we did not know of it or use it. Now, however, the concept is finding increasing use in a wide range of disciplines.[3]

"Experiential knowledge", Borkman wrote, "is truth learned from personal experience with a phenomenon rather than truth acquired by discursive reasoning, observation, or reflection on information provided by others". There is a certainty that what is experienced is "true": "that the insights learned from direct participation in a situation are truth, because the individual has faith in the validity and authority of the knowledge obtained by being a part of a phenomenon".

This kind of knowledge, distinct from professional knowledge, was "a primary source of truth" for self-help groups. Indeed, for Borkman, it is through their reliance on this distinctive kind of knowledge that self-help groups can be distinguished from patient groups controlled by professionals. It is true, of course, that medical professionals also make use of knowledge acquired as a result of their clinical experience. Nevertheless, Borkman argues that the kind of knowledge she is referring to can be distinguished from professional knowledge because it is different in kind. Most importantly, it is holistic and total, rather than being divided into specialized segments as medical knowledge is. And, no less important, it is "oriented to here-and-now action rather than to the long-term development and systematic accumulation of knowledge". In other words, it "is pragmatic, in that it emphasizes obtaining concrete observable results that 'work', as subjectively perceived by the individual who is going through an experience".

Borkman tells us that her sense that such a term was needed, that a distinction had to be drawn from the "truths" underpinning professional practice, followed from her observation of the growing number of self-help groups in the health field. Consonant with this perception, current growth in use of the term may reflect the growing social and political significance of groups which are increasingly evolving from "self-help" to a more outward-directed and political "advocacy".

Boardman (2014) has recently pointed out that, since Borkman introduced the term, its meaning has become less clear-cut. Whereas Borkman saw it principally as a resource, as a guide to action, the emphasis in more recent work is on "its contextual, subjective, unconscious and emotional properties". Boardman reminds readers of a 1998 publication in which Abel and Browner, analysing the sources of women's resistance to, or deviation from, medical advice, relate this to women's "experiential knowledge" (1998). Looking specifically at studies of women's experience of pregnancy, on the one hand, and caring for frail elderly relatives, on the other, Abel and Browner had argued that the experiential knowledge involved in these two instances was different. In the case of pregnancy, the women made use of their experience of previous pregnancies, or their sense of the changes taking place in their bodies. This they referred to as "embodied knowledge". The experiential knowledge involved in their second case they called "empathetic knowledge". It comes from a long and intimate association with the person being cared for. The stock of experiential knowledge on which women can draw, Abel and Browner suggested, is based not only on personal experience but also on the comparable experiences of others with whom the focal person identifies.

In interpreting her own empirical data on reproductive decision-making, Boardman builds on Abel and Browner's distinction. She suggests that family members with different degrees of proximity to an inheritable condition have distinctive perceptions, distinctive claims to having experiential knowledge of it. The result is that potentially conflicting claims may emerge and have to be negotiated. "The familial context of this analysis brings into sharp focus many of the key issues around the uses of experiential knowledge, including what counts as experiential knowledge (both embodied and empathetic), who is entitled to lay claim to it". Because experiential knowledge has become a form of cultural capital, to be used in legitimating one's views or demands, its possession has value. In drawing attention to the contested nature of the concept, to the possibility of competing claims to possess experiential knowledge emerging, Boardman makes an important point. The fact is that such competing claims emerge regularly and systematically. The perspective of parents of children with a given impairment often conflicts with the perspective of adults with the same condition.

In many countries, adult deaf people commonly espouse (and enact) a cultural–linguistic view of deafness. They wish not to be seen as hearing-impaired individuals but accepted as members of a minority culture. On the other hand, parents of newly diagnosed deaf children rarely turn to members of the Deaf community for guidance regarding how best to bring up a deaf child. Instead, they turn to the medical professionals who claim either to "cure" the child's deafness, or at least to enable it to pass for a hearing child. Similarly, I doubt that many parents of children diagnosed as autistic are likely to seek guidance from adult Autists associated with the "neurodiversity movement" (Chamak 2007). What sense does it make to say that one group has experiential knowledge whilst the other does not? Or that one has more than the other? Why do parents of children who are diagnosed as deaf or autistic rarely turn for guidance to adults with the same condition? What we can say is that the knowledge of living as a Deaf person, or as an autistic person – their experiential knowledge – lacks the authority accorded to (bio)medical knowledge.

Mazanderani, Locock, and Powell (2012) have discussed "the mechanisms whereby patients turn other patients' experiences into a source of knowledge and support". They argue that for this to happen, whether what is exchanged is emotional support or the sharing of practical advice, "the person receiving the information must identify with the person providing it. In the health context, this sense of identification is typically premised on the existence of a common diagnosis".

So according to this analysis, it is in the process of "becoming a resource for others" that the epistemological status of an individual's experience is transformed. They see their analysis as in some way an extension of the distinction between embodied and empathetic experiential knowledge: that

> the epistemic validity of other people's experiences as a source of knowledge in the context of peer support is premised, crucially, on managing the simultaneously embodied and empathetic dimensions of experiential knowledge. Indeed, others' experiences would not be considered knowledge if they were not deemed, in some way, as an empathetic (shared) embodiment of a particular condition. (Mazanderani, Locock, and Powell 2012, 551)

People will see the experience of another as relevant for them insofar as they can – and are willing to – identify with that other individual. There are factors which might constrain this "identity work". Specifically, Mazanderani et al. suggest that it might be limited by reluctance to identify with someone whose disease (they are discussing Parkinson and motor neurone diseases such as ALS) has progressed much further. Identifying with that other becomes too painful (especially when there is a photograph), making for what they term an "identity tension" "that needs to be negotiated in order for patients to be able to engage and benefit from experiential information sharing". They suggest that the nature of the condition will, therefore, influence the extent and the ways in which experience is shared. Reading what another person with motor neurone disease had posted regarding their diagnosis, and most particularly when they had posted a photograph of themselves, interviewees focused on what they shared (the diagnosis) but at the same time (if shocked by what they saw or read) on the ways in which they differed from the person whose story they were reading or viewing. People were thus led to see themselves as "both different and the same – *differently the same*" in order to facilitate the (partial) identification that would enable them to benefit from the other's experience.

Pols (2014) who prefers to talk about "patient knowledge" rather than "experiential knowledge" proceeds pragmatically, and in line with Borkman's original use of the term. Her analysis is based on an empirical inquiry into the kind of knowledge patients' use (and produce) in living with a limiting condition on a daily basis: a "knowing in action". She does not follow the line opened up by Abel and Browner and Boardman and distinguish "embodied" from "empathetic" knowledge. Moreover, unlike the other authors I have discussed here, Pols acknowledges that what patients know, the knowledge they put to use in coping, draws on medical knowledge (what they have learnt from their professional advisors) as well as on their own raw experience. She sees "patient knowledge" as articulated solely in its use, as the source of "techniques for living with disease", rather than a body of knowledge. Patients' knowledge is practical knowledge, and cannot be contrasted with medical knowledge because though different, it draws on the latter, and their interrelations have to be part of a comprehensive analysis.

> I suggest we analyze patient knowledge as the patient's equivalent to clinical knowledge with, however, the objective of crafting an acceptable daily life, rather than coaching or treating different individual patients. Patients use and develop this practical knowledge to translate knowledge from different sources and advices they get into usable techniques, and coordinate this with the different aims they have in life. (Pols 2014, 78)

Like the authors I discussed previously, Pols understands patient or experiential knowledge in terms of its utility or use-value for other patients (or perhaps also carers). It is by virtue of its use by others that any claim to be regarded as "knowledge" must be judged.

But this does not quite exhaust the matter since we have already encountered two complications. The first, to which I will return presently, concerns the fact that some people's knowledge, however, rooted in a lifetime of experience, may be ignored by others. I gave the example of Deaf adults commonly ignored by the parents of newly diagnosed hearing-impaired children. The second complication is that experiential knowledge has acquired applications other than in the context of personal coping. It comes into play when representatives of patient organizations are invited to help determine, for example, the quality of care available to people suffering from rheumatoid arthritis, or future priorities in cancer research. Caron-Flinterman, Broerse and Bunders looked at this specifically. Experiential knowledge, for them, arises when the lived experiences of individual patients "are converted, consciously or unconsciously, into a personal insight that enables a patient to cope with individual illness and disability". (Caron-Flinterman, Broerse, and Bunders 2005, 2576). They go on to introduce the idea of "utility in context". If patients' experiential knowledge proves useful in a given context (e.g. "development of individual coping strategies, the mutual understanding and mental support of fellow sufferers, and individual health care decision making"), then it can be considered valid within that context. The evaluative criterion is thus "validity" and this corresponds to utility, though within a given context.

These authors also refer to the possibility of this knowledge being shared. "When patients share experiential knowledge, the communal body of knowledge exceeds the boundaries of individual experiences ... " But what is this sharing? If patient A's experience only becomes a resource for patient B insofar as B can identify with A, in what sense is sharing possible? Is it like adding books to a library, so that a visitor may choose one that he or she feels they might find profitable? Or is more involved ... for example, might it relate to the experiences of individuals rather as a generalization or hypothesis in science relates to the results of individual trials or experiments? Is it like the kind of idealization that goes into drawing a diagonal line through the middle of a cloud of points that are scattered about it, thus ignoring outliers? Madeleine Akrich studied the ways in which experiences related to childbirth were collected and aggregated in internet-based "epistemic communities". Her interpretation is that, indeed, a process of abstraction is involved, independent of the personal identification of A with B.

> The experiential knowledge in question is not a subject's intimate knowledge relating to him/herself, it integrates and questions the relationship between personal experience and its interactions with the medical world. In other words, medicine is already involved with what is considered as "experience". (Akrich 2010)

Howsoever we look at it, is some kind of test involved? Does someone ask (metaphorically speaking) "Is this book good enough to be added to the library?" "Is it interesting/representative/appealing/inspiring enough?" Or in the other instance "Have these readings been obtained with sufficient care?" Is the test to be of replicability? Of authenticity? Or, regularly referred to in this literature, of utility?

Assuming now that experiential knowledge can be deployed in various contexts, Caron-Flinterman et al. pose the question of whether it might be useful in the context of biomedical research (in essence, laboratory research, to be distinguished from health research). What seems to be necessary for a patient, invited to join a research committee, to make a significant contribution? Essential, they suggest, is that the patient has picked up enough of the professional language to be able to participate in the discussions. But this "proto-professionalization" carries the risk that it

> may lead to non-representation of the patient community and to the loss of "pure" experiential knowledge. In the process of professionalization, patients internalise biomedical or other forms of professional knowledge, which they integrate into their own knowledge. Several interviewees stressed that in order to reduce the risk of losing specific patient perspectives, participating proto-professionalized patient representatives should stay in close contact with the patient population they represent. (Caron-Flinterman, Broerse, and Bunders 2005, 2582)

In almost all this literature, it is taken for granted that, given a common diagnosis, everyone's experience is more or less equivalent in terms of its validity or utility. Though rarely made explicit, there seems to be an assumption that in patient collectives, where the experiences of people from different backgrounds are presented, shared, perhaps pooled, the common elements will emerge. The diagnosis is the principal determinant of identity. Missing from the analyses is any mention of the other statuses – age, gender, ethnicity, socio-economic status – which in any society might interfere with this identity work. Yet, the fact is that experiences of living with, or caring for someone with, any chronic illness or impairment are vastly influenced by these other statuses. Analysing accounts produced by parents of children with disabilities in the United States, Cindee Calton concludes that they all reflect the experiences of educated middle-class parents (Calton 2010). A poor working-class family will glean nothing from these accounts that might help it prepare for, cope with, the quite different challenges that it would face.

> The authors who write the memoirs in question are able to do so because of the occupations they have (mostly writers and professors) and wealth and connections that they have because of these occupations ... Thus when the public reads these books, perhaps to gain insight into how to raise their own child with a disability, they only read about how to do so with the financial and social resources available to the middle and upper middle classes. (Calton 2010, 853)

Interviewing parents of children with a hearing impairment in Ecuador, Lourdes Huiracocha and I reached a comparable conclusion (Huiracocha et al. 2015). Like all South American countries, Ecuador is marked by huge inequalities in wealth, social resources and access to health care. There were vast differences in the coping strategies available to educated middle-class parents and poor parents lacking both financial and informational resources. Nor were these differences ironed out in the self-help group that some parents had recently established. Not only was the group limited at the time to parents of children being raised orally (i.e. without access to sign language), but the lives of many parents (often single mothers) did not allow them time or opportunity of participating. The gap in the experiences of these families was far too great to be encompassed by any coherent distillation or useful guidelines. It is not only that some experiences are accorded greater status, means of dissemination, representativeness – but families differ in their ability to draw on the experience of others. They may have no access to it, or they may lack the control over their lives that would allow them to develop experientially informed strategies.

Mazanderani et al. were right to conclude that much remains unclear, and to "suggest that additional theoretical and comparative work that conceptualizes how 'experience' is turned into different forms of knowledge in healthcare is needed". But I am pretty sure that the experiences that come to be seen as "valid" as "useful" – even as authoritative – will be vastly weighted towards the experiences of articulate middle-class patients and families. The experiences of families and patients like these are likely to be far more deeply infused by medical–professional language and insights than are those of the poor, the ill-educated or the marginalized. And although everyone has experiences, not everyone is equally able to articulate or utilize those experiences. In her article 40 years ago, Borkman seems to have been more aware of this than many later writers. So, she introduced as a second concept, the notion of "experiential expertise", to designate

> competence or skill in handling or resolving a problem through the use of one's own experience. While everyone with the same problem may have experiential knowledge, the degree to which an individual has integrated the information and become competent in applying it to a problem varies. (447)

Tensions

Personal experience has no "inherent" authority, and is not "by definition" a source of expertise. Not only has its status changed over time, but also the extent to which it is taken as relevant differs from one society to another and within any society from one decision-making context to another. Where it exists, "relevance" has typically been won through years of advocacy and negotiation. In some parts of the world, experience of living for years with a chronic ailment is now accepted as leading to a certain sort of knowledge. Patients acquire knowledge-based-on-experience (experiential knowledge) of the way their own bodies respond to treatments. In today's health discourse, they are acknowledged as "expert" in their own illness. Doctors who have treated such patients over long periods of time are said to respect their insights and their judgements and to work with them in determining, for example, the optimum dose of a medication. This is the kind of expert, empowered patient (or perhaps better here, "health care con-sumer") policy in many countries now encourages people to become. A patient like this not only understands his or her own illness but also takes responsibility for its manage-ment, in partnership with the physician of course. The unstated assumption is that the patient's understanding has been sufficiently infused with medical thinking that the way he or she deals with the condition is pretty close to what the doctor would advise. It often is like that. For example, in a study of an obesity internet discussion group, it was found that most participants were looking to develop precisely this kind of expertise. "'Official' advice from doctors and others was refracted through the lens of experience, but there remained an underlying commitment to medical models of illness and treatment" (Fox, Ward, and O'Rourke 2005).

I want now to argue that, in general, experience is treated as authoritative, as worthy of being characterized as "knowledge" only to the extent that it appears compatible with medical knowledge and assumptions. A patient who sets off on a radically different road, relying, for example, on some form of alternative medicine, or convinced that her anorexia helps her to cope with life, is likely to encounter anything but respect for the reasoning behind her decision. Healthcare professionals seem frequently to be seen as an obstacle to informed choice, rather than a non-directive source of advice and information. Consider vaccination, now the cornerstone of public health policy in most of the world. In many European countries, paediatric vaccination is voluntary, in theory at least. But that is not how health professionals tend to treat it in practice. The information literature parents are given, in the view of many of them, is not designed to inform and facilitate personal choice, but to induce conformity. It is full of glossy pictures, propaganda, nothing whatever on possible risks or side effects, on the duration of protection, on systemic effects on the child's immune system. It is of no help in trying to make a personal decision since that is not its purpose: something particularly resented by highly educated parents accustomed to making reasoned decisions in most aspects of their lives. The social pressure exerted on parents who ask awkward questions, trying to reason things out for themselves, is deeply resented:

> Well I went to the health clinic to have him weighed. The health visitor sort of came the line "you ought to have him weighed". Anyway I went and they said he was due for his immunis-ation, "if you'd like to go along the corridor you can have him immunised today", and I said "'I don't want him immunised' and there was like this shock horror, I mean they were really shocked. But I was very annoyed. They just tell you to go along the corridor. It is not a choice is it? Even though it is not compulsory, it doesn't feel like that". (Krijnen 2004, 637)

This is all the more so when what is at stake is not *self-management*, but how *in general* a particular condition, or patient population, should be handled. As we move from the private to the public sphere, as organized patient groups publicly question the ways in which a particular condition is treated, the status of experiential knowledge is contested. Parents who are convinced their child has suffered damage as the result of a vaccination, and who try to mobilize others with similar convictions via internet, will encounter more than mere scepticism.

Two challenges for social scientists

Modern consumer culture seems to display a growing obsession with health, with bodily perfection, with the maintenance of youthful vigour despite advancing years. A result is that an insatiable demand for medical "goods" – once thought to be a characteristic of the American middle class (Rothman 1997) – has become a global phenomenon. The future of health care will surely be a future which promises profit (to the pharmaceutical industry), status (to competing purveyors of care) and fulfilment (to wealthy consumers). These developments are more likely to exacerbate than to reduce inequalities in health or in access to health care, both within or between countries. Controversies around the future of health care will no longer be limited to patient groups demanding access to expensive treatments that health economists insist are not cost-effective. With advances in genetics, in proteomics and nanotechnology, in immunology, in reproductive medicine, there will be more and more issues of the kind that have traditionally concerned bioethicists. Given the breadth of its implications, there are good arguments for involving a broad spectrum of "stakeholders" in deliberating the future of health care. Those with the greatest interest in influencing the debate, in shaping its outcome, will be people with intimate (embodied or empathetic) experience of one or other illness or impairment. Insisting that their life or well-being is at stake, they may well demand that their preferences – distilled from their own distinctive (experiential) knowledge – be given particular credence.

Looking at a sample of studies in which social scientists have tried to establish what exactly experiential (or patient) knowledge is, we find little in the way of unanimity. Whilst some researchers have explored how it can best be deployed in decision-making, others have cast doubt on what it precisely entails. Lindsay Prior, for example, has emphasized its limits. Experience leads to the perception only of changes in a patient's state or symptoms. It cannot uncover causes or underlying mechanisms. "So what lay people recognize and report upon is change, and not disease. Theirs is what might be called experiential knowledge. What is not experienced is not known" (Prior 2003, 48). Yet, on the other hand, there is no doubt that in trying to make difficult decisions about treatment, or care, or about how best to bring up a child with an impairment, people attach tremendous value to the experiences of others who have travelled a similar road and wrestled with comparable questions. We may not know *how* people's experiences become valuable for other people, how experiences come to be treated as knowledge, or something knowledge-like …. but the fact is that they do. Despite current conceptual difficulties in attaching a precise meaning to the concept, it is clear that it plays an important role in informing personal choice and in legitimating broad participation in discussion of the future of health care.

As experiential knowledge becomes a more and more important form of cultural capital, the question of who can lay claim to it becomes increasingly salient. We have seen that the possibility of competing claims emerging (as, for example, between parents of children diagnosed as autistic and "neurodiversity" spokespeople) is always potentially present. There is no way of adjudicating between these competing claims in any "objective" manner. But because a great deal is at stake, there may be moves to strengthen claims deemed compatible with (and hence of value to) powerful interests. This has led some sociologists to investigate ways in which industrial corporations have set about influencing patient advocacy in a number of countries (e.g. O'Donovan 2007; Rothman et al. 2011). Though few suggest that the advocacy agenda has been wholly captured, a lack of transparency regarding the extent of sponsorship in each of the countries seems no longer to be in doubt. Going further, there are examples of satisfied "consumers" (users of an implant, for example) being supported by a manufacturer in establishing a "patient association" to lobby for funding, or to argue against existing associations critical of the intervention in question.

Society places various constraints on the authority accorded to one or other set of health/treatment-related experiences. Whose experiences achieve the status of "experiential knowledge"? Compatibility with professional opinion is one source of constraint. Compatibility with the market orientation of a consumer society is another.

Studying marketing of an anti-cancer drug, tamoxifen, a few years ago, Linda Hogle found that breast cancer activists in the United States felt that advertising was misleading (Hogle 2002). They expressed concern that "physicians may just give the drug to women who request it, bowing to pressure from consumers, and expressed considerable concern about women's ability to interpret information presented in the ads ... ". A controversy over an advertising campaign arose as cancer activists mobilized against it, placing their own full-page ad in the *New York Times*. This coalition (Breast Cancer Action) referred to the drug as a carcinogen, and warned women of the commercial interests behind the information that was being given. But many of the women Hogle interviewed objected to what the activist coalition was saying. They had confidence in their own ability to act as informed consumers. Whatever the accumulated expertise of the cancer activists, women interviewed found the drug ads informative and objected to the activists' cries of *caveat emptor*.

Powerful interests thus influence the status of potentially rival articulations of experience: amplifying some, silencing others. So too do socio-economic status differences in a society. Groups and communities which lack status, which lack articulate spokespeople, will find that their experiences are unheard, barred from access to the status of knowledge.

The first challenge for the social sciences that I want to identify flows from this. Mazanderani et al. suggested that additional theoretical and comparative work had to be addressed to the question of how "experience" is turned into different forms of knowledge in healthcare. I would now modify this to "how different forms of experience" acquire (or do not acquire) the status of knowledge, and the filtering mechanisms that come into play. How do these filtering mechanisms work, and whose experiences are in effect discarded? The sociologist too needs to be warned, however, that in examining competing claims, some probably backed by powerful interests (and able to mobilize substantial research funds), he or she might well be treated as partisan, arguments to the contrary notwithstanding (Martin 2016).

The second challenge relates to the implications of trying empirically to uncover and articulate the experiential knowledge of sick or suffering people. What responsibilities do such efforts bring with them? What is going on when we ask people who are, or have been, sick or disabled to tell us about their experiences? Think back to the example with which I opened this paper. How should we distinguish between her *physician* listening to Mrs Flowers' story, and the *ethnographer* listening there too? The physician's obligation is to offer a treatment, a respite, a relief of pain or suffering – though this particular physician clearly fails. The purposes of social scientists, in gathering and (re)writing illness-experiences, are likely to be different. Whether or not they take the patient perspective as their starting point, social scientists are often looking for patterns: in patient–doctor communication, or in generational experiences and expectations, or in how parents experience the diagnosis of a child. Sometimes, they – we – try to find these patterns through juxtaposition of stories. Sometimes, we try to find them by means of quantification and statistical tests.

If anthropologists, sociologists, biographers, journalists can justifiably claim to offer an articulation of the patient perspective, what is allowed and what is not? Does the ethnographer, collecting stories, have obligations analogous to those of the physician? Consider, I visit a patient and ask her to tell me her life story: to tell me what her experience of her illness has been, over the years. I prompt and question her, my tape recorder whirring … Later I edit her text, cutting out repetitions, giving it a little more structure, fitting it a little to the scholarly or other purpose for which I have recorded it. In this reworking of a patient's story, directness and authenticity are lost compared to the original telling, but the authority of science is being added. On the other hand, when stories are collected and codified by sociologists, generalizations established, is what is produced still experiential knowledge … or has it become sociological knowledge? Have sociologists appropriated something properly belonging to their research subjects? What if the person whose story I am (re)telling rejects my interpretation of her experience – perhaps feeling angry and betrayed, as Estroff (1995) reports happened to her?

In my own previous work, I have been confronted with the distressing claim that we anthropologists and sociologists are engaged in turning other people's experiences, other people's suffering, into the stuff of which our own careers are built. In my teaching, I have found that students often take for granted their own right to interview, and to probe matters that might be a source of pain or of grief for those being interviewed. I have tried to convince my students that they have no such right: that there is an obligation on them to consider what – if anything – they should strive to offer in return.

Notes

1. https://en.wikipedia.org/wiki/DIPEx_Charity
2. http://www.healthtalk.org/
3. Web of Science® reports 115 articles with "experiential knowledge" in their titles (as of 12 June 2016). Of these, almost 50% have been published since January 2010. If we search with the same term in "topic" rather than title, we find that slightly more than 50% of the 2300 papers have appeared in the same period. But what does this mean? If we search for "patient perspective" in the titles of articles, then, of the 6400 articles, more than half of these too have appeared since the start of 2010. It is possible that all we are seeing is the growth in volume of publications.

References

Abel, Emily K., and C. H. Browner. 1998. "Selective Compliance with Biomedical Authority and the Uses of Experiential Knowledge." In *Pragmatic Women and Body Politics*, edited by M. Lock and P. Kaufert, 310. Cambridge: Cambridge University Press.

Akrich, Madeleine. 2010. "From Communities of Practice to Epistemic Communities: Health Mobilizations on the Internet." *Sociological Research Online* 15 (2): 10.

Blume, Stuart S., and Geerke Catshoek. 2001. *Articulating the Patient Perspective. Strategic Options for Research*. Utrecht: Patientenpraktijk.

Boardman, Felicity K. 2014. "Knowledge is Power? The Role of Experiential Knowledge in Genetically 'Risky' Reproductive Decisions." *Sociology of Health & Illness* 36 (1): 137–150.

Borkman, Thomasina. 1976. "Experiential Knowledge. A new Concept for the Analysis of Self-Help Groups." *Social Service Review* 50 (3): 445–456.

Calton, Cindee. 2010. "The Obscuring of Class in Memoirs of Parents of Children with Disabilities." *Disability & Society* 25 (7): 849–860.

Caron-Flinterman, J. Francisca, Jacqueline E. W. Broerse, and Joske F. G. Bunders. 2005. "The Experiential Knowledge of Patients: A new Resource for Biomedical Research?" *Social Science & Medicine* 60 (11): 2575–2584.

Chamak, Brigitte. 2007. "Autism and Social Movements: French Parents' Associations and International Autistic Individuals' Organisations." *Sociology of Health & Illness* 30 (1): 76–96.

Csordas, Thomas J., ed. 1994. *Embodiment and Experience. The Existential Ground of Culture and Self.* Cambridge: Cambridge University Press.

Estroff, Sue. 1995. "Whose Story is it Anyway? Authority, Voice and Responsibility in Narratives of Chronic Illness." In *Chronic Illness. From Experience to Policy*, edited by S. K. Toombs, D Bernard, and R. A. Carson, 77–104. Bloomington: Indiana University Press.

Fox, N. J., K. J. Ward, and A. J. O'Rourke. 2005. "The 'Expert Patient': Empowerment or Medical Dominance? The Case of Weight Loss, Pharmaceutical Drugs, and the Internet." *Social Science & Medicine* 60 (6): 1299–1309.

Frank, Arthur W. 1995. *The Wounded Storyteller: Body, Illness and Ethics*. Chicago, IL: University of Chicago Press.

Herxheimer, A., A. McPherson, R. Miller, S. Shepperd, John Yaphe, and Sue Ziebland. 2000. "Database of Patients' Experiences (DIPEx): A Multi-Media Approach to Sharing Experiences and Information." *The Lancet* 355 (9214): 1540–1543.

Hogle, Linda F. 2002. "Claims and Disclaimers. Whose Expertise Counts?" *Medical Anthropology* 21 (3–4): 275–306.

Huiracocha, Lourdes, Liliana Brito, Maria Esther, Ruth Clavijo, Silvia Sempertegui, Karina Huiracocha, and Stuart Blume. 2015. "Su Guagua no Escucha Nada: Ecuadorian Families Confronting the Deafness of A Child." *Disability & Society* 30 (4): 556–568.

Hunsaker Hawkins, Anne. 1993. *Reconstructing Illnesses. Studies in Pathography*. West Lafayette: Purdue University Press.

Kleinman, Arthur. 1988. "Conflicting Explanatory Models in the Care of the Chronically Ill." In *The Illness Narratives*, edited by A. Kleinman, 120–136. New York: Basic Books.

Krijnen, Willianne. 2004. "Conscious Compliance (MA Thesis, University of Amsterdam) Quoted in Stuart Blume 2006. Anti-Vaccination Movement and Their Interpretations." *Social Science & Medicine* 62 (3): 628–642.

Martin, Brian. 2016. "STS and Researcher Intervention Strategies." *Engaging Science, Technology and Society* 2: 55–66.

Mazanderani, Fadhila, Louise Locock, and John Powell. 2012. "Being Differently the Same. The Mediation of Identity Tensions in the Sharing of Illness Experiences." *Social Science & Medicine* 74 (4): 546–553.

Murphy, Robert F. 1990. *The Body Silent*. New York: W.W. Norton.

O'Connor, Erin. 2007. "Embodied Knowledge in Glassblowing: The Experience of Meaning and the Struggle Towards Proficiency." *The Sociological Review* 55 (Supplement 1): 126–141.

O'Donovan, Orla. 2007. "Corporate Colonization of Health Activism? Irish Health Advocacy Organizations' Modes of Engagement with Pharmaceutical Corporations." *International Journal of Health Services* 37 (4): 711–733.

Polanyi, Michael. 1962. *Personal Knowledge. Towards A Post-Critical Philosophy*. London: Routledge & Kegan Paul.

Pols, Jeannette. 2014. "Knowing Patients: Turning Patient Knowledge Into Science." *Science, Technology & Human Values* 39 (1): 73–97.

Prior, Lindsay. 2003. "Belief, Knowledge and Expertise: The Emergence of the lay Expert in Medical Sociology." *Sociology of Health & Illness* 25 (Special Issue): 41–57.

Rothman, David J. 1997. *Beginnings Count. The Technological Imperative in American Health Care*. New York: Oxford University Press.

Rothman, Sheila M., Victoria H. Raveis, Anne Friedman, and David J. Rothman. 2011. "Health Advocacy Organizations and the Pharmaceutical Industry: An Analysis of Disclosure Practices." *American Journal of Public Health* 101 (4): 602–609.

Yaphe, J. M., A. Rigge, A. Herxheimer, Ann McPherson, Rachel Miller, Sasha Shepperd, and Sue Ziebland. 2000. "The use of Patients' Stories by Self-Help Groups: A Survey of Voluntary Organizations in the UK on the Register of the College of Health." *Health Expectations* 3: 176–181.

Seeing the wood for the trees: Social Science 3.0 and the role of visual thinking

Joe Ravetz[a] and Amanda Ravetz[b]

[a]Centre for Urban Resilience & Energy, School of Environment & Development, HBS, Manchester University, Manchester, UK; [b]MIRIAD, Manchester School of Art, Manchester Metropolitan University, Manchester, UK

Social Science is increasingly called on to address "grand challenges", "wicked problems", "societal dilemmas" and similar problematiques. Examples include climate change, the war on drugs and urban poverty. It is now widely agreed that the disciplinary structure of academic science, with its journals, curricula, peer communities, etc., is not well suited to such trans-disciplinary, ill-bounded, controversial issues, but the ways forward are not yet clear or accepted by the mainstream. The concept of a next generation paradigm of "Science 3.0" has emerged through work on sustainability systems analysis, and for this multiple channels for learning, thinking and communications are essential. Visual thinking in its many forms (from technical representation or mapping, to photography or video, to design or illustration, to fine art) can bring to the table tacit and "felt" knowledge, creative experience and links from analysis with synthesis. This paper first sketches the contours of a Social Science 3.0, and then demonstrates with examples how visual thinking can combine with rational argument, or extend beyond it to other forms of experience.

Introduction

The "Urban Living" UK research programme recently called for "holistic diagnosis of challenges... a breadth of expertise and knowledge... co-create[d] innovative understandings... integrated pathways to future solutions" (RCUK 2015). Like many others, this programme had aspirations to connect social technology, industrial ecology, organizational learning, urban planning, civil engineering and behavioural economics, to name but a few fields involved.

In a similar vein there are high aspirations from research sponsors, such as the world's largest research and innovation (R&I) programmes at the European Commission. They call on foresight and prospective studies, with communities of "high level experts" comparing notes on "megatrends". They frame a set of "Grand Societal Challenges", "wicked problems" or nexus type dilemmas, that is, research agendas beyond a single analysis, without clear definitions, with the solutions understood as part of the problem. They then call for "integrated projects", to combine theory with case studies, technical analysis with policy deliberation and academic rigour with creative practice.

In reality much of this rhetoric falls short of expectations; with large public funds involved, risks are minimized, outputs are fixed 5 years in advance, coordinators have a near-impossible task of holding disparate elements together and multi-national consortiums are formed by political necessity as much as scientific logic. At the same time it seems that most of the science establishment (with some exceptions) is pointing in the opposite direction, along with the wider community of "R&I" (ERA Expert Group 2008; Duckworth et al. 2016). Too often, specialist knowledge is arranged into silos, disconnected from users, with an almost medieval regime of insider peer-group reviews and self-legitimizing academic league tables. The UK Research Excellence Framework is a classic example, consuming huge efforts by leading academics, and argued by some to be destructive of real innovation, creative collaboration and inter-disciplinary thinking (Sayer 2014).

Given this picture, how possible is it to work with more diverse forms of knowledge in a synergistic "social-mind-scape"? In what follows we suggest ways in which visual thinking might help to connect cultural, ethical, emotional, spiritual, aesthetic, felt and other knowledges, and bring these into constructive counterpoint with more so-called "objective" science. Rather than drawing hard lines between objective or subjective, we can ask whether such knowledge is "useful", in the sense of public, creative and collaborative.

This paper is a brief review of a complex argument. First we sketch the contours of an emerging scientific paradigm which is framed as Science-3.0. Next, the example of climate science provides a demonstration. Third, we look beyond "post-normal science" into new territories of multiple knowledges. Fourth, we look at how visual thinking can extend and work in combination with rational thinking. Fifth, we look at other forms of visual thinking on the art-anthropology interface working "beyond" rational thinking. Finally a brief conclusion asks about future directions.

An emerging Science 3.0

The aim of the co-evolutionary 3.0 framework is to help with mapping of current issues for social science, and to design or navigate future pathways.

The grand societal challenges above show how "useful knowledge" concerns not only technical problems, but conflicts of power and ideology and personalities, and more so, dilemmas (or "trilemmas") of wicked, problematic, "post-normal" types of knowledge. One manifesto for climate-related science calls for:

> societal agenda setting, collective problem framing, a plurality of perspectives, integrative research processes, new norms for handling dissent and controversy, better treatment of uncertainty and diversity of values, extended peer review, broader and more transparent metrics for evaluation, effective dialog processes, and stakeholder participation. (Cornell et al. 2013)

These features can be summarized as a "Science 3.0" agenda, which pushes at the conventional boundaries in several ways:

- *wider*, looking towards whole systems' synthesis, with a *collaborative* approach, in contrast to reductive component-based analysis;
- *deeper*, in combining different worldviews and value-systems, with a *cognitive* approach; for example, social, technical, economic, ecological, political and cultural and
- *longer*, looking beyond linear solutions to defined problems, with a *co-creative* approach, towards a reflexive deliberation and inter-subjective learning, better suited to wicked, messy, unbounded challenges.

The "3.0" framing as used here is drawn from a methodology and framework that are emerging currently (Ravetz 2015; Ravetz and Miles 2016). (Note the same term, Science 3.0, is used in a similar but distinct way by Pielke (2014)). The core concept is the capacity of any system to learn and think in synergy, where the whole is greater than the parts. We can identify several levels of synergy, each with its "model" or paradigm of system activity and change:

- *1.0 – linear model:* the synergy works as a *"functional system"*, to be analysed as a "problem of simplicity". The system follows instructions and responds to direct short-term change (with an image of a large or complex *machine*).
- *2.0 – evolutionary model:* the synergy works as a "complex adaptive system", evolving in a biological autonomous model of adaptive self-organization. This can be framed as a "problem of disorganized complexity" (with an image of *a wilderness or jungle*).
- *3.0 – co-evolutionary model:* the synergy works as a "cognitive-creative-collaborative", social-mind, collective intelligence system. This can be framed as a "problem of organized complexity". This is shaped more by human qualities – learning, thinking, questioning, creating, strategizing – with a process of cognitive collaborative co-evolution (with an image of a *human community or personal development*).

This "3.0" model can help to explore and understand almost any kind of human problem or challenge (e.g. in social, technical, economic, environmental or political domains). It can also help to design responses which are suited to the level of the problem. For example, if we take the RCUK "urban living" programme above, which called for research on the national housing crisis, a linear frame and model would focus on numbers of units; an evolutionary model would look at markets, incentives and behaviour models; and a co-evolutionary model would explore the collective intelligence, the learning and thinking capacity of the combined housing ecosystem, including public, private, civic and community sectors.

In response to this, a co-evolutionary model for Science 3.0 (including many varieties of R&I) is not only inter-disciplinary (bilateral), but trans-disciplinary (multi-lateral). It starts with more systemic and inter-connected problems and responses, questions the concept of a "thing" or "unit of analysis", and works back to the knowledge domain (Ingold 2010). It is part of a shift from a reductivist approach which looks for "problems of simplicity", towards a holistic approach to "problems of organized complexity", in which human experience is at the centre (Weaver 1948).

Such knowledge is then more than information in a paper or text-book, becoming similar to an active component of a cognitive (i.e. "cognostic") co-evolution, towards a synergistic social-mind model, involving all kinds of actors in all kinds of domains in co-learning and co-creation. Science 3.0 does not suggest that we can get all the data on the ultimate super-computer, though it may use big (or "huge") data as part of a decentralized, networked, creative-heuristic process, on the path of synergistic design of the open-mind 3.0-type models for economies, technologies, energy systems or city systems. Overall, a Science 3.0 model combines analysis and modelling with synthesis and design, bringing in the normative as an integral part of the design thinking for wicked problems (Conklin 2005).

Example – climate science

Climate change is a good example for exploring new directions in science. Scientific analysis of risks, impacts and adaptation over 20 or 40 years has to assume that everything else will stay the same, *ceterus paribus*. But in reality nothing will stay the same, many things will be inter-connected, and there is no scientific-technical model which can even guess at the combined uncertainties. What role is there for science, in such existential ignorance, even in our own backyards?

Globally, the climate change challenge shows fragmentation and conflict on an existential scale. Many scientists see gaps and fractures in the physical science, even while the physical world appears to move closer to catastrophic tipping points (Smith and Stern 2011). The 2015 Paris Agreement was a great achievement of aspiration, but the stated emissions targets ("national intended contributions"), if they could be achieved, are estimated to result in 2.7° temperature rise which is into the danger zone. There are raging battles between earth science, economic investment, political strategy, social divisions, together with many related issues of adaptation, disinvestment, international transfers, social justice and so on (Pielke 2014).

The physical science of earth systems, with measurable effects of radiative forcing among others, generally seems framed as a linear, 1.0-type problem of physics and chemistry. The system is hugely complex and dynamic, with multi-level feedback and regulating loops. But in principle, with better data, better models and better calibration of stochastic effects, the earth system could be analysed and forecast by a technical "model" (subject to the usual uncertainties), and we might then give better advice to policy-makers, as in *Science-3: Example,* left side (Figure 1(a)).

A more evolutionary view sees a multi-level "complex adaptive system" or 2.0-type model of knowledge. Climate science looks at how countless bio-physical cycles have evolved into fractal-like niches and habitats, from global scale oscillations to single-

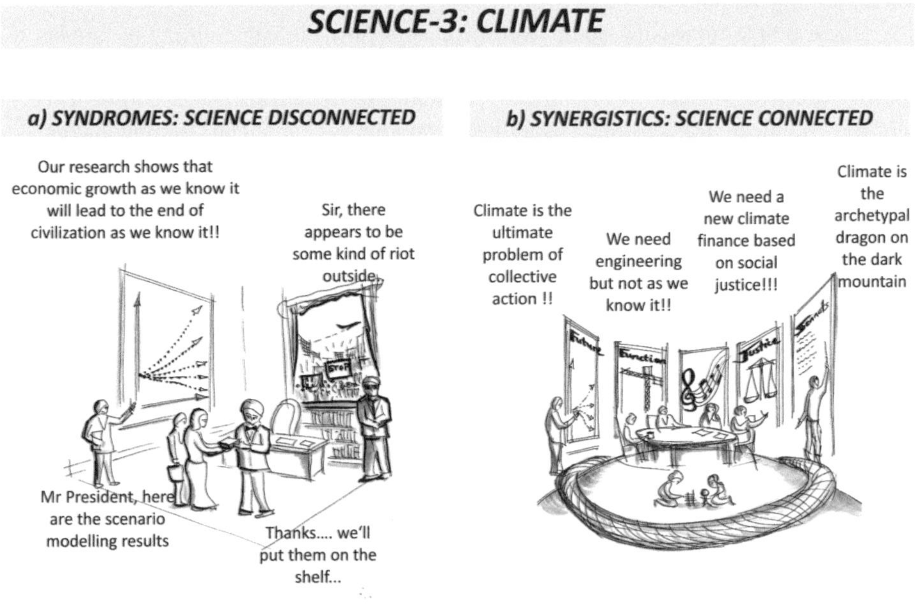

Figure 1.   Science-3: climate example.

celled algae. We then add in complex economic or political models, and as long as the parameters are clear and stable (for instance, what is economic "production"?), in principle we can get the data and build the models. But in practice such parameters are not often clear or stable. To keep the show running, the global "integrated assessment" models and studies stay with the safer 1.0- and 2.0-type knowledge zones. If we assume physical disruptions and tipping points, combined with socio-cultural-political "surprises" (and history tends to be shaped by surprises), then we are beyond the models and into existential uncertainty. For example, the link between climate change and the Syrian civil war appears to be a question of profound disagreement; whether by data analysis, interviews with farmers or agent-based modelling, the ultimate analysis of such a problematic reality seems impossible (Kelley et al. 2015; Selby and Hulme 2015).

Once we add in the human capacity for disruptive or chaotic behaviour, this begins to look like a "cognitive-collaborative-co-evolutionary" system of knowledge, in other words, a synergistic Science-3.0 model. If we try scenario modelling of emissions and climate impacts, we have to think about citizens and livelihoods, consumers and lifestyles, urbanization and migration, conflicts in Syria and elsewhere, and other societal challenges on a grand scale. As for the human qualities, there is shared learning, creative collaboration and social intelligence, alongside corruption, denial, profiteering and expropriation. In systemic terms, climate is a "threat multiplier" or "trigger" in an already hyper-stressed global system of hyper-complexity. And this is not just about the content but the scientific process itself, as the "climate-gate" fiasco showed (Nerlich 2010).

So for these kinds of problems, which are more like 3.0-type societal challenges, we can revisit the boundaries of what is "useful knowledge", how it can be generated and where it can be applied. Here, useful knowledge is not only the physical lab results, but a moving frontier of analysis, experience, communication, strategy and action. Such "useful knowledge" is spread around different sectors and actors, global or local, powerful or dependent, scientists and citizens and everyone between; and it was distributed around the inter-connections and conflicts between different domains – social, technical, economic, ecological, political, cultural and so on.

One example from New South Wales concerns how the vulnerability of farmers was framed not only as a physical climate issue, but as a human 3.0-type issue, beyond simplistic or reductive models of land-use or economic development. As a consequence the climate "problem" was reframed as a rural "opportunity" for social learning and creative collaboration, which could be mobilized by a travelling museum-in-a-bus (Vanclay et al. 2004). Another example is the first image of "earthrise" in 1969, as in Figure 2; the scientific information on our planet was already known, but the image had a huge influence as a cultural tipping point in global ecological awareness (Ravetz 2013).

Overall, this approach calls for a reframing or resetting of climate change science, as potentially "useful knowledge" which extends beyond the physical science or simple economic impacts. In this wider field, useful knowledge is as much creative-synthetic as analytic; useful knowledge is part of the solution with a mutual "action learning" approach; useful knowledge crosses as many boundaries as it needs to. This starts to look more like development process work (with possibly therapeutic and spiritual dimensions), on a collective and global scale. A "climate-therapeutic process" would work on inter-connections between facilitators (scientists) and co-producers (other actors in the role of "client" or active equal participant), in a process of collective re-evaluation and self-empowerment. A vignette is in SCIENCE-3: CLIMATE EXAMPLE, right-hand side (Figure 1(b)). We still need the physical models, impact analysis and socio-economic cross-sections, but we also need much more.

SCIENCE-3: THE ROLE OF VISUAL THINKING

Adapted from: https://urban3.net/visual-thinking/ & based on Ravetz (2013)

Figure 2. Science-3: visual climate thinking.

Mapping the Science-3.0 landscape

From its origins, modern science was constructed around the search for fundamental laws, deduced from empirical observation, which increase predictive powers, with elegance and "parsimony". But, in the climate change case, alongside other grand societal challenges, the uncertainties multiply up, the debate is conflicted and controversial, and the rational-objective-parsimonious version of the science model does not seem adequate. In fact much of current scientific activity is argued to be "on the verge" of fraud, manipulation and corporate corruption (Benessia et al. 2016).This is not all new to the critics, but it often seems easier to criticize than propose. In response, can we overlay the synergistic thinking and co-evolutionary "1-2-3" model on current concepts of science, both regular and heterodox, looking beyond problems and towards opportunities?

This starts with the notion of multiple intelligence, as in development psychology, framed here as STEEPCU (social, technical, economic, environmental, political, cultural, urban, etc.). Again, these categories are not fixed or "objective", but they seem to be useful for this kind of problem. Many researchers are pressed to summarize 5 years of research into three bullet points, then hand it to the "policy-maker", who puts it on the shelf (Figures 1(a) and 2(a)). It was easy for frustrated researchers to overlook how politicians and policy-makers play an equally complex game with its own logic, as do entrepreneurs, creative artists or so-called non-expert "lay people". If we follow through the climate example, or other similar challenges, then each of these domains of knowledge, values, worldviews and systems of logic needs to communicate and collaborate with others.

This is visualized as a 3.0-type knowledge system on the right-hand side, MULTIPLE DOMAINS (Figure 2(b)). Here we map the mutual exchange and inter-subjective social learning between different domains, each with its different worldview and logic. Some examples include: we could link earth science to the political process, or social/community knowledge to technical analysis or creative culture to new forms of entrepreneurial finance.

Beyond these bilateral links, we could look for a synergistic learning process which travels right around the landscape, and weaves the many inter-connections into a greater whole. One early example was the Georgia Basin Futures Project in British Columbia, which set out to build some of these wider inter-connections and learn from the experience (Robinson et al. 2006).

And if we enquire further into what is this knowledge, in all of its domains, we get into deeper levels of uncertainty and controversy. This is mapped in *BEYOND POST-NORMAL*, left side (Figure 3(a)), with a key concept graph, showing the uncertainty of "facts", versus controversy of "values" or "outcomes". These axes can be framed as "post-normal science", and there are many similar interpretations such as wicked problems, problematic knowledge or the classic "known-unknowns" of Donald Rumsfeld (Ravetz 2004; Stacey 2011; Leach, Scoones, and Stirling 2010).

In the bottom corner of Figure 3(a), we see normal "disciplinary" type science, on a linear 1.0 basis, where uncertainties can be quantified, and controversies can be managed; classical physics or neo-classical economics are each in their own way reductive and deterministic. Such *known-known* type knowledge works (at least with internal coherence), where the system is measurable and the dynamics of change are predictable. However, real life is not always so straightforward. If our uncertainties multiply up along the x-axis, into "technical challenges" and *known-unknowns*, this is more like a consultancy model, of expert best guesses and due diligence. If the controversies multiply up on the y-axis, with ethical dilemmas or social conflicts, this looks more like "societal problems" for politics or journalism. Scientists might advise but the major decisions are out of their hands.

And if we push the boat towards "societal challenges" – of which climate change is just the start of a long list – each has massive uncertainties and controversies, ethical dilemmas, wild-cards, tipping points and discontinuities, and altogether *unknown-unknowns*. At this point, "normal" linear scientific knowledge breaks down and we need to look beyond. Here the post-normal literature calls for "discursive inclusive participative" types of extended

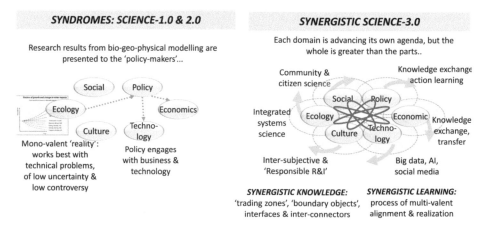

Figure 3.   Science-3: multiple domains.

peer review, but this hardly seems adequate in the face of existential challenges such as climate change (Defra 2011).

In response, we can set up a mapping of "synergistic" knowledge (Figure 3(b), right-hand side). This shows the same corners as before – technical problems and technical challenges, societal problems and societal challenges. We have the "societal challenge" corner of high uncertainty/controversy, framed as a "post-normal science" or "wicked problem". But instead of a single axis for technical uncertainty, we have a bundle of the multiple knowledge domains, or a similar range of multiplicity, where it seems that a technical type of uncertainty is not the same as a political or cultural uncertainty (Figure 4).

If we follow up the societal challenge/post-normal type agenda of climate change, the physical science is accepted (more or less) but with highly uncertain predictions; the political situation may be more tangible but highly controversial; the cultural-ethical wisdom may be controversial but less tangible and so on. So here we can visualize the role of "synergistic knowledge", to navigate the different corners and combinations of certainties and controversies, and to mobilize the exchange and learning between different knowledge domains. This is visualized on the mapping as a circular pattern of movement. It also includes a possible "back-loop" or trade-off between uncertainty and controversy. Note that this kind of mapping is only a metaphor, not to be taken too literally. The point is to visualize a multiplicity of knowledge, not so much as a "thing", but more as a "process". Within this multiplicity the configuration of values and uncertainties can be constructive or "useful". If climate science has technical uncertainty then political action might resolve it; or if social models are fragmented then an ecological awareness can fill the gap and so on.

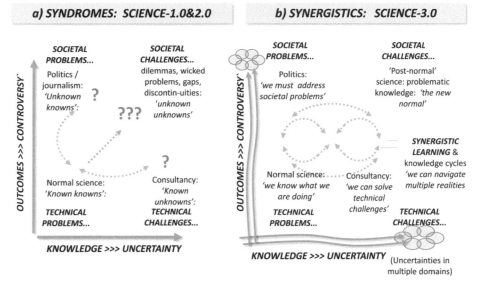

Figure 4.   Science-3: beyond post-normal.

Finally, we should note that this is not a definitive or objective "answer" on the table. Each of these domain bubbles as drawn here is in reality a cauldron of conflict and controversy. In the economic bubble for instance, we have corruption and expropriation, global trade injustice, neo-liberal outrage and systemic vulnerability, to name but a few tensions. Our synergistic knowledge pathways need to understand such forces, find ways to work with them and inter-connect with other domains. It seems inevitable that such knowledge will be entangled, co-opted or subverted. So we look for ways to enhance deliberation and transparency through channels for "knowledge democracy". It also seems inevitable that the institutions of knowledge have a huge inertia which produces the myopic/autistic approach to science, as above. So this knowledge is not some abstract thing written in a paper, it is a hands-on process and pathway for institutional learning and renewal.

Overall, synergistic science – *SCIENCE-3.0* in the language of this paper – calls for creative responses for complex inter-connected problems. For each "societal challenge" there is an equivalent "knowledge challenge" – a synergistic knowledge model, which combines problems and responses, conflicts and controversies, uncertainties and ignorance, opportunities and risks. In this way we see scientific research producers and users in a wider community of learning, thinking and social-mind intelligence.

Visual thinking combined with rational thinking

To respond to this multiplicity of knowledge, multiple channels and media for learning, thinking, reflecting and communicating are essential. The performing and visual arts have their own traditions that connect in diverse ways to synergistic thinking, inter-personal communication and creative experience. But visual thinking, as a particular field, with its many forms (from technical mapping, to design or illustration, to visual arts), is the medium that perhaps most easily links with written text (Ravetz 2011). Visual thinking brings several things to the table:

- Mobilizes tacit and felt knowledge, the unconscious mind and the numinous.
- Focuses on the creative, experiential and personal level.
- Helps to bridge the gap between analysis and synthesis.
- Offers a design thinking approach for complex problems.

Generally, visual thinking (and/or visualization) can be a powerful enabler for new insights on complex problems (Tufte 1983; Horn 1998). There is a more technical-analytic approach which can focus on human–computer–information interfaces (Huang, Nguyen, and Zhang 2010). In parallel there is a more experiential and creative approach, which uses the visual medium to access the unconscious, experiential and inter-subjective kinds of thinking (Nachmanovitch 2007) Such visual thinking then points the way towards more holistic ways of "complex adaptive thinking", which might be more responsive and flexible and better equipped than "linear rational thinking", for the inter-connected and multi-scale challenges around us (Waltner-Toews, Kay, and Lister 2009). Through many diverse channels, techniques, audiences and cultural platforms, visualization can offer the following to the research task: firstly a trans-disciplinary perspective, grounded in social experience, with open and inclusive cognitive processes; and secondly, a spectrum from systems analysis and problem mapping to experiential envisioning and creative policy design and synthesis.

This suggests a field of visual thinking possibilities with two main axes (Ravetz 2011): (Figure 5)

- From analytic/mechanical (focusing on abstractions) to synthetical and holistic (focusing on figurative substance).
- From discreet/disaggregated (specific purpose) to fuzzy/embedded (general purpose or aesthetic communication).

This analytic approach can be useful for mapping the possibilities. But there is an alternative approach where the visualization thinks and speaks for itself, rather than as an explanation of text. In the visual arts, there are many interpretations and levels of analysis, but the primary purpose is clearly aesthetic, affective and experiential. Likewise if we approach societal challenges as "experiences" as much as technical problems, then a visual art approach can be more significant than rational analysis. This can be applied to process-oriented deliberation, which again is about experience as much as technical information. For instance, "graphic facilitation" is now established as a valuable technique in process-focused workshops, with an active training and practitioner network (http://graphicfacilitation.blogs.com/). In parallel the method of "visual synergistics" emerged from sustainability and foresight methods, where visual material (from on- or off-site) can be a powerful catalyst to creative group thinking (http://urban3.net/visual-thinking/). To summarize, there are three parallel strands of visual thinking in combination with rational thinking:

- visualization IN process – that is, used in workshop or discussion situations – visioning, consensus building, conflict mediation, strategy forming, negotiation and bargaining;
- visualization OF process – that is, directly capturing dialogue, debate, argument and even conflict. The classic cartoon strip is one example where a dialogue can communicate a nuance of thinking and multiple meaning, which is hardly possible in any other way and

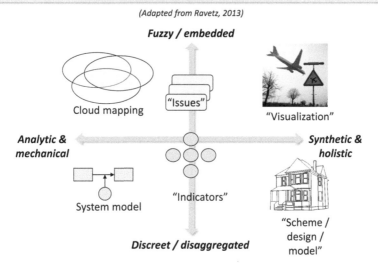

Figure 5. Mapping visual thinking.

- Visualization AS process – that is, harnessing everyday creativity, surfacing topics of public concern, giving voice and visibility to marginalized communities, co-producing research, preserving heritage.

Faced with a wicked problem, a crisis or catastrophe, as humans we need not only "know about it", but "see" it and "feel" it. As such, visual thinking is not only about technical information on risks or responses, but a multi-level, multi-channel lived experience which resonates with different parts of the human experience and psyche.

Visual experience beyond rational thinking

It was clear that the visual arts have long demonstrated to us the diversity of what it is to be human, but the yoking of the visual arts to institutional forms of research is a more recent and contested phenomenon. Here we review this landscape, and highlight one recent example which looks "beyond the rational".

During the twentieth century, science, the humanities and the social sciences used a variety of visual tools to augment established methodologies and communication strategies. Photographs, moving images, diagrams, drawings and graphics were all applied, sometimes sparingly, sometimes more enthusiastically, to questions of science and social science. Over the same time frame, the visual arts moved from doctrines of separation from the social to those of being fused with critical understandings of the social and the everyday. During the latter part of the twentieth century, however, the visual arts began to be viewed differently in third-tier educational contexts – as knowledge-producing modes of research. In the sciences, the visual arts and visual representation were recognized as reflecting the partial views of those who used them rather than neutral "evidence"; in positivist circles this confirmed the visual as suspect and problematic; but for others the affecting, experiential and expressive qualities of the visual suggested newer sensory forms of social enquiry (see e.g. Pink 2007; Ravetz 2005). In art and design meanwhile, the partial, subjective and experiential qualities of the visual were already well understood; what was new was the reframing of the arts not simply as ways of knowing, but as knowledge producing in ways comparable to the sciences.

Arguments for visual arts *as* research – with monikers such as artistic research, sensory anthropology, visual anthropology, arts-based research, practice-based research – come from at least two sides. From the social sciences perspective, the benefits are presented as having to do with

- the *extended reach* lent by visual arts to research practices including methodological, analytical and experiential;
- the *engagement and impact value* of the visual arts (see e.g. https://www.publicengagement.ac.uk/ for case studies of projects invested in visual arts) and
- the *different dimensions of experience* opened up by visual modes as opposed to heavily text- or language-based approaches.

From the visual arts research perspective, value has to do with

- *generative* capacity: allowing research to be co-produced through a genuinely shared engagement in making;
- valorization of an "anti-reductionist" research output (Lesage 2009) and
- sensual and physical, "embodied knowledge", *a felt knowledge* (Klein 2010).

What both sides share, despite their different starting points, is an acknowledgement of the power and necessity of incorporating *sensual* knowledge into the research landscape. Klein defines this as the means to "have a look from outside of a frame and simultaneously enter into it" (2010); a kind of liminal state in which our perception is comparably sensible and present (Klein 2010).

The implications of felt knowledge for social science, and of visual arts more widely, reflect the broader problems attending any kind of knowledge incommensurablity. The experiential knowledge associated with the visual arts has conventionally been eschewed by the sciences, with the visual most often limited to illustrative and communication purposes. Arguments for the inclusion of visual arts into humanities and social sciences are frequently presented in binary terms. Visual art that intentionally goes either "beyond" or "around" the rational is expected/asked to assimilate to scientific research, by providing quantitative measures of its efficacy, as has happened in arts for health research. Or, it is judged by and within its own (rigorous, but different) standards. In some recent research by a team including Amanda Ravetz, looking into the inclusion of art and artists in Arts and Humanities Research Council (AHRC)-funded "connected communities" projects, a less polarized approach was established. Reporting on the different legacies of the involvement of artists in a number of co-produced research projects across a wide range of topics and situations, Pahl et al. (Forthcoming) argued that artists' epistemological approaches in AHRC-Connected Communities research often went unrecognized by different disciplines. They nevertheless produced "subtle shifts in the [research] atmosphere or layout, [which] could then alter what happened in that space". Tracing the legacies of artists' contribution using mixed methods, the findings recognized the potential of the arts to productively unsettle or disorientate standard academic practices, to contribute to the conceptualization of research questions, to widen outcomes and the diversity of outputs and to re-orientate and change how things were understood. (Pahl et al., forthcoming).

An experiential approach was used to trace the experiential dimension of some of these legacies. "Close up" analysis of three projects was conducted that involved "slowing down the action", as a way of understanding the processes and practices of the artists involved. Some of these investigations revisited a past project through a new action. In the research involving Amanda Ravetz three participants (Douglas, Genever and Ravetz) became immersed in drawing while also distilling and articulating their experiential knowledge (Douglas et al. 2014).

The experiment yielded a set of reflections with pertinence to "felt knowledge", including not chasing goals or worrying if something looked like art or not, but allowing unexpected things to happen, valuing what was here and now, being able to grow something from small beginnings rather than trying to match the experience against anything beyond itself, seeing what came to the surface and noticing what was happening, learning to be responsive to the pressure points within the drawing and social experience, not following a blueprint but responding to things as they unfolded, using a framework to hold open a space of "not knowing", going beyond happenstance to a more refined activity of drawing as a way of trying to reach what might become a new kind of experience and understanding.

In summary the felt experience, in this case of drawing, put the researcher-participants in touch with a sense of becoming, rather than with something pre-formed. The approach challenged the idea that what artists should be doing when they work in communities is proposing new forms of access, technique, conviviality or modes of data elicitation.

Instead the researchers proposed that the "community credentials" of their experiment of three (later four, when joined by interlocuteur Johan Siebers) should be judged on quality not quantity – the qualities of drawing, its immanence, its hovering between determined and indetermined states of being (Douglas et al. 2014, 128) and the relationship between these and experiences and constitution of community. Rather than drawing encouraging participation, participation might be considered integral to drawing – a social practice that is not manufactured but given (Nancy 2013, 35). Drawing then was found to be a means not of manufacturing community – the more people the better – but of becoming attuned to community as our human condition (Nancy 1991, 22).

This experiential and qualitative artistic investigation was developed during follow on AHRC-funded research led by Amanda Ravetz with partners Portraits of Recovery (Founder Mark Prest) and people in recovery from substance misuse (see https://wonderandrecovery.wordpress.com/).

"Wonderland: the art of becoming human" aimed to bring together experiences of recovery from substance misuse, with artistic research methods. The idea was to explore how the recovering person's inner landscape and journey mirrors wider utopian impulses. Lens-based self and co-authored representations of recovery were used to communicate participants' lived experiences. A further aim was the development of recovery as a social movement, with new organizational links.

The research hypothesis was that the path of recovery is inherently utopian, fuelled by a desire for change that requires constant transformative renewal. From 2010 the substance misuse agenda moved away from harm-reduction towards recovery-focused outcomes, self-empowering the recovery community to become more active and visible. Addiction is increasingly being seen as a "feelings illness" that rarely resolves itself with the end of active using – "from time to time, self-destruction still tries to seduce me". The recovery movement espouses collective emancipatory principles; for example, "I can't, but together we can get well" and "FEAR – face everything and recover" (rather than "f**k everything and run"). The research set out to explore this "connective" impulse, asking: "How can an understanding of the utopian aspects of recovery experiences, in association with artistic research, contribute to mutually supportive, resilient and connected communities?"

Artist Cristina Nuñez was invited to run two three-day intensive workshops, with 10 participants in longer-term recovery, and these workshops were punctuated by further peer-led meetings between the participants and the research team during which associated visual arts activities were shared. Nuñez, herself in recovery, used her honed and well-tested methodology, rooted in photographic self-portraiture, with the participants. Between the two workshops she set various photographic activities for them to study alone and in supportive groups.

A film documenting the process of the research was directed by the PI (https://vimeo.com/171903022). This shows the progression of the workshops. It begins with people being instructed on how to take self-portraits in a lit studio against a black backdrop focusing on a difficult emotion, and follows through with group assessments of the images using a mixture of aesthetic and affective criteria – what is visually powerful about the images, what is affecting about the images? (Figure 6)

During evaluation interviews, conducted as conversations between participants, several characteristics and benefits of the project were identified, including:

- working with visual media and at times without words allowed emotions denied verbally to be identified and expressed;
- working with an artist who was "part of the tribe" (i.e. in recovery) made people feel safe, understood and able to take more risks in what they were able to achieve and gain from making the artwork;
- working with an artist with a tested methodology, who was very skilled in "unwrapping" people, helped participants to experiment photographically and emotionally;
- the project left people feeling "normal" and "grown up" – rather "ghettoized" and "infantilized" (a familiar and uncomfortable state). This was put down in part to the reframing of recovery as something utopian rather than within medical or criminology discourses – the idea that illness might be a social asset rather than a deficit;
- working with visual media allowed participants to connect to feelings, to make something of these feelings and to re-evaluate them and
- working in a group that built trust via the sharing of visual images allowed people from different backgrounds and communities to connect, and to recognize both their differences and the things shared.

The implications of this work with visual arts for research of various kinds are about the need to allow felt aspects of knowledge to occupy their proper space without suffering over-constraint from science-based models and funding regimes. Artistic research is currently debating its place in research and the public world – should the research content of the visual arts be explained using external words and text; or is translation a denigration

WONDERLAND: THE ART OF BECOMING HUMAN

Copyright Amanda Ravetz

Figure 6.   Wonderland: the art of becoming human.

of the knowledge that is properly inseparable from art itself – lived experience which is partial, situated, contested but fused within the art? The Wonderland project and the research that preceded it about the legacies of artists working on a variety of AHRC-Connected Communities projects suggests that both approaches should be allowed to co-exist. If a dominant language of scientific research is allowed to replace artistic epistemologies enunciated in their own forms, much of what characterizes the visual arts will be lost; but the visual arts can make important contributions to other research paradigms, at times using explication and translation by necessity, without having to lose what is specific and powerful.

Conclusions

So, what are the next steps and future directions for the visually enabled, social-mind-thinking, social science multiplicity of the future? There are global-level tipping points in all directions, and the technical evidence for an existential crisis for our civilization seems overwhelming. Yet to generate any kind of response needs many foundations – political legitimacy, economic viability, behavioural change, collective responsibility, psychological resolve and, particularly, cultural resonance. Few of these are purely technical in nature or respond only to technical stimulus; rather they are socio-cultural hubs and dynamic spaces of learning, creative action and social-mind collective intelligence. So, the role of visual thinking and other types of media is crucial in appreciating the problems and designing meaningful responses. As above, visual thinking is one part of a boundless landscape of opportunity, including theatre and role-play, music and opera, dance or performance. But the visual is arguably the most easily integrated to text-based material. We end with some speculations on possible future directions for the visual art–visual science relationship, taking some cues from FutureEverything (Lima 2011)

- Big data combined with "Internet-of-things": mashups of geo-located data, with complex user-feedback networks, with algorithmic co-creation, with new forms of remote sensing.
- Gaming approaches: the building of virtual mirror cities as in Grand Theft Auto, now enabling inter-penetration of real places with virtual characters, as in Pokemon-Go.
- Activist art approaches: combinations of visual art with political activism, with urban design and the "science of cities", or in social innovation and grassroots "zines", as seen in the art of Banksy in the UK, and similarly in Colombia, Yemen, Mexico and elsewhere.
- Combinations of the above with new science channels, for example, citizen science, crowd-science, artificial intelligence/neural network based action-experience-research.

All this suggests new cognitive-aesthetic landscapes and frontiers, yet to emerge. Science-/technology-enabled art and aesthetic experience will combine in new ways with art-enabled scientific research. Grand societal challenges such as climate change may rely on visual arts to understand the human condition and design its potential, as much as on technical data or modelling. And looking towards a global "cognopolis" of co-learning and co-creation, these domains could be part of a larger whole.

Funding

"Wonderland: the art of becoming human" was supported by the Arts and Humanities Research Council under the Connected Communities strand.

References

Benessia, A., S. Funtowicz, M. Giampietro, A. Guimaraes Pereira, J. R. Ravetz, A. Saltelli, and J. P. van der Sluijs. 2016. *The Rightful Place of Science: Science on the Verge.* Tempe, AZ: Consortium for Science Policy & Outcomes.

Conklin, J. 2005. *Dialogue Mapping: Building Shared Understanding of Wicked Problems.* New York: Wiley.

Cornell, S., F. Berkhout, W. Tuinstra, J. D. Tàbara, J. Jäger, I. Chabay, B. de Wit, et al. 2013. "Opening up Knowledge Systems for Better Responses to Global Environmental Change." *Environmental Science & Policy* 28: 60–70.

Defra. 2011. *Participatory and Deliberative Techniques to Embed an Ecosystems Approach into Decision Making: An Introductory Guide.* Project NR0124. London: Defra.

Douglas, A., A. Ravetz, K. Genever, and J. Siebers. 2014. "Why Drawing?" *Journal of Arts and Communities* 6 (2/3): 119–131.

Duckworth, M., D. Lye, J. Ravetz, and G. Ringland, eds. 2016. *Strategic Foresight: Towards the 3rd Strategic Programme of Horizon 2020.* Brussels: Research and Innovation. http://bookshop. europa.eu/en/strategic-foresight-pbKI0215938/.

ERA Expert Group. 2008. "Challenging Europe's Research: Rationales for the European Research Area (ERA): ERA (European Research Area) Expert Group, Brussels." http://ec.europa.eu/ research/era/pdf/eg7-era-rationales-final-report_en.pdf.

Horn, R. E. 1998. *Visual Language: Global Communication for the 21st Century.* San Francisco: Macro VU Press.

Huang, Mao Lin, Quang Vinh Nguyen, and Kang Zhang, eds. 2010. *Visual Information Communication.* Berlin: Springer.

Ingold, T. 2010. *Bringing Things to Life: Creative Entanglements in a World of Materials* (Working Paper 5/10). Swindon, UK: ESRC National Centre for Research Methods.

Kelley, C. P., S. Mohtadib, M. A. Canec, R. Seagerc, and Y. Kushnirc. 2015. "Climate Change in the Fertile Crescent and Implications of the Recent Syrian Drought." *PNAS* 112 (11): 3241–3246.

Klein, J. 2010. "What is Artistic Research?" *Research Catalogue.* Accessed 19 August 2016. https:// www.researchcatalogue.net/view/15292/15293/0/0.

Leach, M., I. Scoones, and A. Stirling. 2010. *Dynamic Sustainabilities: Technology, Environment, Social Justice.* London: Earthscan.

Lesage, D. 2009. "Who's Afraid of Artistic Research? On Measuring Artistic Research Output." *Art and Research: A Journal of Ideas, Contexts and Methods* 2 (2). http://www.artandresearch.org. uk/v2n2/lesage.html.

Lima, M. 2011. "Complexity and the Enthralling Power of Networks." In *the Future Everything Manual*, edited by D. Hemment. Manchester: FutureEverything. www.futureeverything.org.

Nancy, Jean-Luc. 1991. *The Inoperative Community.* Edited by Peter Connor and translated by Peter Connor, Lisa Garbus, Michael Holland, and Simona Sahey. Minneapolis: University of Minnesota Press.

Nancy, Jean-Luc. 2013. *The Pleasure in Drawing.* Translated by Phillip Armstrong. Fordham: Fordham University Press.

Nachmanovitch, S. 2007. "Bateson and the Arts." *Kybernetes* 36 (7/8): 1122–1133.

Nerlich, B. 2010. "'Climategate': Paradoxical Metaphors and Political Paralysis." *Environmental Values* 14 (9): 419–442.

Pahl, K., H. Escott, H. Graham, K. Marwood, S. Pool, and A. Ravetz. Forthcoming. "What Is the Role of Artists in Interdisciplinary Collaborative Projects with Universities and Communities?" In *Valuing Interdisciplinary Collaborative Research: Beyond Impact*, edited by K. Facer and K. Pahl. Bristol: Policy Press.

Pielke, R. A. 2014. *The Rightful Place of Science: Disasters and Climate Change.* Tempe, AZ: Consortium for Science Policy & Outcomes.

Pink, S. 2007. *Doing Visual Ethnography: Images, Media and Representation in Research.* 2nd ed. London: Sage Publications.

Ravetz, J. R. 2004. "The Post-Normal Science of Precaution." *Futures* 36 (3): 347–357.

Ravetz, A. 2005. "News from Home: Reflections on Fine Art and Anthropology." In *Visualising Anthropology*, edited by A. Ravetz and A. Grimshaw, 69–80. Bristol: Intellect Books.

Ravetz, J. 2011. "Exploring Creative Cities for Sustainability with Deliberative Visualization." In *Creativity and Sustainable Cities*, edited by L. F. Girard and P. Nijkamp, 339–366. Oxford: Heinemann.

Ravetz, J. 2013. "Beyond the Linear: The Role of Visual Thinking and Visualization." In *Addressing Tipping Points for a Precarious Future*, edited by T. O'Riordan and T. Lenton, 289–299. Oxford: Oxford University Press for the British Academy.

Ravetz, J. 2015. *The Future of the Urban Environment & Ecosystem Services in the UK*. Report to the Government Office of Science, Future of Cities. London: Government Office of Science.

Ravetz, J., and I. D. Miles. 2016. "Foresight in Cities and the Possibility of a 'Strategic Urban Intelligence'." *Foresight Journal* 18 (5): 318–336.

RCUK (Research Councils UK). 2015. *Urban Living Partnership – Pilot Phase*. Swindon: RCUK. https://www.epsrc.ac.uk/funding/calls/ulppilotphase/.

Robinson, J., J. Carmichael, R. VanWynsberghe, J. Tansey, M. Journeay, and L. Rogers. 2006. "Sustainability as a Problem of Design: Interactive Science in the Georgia Basin." *The Integrated Assessment Journal* 6 (4): 165–192.

Sayer, D. 2014. *"Five Reasons Why the REF Is Not Fit for Purpose." The Guardian*, December 15. http://www.theguardian.com/higher-education-network/2014/dec/15/research-excellence-framework-five-reasons-not-fit-for-purpose.

Selby, J., and M. Hulme. 2015. "Is Climate Change Really to Blame for Syria's Civil War?" *The Guardian*, November 29. http://www.theguardian.com/commentisfree/2015/nov/29/climate-change-syria-civil-war-prince-charles.

Smith, L. A., and N. Stern. 2011. "Uncertainty in Science and its Role in Climate Policy." *Philosophical Transactions of the Royal Society A* 369: 1–24.

Stacey, R. D. 2011. *Strategic Management and Organisational Dynamics: The Challenge of Complexity to Ways of Thinking about Organisations*. London: Pearson Education.

Tufte, E. R. 1983. *The Visual Display of Quantitative Information*. New York: Graphics Press.

Vanclay, F., R. Lane, J. Wills, I. Coates, and D. Lucas. 2004. "'Committing to Place' and evaluating the higher purpose: Increasing engagement in natural resource management through museum outreach and educational activities." *Journal of Environmental Assessment Policy and Management* 6 (4): 539–564.

Waltner-Toews, D., J. Kay, and N. Lister. 2008. *The Ecosystem Approach: Complexity, Uncertainty and Managing for Sustainability*. New York: Columbia University Press.

Weaver, W. 1948. "Science and Complexity." *American Scientist* 36 (4): 536–537.

Maps of the uncertain: a new approach to communicate scientific ignorance

Christoph Henseler and Hans-Liudger Dienel

Chair Work and Technology, TU Berlin, Berlin, Germany

While uncertainty and the unknown are not only accepted but favoured within scientific debates, these concepts are less tolerated in instances of exchange with society. In scientific communication, definitive statements are expected and thus delivered; and this societal expectation of the scientific community has obviously been internalized by the scientists themselves. After giving an overview of the lively discussion about scientific uncertainty and nescience (landscapes of the uncertain), this paper presents a new tool for the communication of scientific uncertainties: *Maps of the Uncertain*. These maps take the form of infographics, which allow a different kind of communication of uncertainties, and thus a different relationship between science and society. The paper presents and discusses examples of six maps.

"I have noticed", said Mr. K., "that we put many people off our teaching because we have an answer to everything. Could we not, in the interests of propaganda, draw up a list of questions that appear to us completely unsolved?" (Brecht 2001)

Introduction

In his book *Uncertain Science ... Uncertain World*, the geophysicist and climate researcher Henry Pollack remarks: "The uncertainties that scientists face are really not so different from the uncertainties we encounter in daily life. ... Ironically, people who are not scientists often equate science with certainty, rather than uncertainty" (Pollack 2003, 6). The project *Maps of the Uncertain* aims to change this perception.

The objective of *Maps of the Uncertain* is to communicate forms of uncertainty and ignorance from the realms of research and science to the public. By informing the larger public about the limits and uncertainties of science and its methods, the goal of the project is to foster transparency between the two realms in order to further support the legitimacy of the sciences. The project was funded as part of the Volkswagen Foundation's programme on "Extreme Events", and as such focuses on extreme events from the recent past. This subject matter should interest a large public, as the events are still fresh in the minds of the people. The individual events were chosen specifically to serve as archetypal examples for larger issues.

Uncertainty, ignorance, and non-knowledge in science and media

Modern society's experiences with technological innovations causing unexpected, harmful side effects led to increasing attention towards uncertainty and ignorance in science and policy-making. Starting with the implicit assumption that if we do not know what will happen, it might also be something bad, uncertainty and ignorance gained the most traction as research topics in the fields of technology assessment and Science and Society Studies (STS). Starting with the now almost canonical example of CFC (chlorofluorocarbon), the question how the outcomes and side effects of scientific innovations might do unexpected damage to humans, society, and the planet looms large (Wehling 2006, 83ff.). In *Risk Society* and his subsequent works, Beck (1992) and Beck, Giddens, and Lash (1994) put uncertainties, risks, and how society deals with them at the centre of his concept of reflexive modernity.

This increased interest in the topic lead also to the insight ignorance is not just the negative side of knowledge but a phenomenon deserving an attention as its own research topic alongside the study of knowledge (Smithson 1985, 1989). This lead to an own strand of research, studying the nature, role and production and use of uncertainty and ignorance in science and society (Proctor 2008; Ravetz 1987; Smithson 1985, 1989; Wehling 2006, 2009, 2015; Böschen et al. 2008; Wehling and Böschen 2015).

Smithson pointed out that ignorance is not something objective which science is bound to eradicate; but rather it is itself – sometimes intentionally – constructed and serves different purposes (Smithson 1989). In science, ignorance has very positive connotations. As Merton pointed out, the "socially defined role of the scientist calls for both the augmenting of knowledge and the specifying of ignorance" and also serves the very interest of scientists, as it provides the rationale for new research and funding (1987, p. 10). Schatz provides an illustrative example for this self-image, claiming in a recent article directed at the general public that "creating new ignorance, discovering something we did not know that we did not know" is the "highest goal in science" (2012, p. 16).

But while uncertainty and ignorance might be a good thing in itself for science, for the policy process, it has to be transformed into "usable ignorance" and compliment usable knowledge (Ravetz 1987). However, as the example of evidence based policies shows, providing usable knowledge is already quite difficult, and working with ignorance in a useful way is even more so. Ignorance can be useful for many purposes. Making claims of scientific uncertainty and ignorance is a known and well-documented tactic in discourses on risks which affect the economic interests of powerful interest groups: be it the tobacco industry manufacturing doubts on the cancer risks of smoking (Proctor 1995) or the production of perceived scientific ignorance in the debate on climate change, probably the most egregious example of divergence between science self-assessment of certainty and public's change (Corbett and Durfee 2004; Oreskes, Conway, and Shindell 2008; Wilson 2000) or the public representation and debate of genetic engineering (Böschen et al. 2006), biotechnology (Böschen et al. 2010), or mobile phone risks (Böschen et al. 2010; Stilgoe 2007), the production and use of ignorance in public debates are so numerous, that this phenomenon gave rise to its own term and field of study: agnotology (Proctor 2008).

The media plays an important role in the creation of such doubt, not so much by following its own agenda, but by giving minority or even fringe positions in science undue prominence, thus misrepresenting even broad scientific consensus. The role of the journalist is generally understood as one of a neutral disseminator of information. Journalists are therefore especially susceptible to such misrepresentations, as they cater to the professional habit of presenting competing views with equal weight (Stocking and Holstein 2008). This practice turns the traditional strength of the journalistic profession into a weakness (Christensen 2008). The media serves as an important transmitter and amplifier in the construction of ignorance especially in contested political situations.

This strategy is especially effective as science is often overestimated in its presentation to the public. Because generally media tends to overstate the certainty of scientific findings, by leaving out uncertainties. In a study based on 21 cases of journalistic decision-making in reporting on scientific findings, Lehmkuhl and Peters found that the journalists' decisions on if and how to report on uncertainties in scientific findings were mostly driven by the needs of the story. Only if ignorance, uncertainty, or controversy were at the centre of the story's narrative, were those topics covered. Otherwise, they were omitted (Lehmkuhl and Peters 2016).

Thus, contrary to what the above-mentioned examples of agnotology might imply, in general, the media tends to overstate the certainty of scientific findings and knowledge, thereby creating a skewed public perception of science. This pattern applies across disciplines and can be found in the reporting on the natural sciences (Singer and Endreny 1993, 150–159) and on social science, where Weiss and Singer (1988, 132–150) found that "undue certainty and closure" were among the most common inaccuracies. This phenomenon occurs not necessarily due to active misrepresentation, but rather due to the omission or playing down of caveats and qualifiers found in the original scientific publications (Fahnestock 1986; Singer and Endreny 1993).

This situation does not sit well with scientists. Parascandola, writing about medical research, voices the fear that omitting these caveats might undermine the credibility of the profession. When their misreported claims do not come true, they risk becoming a laughing stock (Parascandola 2000). And indeed, pointing out uncertainty in media accounts can also serve to strengthen science's perception as credible and legitimate. As Zehr (2000) showed in an in-depth analysis of media representations on global warming in the popular press, stating the incompleteness of results and pointing out the uncertainty of knowledge served to mark the difference between a more prudent science and an activist and misinformed public. This is matched by the public perception of credibility: Jensen conducted a study with 601 participants who received information on scientific results with or without qualifiers and caveats. He found that the more hedged statements were perceived as more credible (Jensen 2008).

In conclusion, it can be said that there is general overrepresentation and overestimation of scientific certainty outside of the sciences themselves, and there is a clear need to counter this perception. *Maps of the Uncertain* aims to provide a tool to counter this perception by refurbishing a form currently used in successful knowledge communication. Driven by new design and publication technologies, most notably the Internet, the last several years have witnessed the rise of the infographic. Straying away from the Tuftian paradigm of simplicity, these embellished and integrated visual diagrams aid in the communication of data and knowledge (Bateman et al. 2010; Borkin et al. 2013; Harrison, Reinecke, and Chang 2015). Now almost every newspaper and magazine regularly presents current facts and figures in an infographic-like format, making the form an almost iconic tool of communicating data and evidence.

By using infographics to map – thus the metaphorical reference to maps in the project's title – and point out ignorance and uncertainties, we hope to subvert and counter the perception of scientific omniscience.

The project

Method

Scientific disciplines deal differently with matters of uncertainty and ignorance. Not only are there different epistemic cultures in dealing with scientific knowledge (Knorr-Cetina

1999), as Böschen et al. point out, there are also different epistemic cultures regarding ignorance. In sciences with a focus on *in vitro* experiments and controlled parameters, ignorance is an actively managed ("controlled") and therefore avoided entity. The complexity-oriented systems sciences tend to have a more open attitude towards "unavoidable" ignorance, while more qualitative, case-based approaches are satisfied with knowledge only certain for a single case (Böschen et al. 2010).

In choosing the subject matter for the infographics, the aim was to represent different epistemic cultures and thus link different academic disciplines (engineering, social sciences, economic sciences, and natural sciences) with different dimensions of ignorance and uncertainty.

This required a selection of topics – that is, extreme events – representing a diverse set of uncertainties and research fields. Before arriving at the final selection of topics, the project team first put together a list of extreme events which had occurred over the last few years, and subsequently sought out those events which seemed well suited to the anticipated forms of ignorance. The team then conducted exploratory research before narrowing down the field even further. This process was in itself an exercise in the uncertain, as hypotheses about the nature of non-knowledge surrounding an extreme event had to be drawn – otherwise not even a tentative selection could be made.

After selecting and developing the first three topics, the project team conducted an interim evaluation, in which the scientific models represented in the first three maps were determined. For the second part of the project, those disciplines whose main means of knowledge accumulation differ from those already represented (observations, interpretations, experiments, hermeneutics) were sought out and focused on.

The diversity of the subject matter made *Maps of Uncertain* an extremely interdisciplinary project from its conception. This was mirrored in the subject fields represented by the maps, which ranged from volcanology and aviation, to economics, political science, geography, and demography. As such, the project required cooperation with external experts and partners. This was also necessary from a methodological point of view: *Maps of the Uncertain* explicitly aimed at communicating knowledge (about ignorance and uncertainty) available in various scientific disciplines to the public. This required the active participation of experts from the different fields. It has to be noted that these experts, regardless of discipline, replied to our requests with overwhelmingly positive feedback about the fundamental premise of the project. Clearly, the topic of uncertainty within one's own field is an interdisciplinary issue.

Based on our initial research, the selected topics were further analysed and research questions and initial hypotheses were developed. These were discussed in small workshops and corresponding interviews with experts in the respective fields, during which the central fields of uncertainty were developed and summarized into succinct statements. These ideas were then developed further in several steps of research, consultation with, and verification by the experts. The topics were then given to the graphic designers, who drafted several designs of the maps, and after consultation with the teams, finally unified the designs.

Examples and challenges

The process of creating the *Maps of the Uncertain* was not always straightforward. The project posed diverse challenges and led to surprising insights. The largest challenges were posed by the chosen format (infographic) on the one hand and the chosen subject matter (extreme events) on the other.

One of the main challenges was a result of the form of presentation itself: the info-graphic. To achieve the highest potential visual knowledge communication, the graphics need to be simple, on point, and tell a story. This is often in direct contradiction to the needs of the subject matter. Although extreme events are a great lens through which to see situations of uncertainty, the forms of uncertainty which they represent are tightly linked to – or a direct result of – their complexity.

This was compounded by the fact that the infographics needed not only to depict uncertainties and ignorance, but also give some contextual information about the extreme event itself. Thus, the desire to depict the situation of uncertainty had to compete for space with the desire to depict the extreme event.

In addition, over the course of the research and interviews with the experts, it became clear that the interesting aspects of such events often take place within fields where uncertainty is actively and intentionally produced. While interesting, these examples of agnotology were beyond the scope of the project.

To deal with these challenges, the project team had to flexibly adapt and make compromises on what to communicate. Two in-depth examples give some insight into the internal process of the map development.

Example 1: eruption of the Eyjafjallajökull and closure of European airspace

The 2010 eruption of the Eyjafjallajökull volcano created an ash cloud which led to the closure of most of the European airspace from 15 to 20 April 2010. It caused the highest level of air travel disruption since the Second World War and affected over 100,000 travellers. The International Air Transport Association stated that the total loss to the airline industry was approximately €1.3 billion.

Volcanic ash is a major hazard to aircraft (e.g. sandblasting effect on windscreens and turbine blades, melting of ash particles in the heat of turbine engines, plugging of air intakes and blocking of sensors, resulting in unreliable airspeed indications). Following some serious incidents during the 1980s, the International Civil Aviation Organization (ICAO) set up a network of Volcanic Ash Advisory Centers (VAACs). Their role is to issue volcano advisories to the meteorological offices, airlines, air navigation service providers, and governments.

Although the safety risks were not disputed in general, the airspace closure was widely criticized. Especially the airlines and the International Air Transport Association considered the closure to be unnecessary and exaggerated. The continuing public and media critique of the "inappropriate" safety measures generated a dominant public (mis-) interpretation of the "cluelessness" of the scientific disciplines. In fact, the problem was much more complicated.

Main problems and areas of uncertainty. Disagreement over the most proper risk assessment and management resulted from (at least) four core problems or "areas of uncertainty":

(a) *Forecasting*: Atmospheric dispersion models are well proven and can be used to predict the spread of pollutants following a chemical or nuclear leak or – as in our case – the spread of volcanic ash plumes. Despite ongoing technological advances, certain fields of uncertainty remain. In order to provide accurate forecasts, dispersions models require the input of data regarding the "source" of the eruption (e.g. the amount, size and character of the particles, release speed, release height, height of the top and bottom of the plume). However, the ejection of volcanic ash differs from case to case and is contingent on various surrounding conditions (e.g. temperature, humidity, existence of ice). It is almost impossible to estimate concrete "eruption profiles" in advance.

(b) *Missing criteria for airworthiness*: Before the Eyjafjallajökull eruption, airframe/ engine manufacturing groups had made no serious attempts to work out reliable criteria for airworthiness in the event of volcanic ash contamination. Regardless of some methodological difficulties in forecasting (e.g. atmospheric dispersion models are not suitable for predicting crucial parameters such as the chemical/ physical properties of the particles or the local distribution), the main problem was the unwillingness of the aircraft industry to provide concrete proposals, mainly for liability reasons and prestige. Here seems to lurk a classic example of agnotology.

(c) *Lack of a risk management approach for individual flight operators*: Before 2010, there were no internationally recognised practices which states could recommend to operators and regulatory authorities in the case of volcanic ash distribution. If one considers the continuing technological progress in the field of forecasting and remote sensing (Point A), and the missing criteria for airworthiness (Point B), an unfavourable imbalance of "the known" and "the unknown" was present in 2010.

(d) *Communication of knowledge*: As a result of the strong institutionalization of communication technology, air traffic control agencies, airlines, and decision-makers reverted to simplified and vague forms of representation of volcanic ash cloud dispersion: VAAs (Volcanic Ash Advisories – in alphanumerical and graphical form) produced by the VAACs. These served as the primary source of information in the case of volcanic ash distribution. However, such VAAs contain only broadly scaled and binary information about the projected ash dispersion. In comparison with the newest possibilities of modelling/remote sensing, these seem almost anachronistic. These crude maps, showing large areas of Europe covered by ash, complemented by the tendency towards binarisation and yes–no decisions in situations of crisis, and rhetorical safety-first approach led to a situation in which the airspace of most European countries was closed.

In the case of this map, this wealth of sources for ignorance and uncertainty could not be represented in a single infographic without losing readability and message. This meant that only one of the four aspects could be addressed in the final map. This decision required deliberation, which took into account the importance of the different factors, as well as the possibilities and strengths of the visual format. We identified the issues of model-based forecasting (a) in tandem with major uncertainties in crucial parts of the model (b) on the one hand and the problems of communicating state-of-the-art information (with its inherent uncertainties) to policy-making (d) as the most important factors. As the project was explicitly not focusing on cases of actively produced ignorance, the question of airworthiness was dropped from the list. As the issues with models and simulations were also topic of other maps, and because of the more interesting visualization possibilities, the choice fell in the end on depicting option.

The "loss of quality" in the communication of information on uncertainties (from expert disciplines to the public and political decision-makers) could elegantly be communicated and explained by overlapping the visual material:

(a) *Dispersion via real-time satellite image*: infrared imaging by geo stationary satellites provides the highest resolution images of area detection. However, these images provide no forecasting and can only be interpreted by experts in the field.

(b) *Graphic output of a common dispersion model*: Weather models are also used for forecasting the dispersion of atmospheric particles. In the short and medium term they provide very reliable results and additionally provide information on ash density and dispersion height.

(c) *VAAs (in graphic form)*: contain only broadly scaled and binary information (ash/no ash) on the projected ash dispersion for three different altitude ranges.

(d) *Map of airspace closures*: due to the lack of consensus, national air spaces were completely closed.

Example 2: Arab Spring

For many years, the analysis of breaks and transformations within political systems has been one of the main research focuses in political science. In comparison to the time and effort invested in this type of research, however, there are very few concrete results. Any predictions that have been made so far in this realm have fallen victim to chance and fate. Prominent events of the recent past have either not been predicted at all (e.g. the collapse of the Soviet Union and the Eastern Block) or have been falsely predicted in terms of their actual development (e.g. no real democratization in parts of the post-communist states); or, thirdly, recommendations by experts have turned out to be completely wrong (no or too late intervention in Ruanda and Yugoslavia, support of current or later authoritarian rulers).

What does that mean for us?. The Arab Spring is a good example of the possibilities and limits of accurate scientific consulting for policy-making and understanding processes of political change and rupture. Before the events coined 'Arab spring', social scientists have been underestimating the potential of non-Islamist civil revolts. This is due to a fog of uncertainty or just ignorance about many important factors which shape the political developments in this region. An ignorance, which even increased over time, as the development did not confirm the normative assumptions of secularization and modernization. Thus, for western researchers many aspects of the Middle East society and their tensions and currents are terra incognita. In the following, we will look closer into three other factors that triggered this faulty knowledge feedback.

Factor I – actors: Key actors of social change in the Middle East are hard to identify correctly from the outside. But even if identified, the actors are often hard to get in contact with (a prominent example being women). And even if one can establish contact with such actors, the sources might not be able communicate their real insights to the researcher due to cultural barriers, political climate, or other considerations.

Factor II – Political transparency: The closed and non-transparent character of the researched regimes also makes typical official sources like political documents and the media untrustworthy and useless. Most often, the written constitution clashes with the political reality. The media is typically tightly controlled and the information that is general published just tells a very small part of the story, being mostly another communication channel for the regimes. While such sources are in western democracies a major source of "hard facts" for the social sciences, in totalitarian regimes they are mostly useless for scientific insight.

Factor III – Academic discourse: Asking researchers directly and informally about the origins of non-knowledge sometimes brings unexpected insights. Our exchange with political scientists from different subfields revealed and interesting example of closed discourses and cultural barriers. Most interestingly, the issue of knowledge accessibility is not confined to on the ground contact to informal actors and citizens. It also affects the scientific community, as not even local and international researchers from the social and political sciences are in direct and seamless contact with one another.

The first and most simple reason for this communication problem is the language barrier: most researchers from the Middle East, particularly in social science, publish in their native languages especially when the discourse is a regional or local one, as these discourses are often not understood or even recognized by the international community. For this very reason, local researchers typically do not publish their findings in international journals and are underrepresented at international conventions, talks, and conferences. And if they do present at international conferences, they are often not taken seriously. This is in part because the scientific traditions, customs, methods, and texts are different across cultures. By not conforming to the customs and styles of the international (western) community, Middle Eastern researchers tend to be not taken seriously and their results not taken up – which intensifies the separation of discourses even more.

Taken together, these factors put the inner workings of Middle Eastern society mostly in a cloud of ignorance and make them a terra incognita for western scientists. This almost classical form of ignorance, stated by researchers from very different strands of social science research spanning from quantitative modelling to index development and qualitative country studies, came as a surprise to us.

The maps

This process led to a set of six infographics, each representing one academic discipline and one archetypal situation of uncertainty. Taken as a whole, these graphics build a narrative of the forms non-knowledge in the sciences and how these are transmitted to and dealt with in society. This larger narrative is depicted in the first map, which serves as both a guide for reading the other maps and a map of the project as a whole (Map 1).

The next three maps are dedicated to the archetypal situations of uncertainty in the sciences which make the prediction of extreme events difficult or impossible.

Using the example of the global financial crisis (and the discipline of economics), Map 2 looks at one of the most central characteristics of science: disputed knowledge. By examining contesting opinions within the discipline, this map shows the branches of uncertainty or not-yet-certainty in the field.

Both the challenge and the impetus of all scientific pursuits – the not yet certain or not yet attainable knowledge – is questioned in Map 3. This map takes as its subject western knowledge about the causes of the Arab Spring.

Using the example of the fateful evacuation of the Loveparade in Duisburg, Map 4 is dedicated to the basic problem of all model-based forecasting: the discrepancy between models and reality, and the enormous dependence of these models on the sample size at hand.

The final two maps focus more pointedly on the second aspect of the project: how society deals with knowledge gaps. By investigating the closure of European airspace after the eruption of Eyjafjallajökull, Map 5 shows the typical handling of openly communicated uncertainties in science. Such uncertainties are interpreted exclusively as hazards

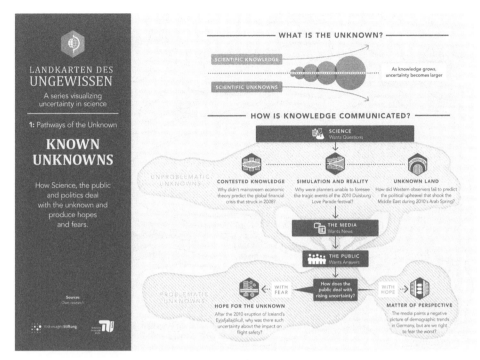

Map 1.   Pathways of the unknown. Meta-map of series.

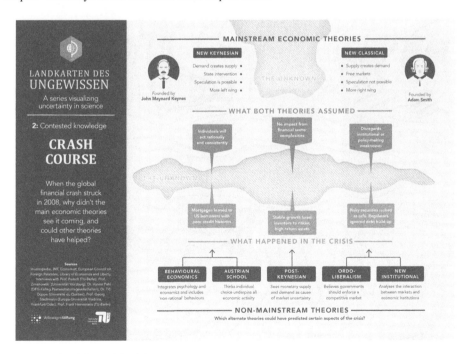

Map 2.   Global financial crisis.

Notes: Many thanks to Prof. Dieter Peitsch (TU-Berlin) Prof. Bernd Zimanowski (Universität Würz-
burg), Dr Hanno Pahl (DFG-Forschungskolleg "Postwachstumsgesellschaften"), Dr Till Düppe (Université du Québec), Prof. Georg Stadtmann (Europa-Universität Viadrina, Frankfurt/Oder) und Prof.
Frank Heinemann (TU Berlin) for their valuable input and advice which allowed us tackle this topic.

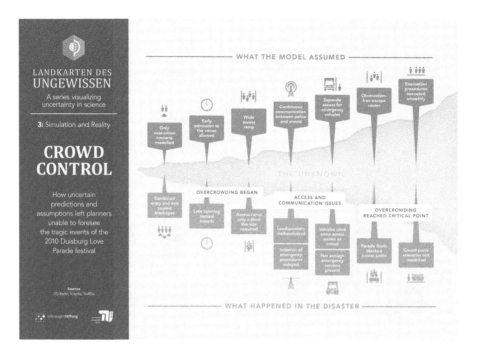

Map 3. Loveparade.
Notes: Many thanks to Dr Hugo Klüpfel (TraffGo) for providing us the original report and his willingness to answer our questions and provide us with insights on the process.

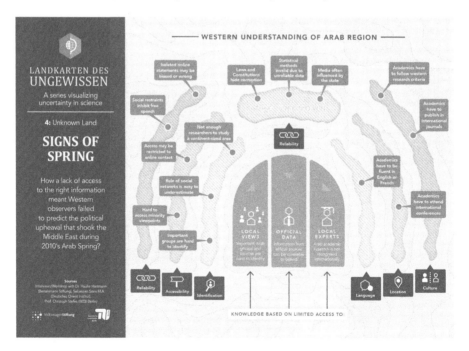

Map 4. Arab Spring.
Notes: Many thanks to Dr Hauke Hartmann (Bertelsmann Stiftung), Sebastian Sons M.A (Deutsches Orient Institut), Prof. Christoph Stefes (WZB Berlin) for their valuable input and advice which allowed us tackle this topic.

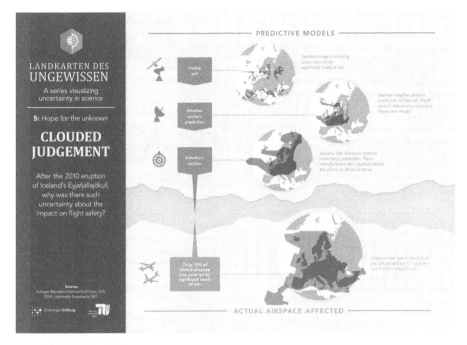

Map 5.   Eruption of the Eyjafjallajökull and closure of European airspace.
Notes: Many thanks to Dr Armin Aulinger (Helmholtz-Zentrum Geesthacht), Dr Hermann Manstein (Deutsches Zentrum für Luft- und Raumfahrt – DLR), Dr Jochen Förstner (Deutscher Wetterdienst – DWD), Kaspar Graf (Deutscher Wetterdienst – DWD), Chris Tyson (Met Office) for their valuable input and advice which allowed us tackle this topic.

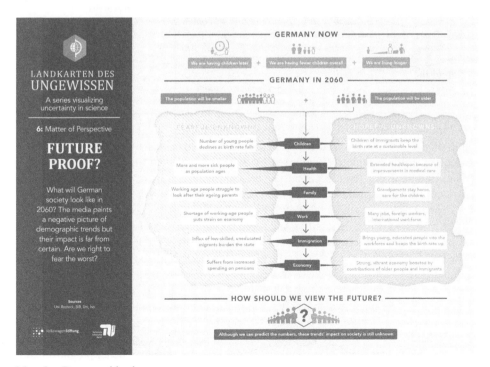

Map 6.   Demographic change.

and applied to clear binary structures (to flee/not to flee) in order to avoid the active dispute of uncertain states of knowledge.

The sixth and last map offers a contrasting vision of uncertainty in science. Using the example of the uncertainty surrounding the implications of demographic change in Germany, the typically presented horror scenarios are juxtaposed with positive ideas for the future. This map also attempts to convey the message that even when there is a level of certitude surrounding events, their interpretations can remain debatable.

The maps were produced in both English and German and are suitable for printing/publishing on a large-scale, in magazines, or online. Because of the chosen medium (infographics) and the topic (uncertainty in the sciences), these infographics are particularly appropriate for a heterogeneous, non-academic target audience and allow diverse uses in science communication.

Topic		Content	Discipline(s)
Map of the Uncertain	*Overview*	*What kind of uncertainties are there in science and how do we cope with them*	Science communication
Global financial crisis	*Disputed knowledge*	*Competing and coexisting truths (different assumptions as indicators for areas of uncertainty)*	Economics
Love Parade Duisburg 2010	*Simulation and reality*	*Low accuracy of models (model vs. "reality") and limitations of models*	Simulation and modelling in general
Arab Spring	*Terra Incognita*	*Limits to the knowledge about other countries due to lack and impossibility of communication*	Political and social science (transformation and democratization research)
Eruptions of Eyjafjallajökull	*Uncertainty as a threat*	*"Binarisation" of complex information from the scientific disciplines to decision-makers/the public*	Natural science (meteorology, volcano research)
Aging of the society	*Uncertainty as a chance?*	Certainty of the data vs. uncertainty of their interpretation	Social science

Topic: The outbreak of the 2008 global financial crisis called many established economic models into question. It seems as though the major differences in opinion within economics went completely unnoticed by a larger public up until the outbreak of the crisis. How is it that these economic models did not warn us of what was to come and why could they not provide us with adequate solutions?

Content: This infographic depicts a map of the principal schools of thought in economics, as well as where these differ, and potential blind spots in the discipline. Differences of opinion are shown between the two mainstream schools of thought within this discipline – the DSGE model (Dynamic Stochastic General Equilibrium) and the so-called heterodox economics. By showing how these two currents diverge, the map reveals where the main blind spots in economics lie and why the causes of the crisis were not observed in the standard models. The map thus shows that the uncertainty surrounding the global financial crises was borne within the economic discipline itself. Indeed, the most prominent models hardly took the most important factors in this crisis into account. By depicting these knowledge gaps, the map shows that there is a clear need for better prognosticating models of crisis market situations.

Topic: The 2010 Loveparade was held for the first time in an enclosed arena. This arena, the former freight depot in Duisburg, was only accessible via tunnel. Due to the high volume of foot traffic, a traffic jam formed at the entrance ramp to the tunnel. Chaos ensued, eventually causing 21 people to lose their lives. In order to receive an event permit for the arena – despite it not conforming to the standard rules dictating necessary escape routes – the event organizers had commissioned an evacuation plan for the area. In the aftermath of the disaster, those in charge of creating this evacuation plan came under massive pressure to explain the situation. The debate remained active in the public discourse until a detailed investigation report of the event was released.

Content: Using the example of the evacuation plan, this map shows the fundamental limitations of simulations and their tremendous dependence on basic assumptions. As a rule, these limitations are openly communicated in such disciplines (as was the case in this example). However, as models become open for public debate, this concept of "knowing what we don't know" is often lost.

The example is particularly adept for showing the large discrepancy between the basic assumptions presumed in a simulation model and the events as they occurred in reality. In this case, the model had two major short comings: (1) it was limited to only a few scenarios and put its emphasis on the wrong one (evacuation instead of regular entrance/exist currents); and (2) it presumed factors which did not come to pass in reality (that there would be a continuous stream of visitors, and that the arena would open early).

This discrepancy between simulation and reality, as well as the resulting gulf between prognosis and incident, is an archetypical and often occurring phenomenon of nescience. The phenomenon is allegorized on the infographic as two divergent forces.

Topic: In 2010/2011 in various nation-states across the Middle East and North Africa, longstanding autocratic systems were destabilized, leading to mass citizen protests and revolts. The uprisings varied in both their size and progression: While a transformation process is currently underway in Egypt, Tunisia, Libya, and Yemen, civil war rages on in Syria. Protests in Bahrain were suppressed by the government with help of the Gulf Cooperation Council countries; and major pressure is building in other nations in the region. However, neither these massive protests and movements for democracy nor their successful counterrevolutions were accurately predicted by experts. How could these events have taken so many prognosticators by surprise, despite the high level of interest in the Middle East?

Content: After much exchange with scientists of various disciplines (regional geography, quantitative international political science, index development), we were able to determine that the main problem here lay not with a lack of knowledge, rather with a lack of access to the right knowledge. This issue becomes especially clear when examining the problem of identifying and talking to relevant on-site actors. As an outside researcher, it is difficult to first identify and second gain access to such actors. And third, it cannot be assumed that in the context of such repressive regimes, relevant actors will talk openly with an outsider. In other words, there is a significant problem of access in such situations.

This problem is mirrored in the academic discourse itself. The regional/local researchers, who would have the most knowledge about such a situation, often do not have access to the international scientific community because of language barriers or "cultural" differences. This leads to a limited exchange between foreign and local researchers: Researchers with the most knowledge tend not to be able to publish internationally, whereas researchers with lesser knowledge of the situation at hand can. Lastly, typical methods of text and data analysis are limited in these situations. The necessary amount political transparency to be able to decisively rely on official documents (laws, etc.) is often lacking in this region. As such, researchers must assume that that which is written in such documents does not always reflect the political reality. Map 3 depicts this three-fold barrier to western researchers using a visualization of a landscape of hills and valleys between viewer and insight.

Topic: The eruption of the Icelandic volcano Eyjafjallajökull in Spring 2010 produced an ash cloud that lead to the longest closure of European airspace since the end of the Second World War. Although a relatively large body of information concerning the safety risks involved with volcano ash and air travel was available at the time, the decision to close the airspace over such a large area was heavily critiqued in the media and by aviation trade associations and operators. The seemingly excessive and chaotic decision led to a loss of trust in the capabilities of both crisis management experts and the involved scientific disciplines.

Content: Questions of knowledge transfer and the handling of uncertainty in society are the central problems depicted on the fifth map. Although there was a good amount of information known in particular disciplines (measurement engineering, modelling, and remote sensing) about the dispersal of volcanic trace substances, these highly complicated information models were difficult to translate to the highly standardized decision-making and communications processes in the aviation sector. Thus, the supervising authorities turned to simplified models, which only delivered binary solutions. In this way, the comparatively small ash clouds (which could be seen on satellite photos) led to a closure of the airspace over all of Europe. Map 5 visualizes the accumulation of misinformation by overlapping (1) real-time satellite photos, (2) the output graphics from dispersion models, (3) VAA data, and (4) a map of the airspace closures.

Topic: *Demographic change* has been a hotly contested issue for the last several years. Almost every academic discipline tackles this issue in some way or another. It is on the agenda of most politicians and is regularly covered in the media. However, each of these different actors represent different interests and present the issue differently, leading to an unclear and often thorny public discourse. What is this demographic change exactly and what are its consequences? A review of the relevant discourses reveal that this demographic change is not at all a predetermined catastrophe, but a megatrend with different possible outcomes.

Content: The term *demographic change* denotes the structural and measurable change in the composition of the population. In Germany, this change is due largely to the changing age distribution of the population, as well as migration to and away from particular regions in Germany and abroad. Despite the fact that the death rate is currently higher than the birth rate, the increase in older people (over 60 years old) compared to those under 30 is characteristic of demographic change in Germany. This is because life expectancy is steadily increasing due to the advancements of medical care and other factors.

The term demographic change is regularly negatively connoted in public, political, scientific, and economics discourses. It is often seen as a threat and a phenomenon which must be stopped. However, it is difficult to draw any concrete consequences from this demographic change, as there has only ever been one society in the history of man with such a demographic make-up. In fact, interpreting the consequences of these changes is relatively simple: they are unknown and allow for other, more positive analyses. Map 6 thus proposes positive counter-narratives within the subject areas children, health, family, work, migration, and economy. In doing so, this last map closes this series of catastrophe, crisis, and the unknown on a positive note.

Conclusion

In order to counterbalance conventional science communication, *Maps of the Uncertain* used extreme events as examples for exploring uncertainties in science. By discussing these events with experts in the respective fields and condensing the information into succinct statements, the project aimed to clearly communicate the limits of science and research. These *Maps* facilitate a public discussion about how to handle situations of uncertainty.

Mapping out the uncertainties and ignorance in a particular field and communicating these alongside the field's knowledge and insights strengthens the credibility of the sciences and might help bring public expectations more in line with science's self-perception. Infographics (and their development process) proved a promising tool to identify and communicate uncertainties and ignorance in science to the public and should become part of science communication. Although this form has inherent limitations regarding the amount of information and complexity, they can be a useful tool in countering the overrepresentation of certainty in popular science communication.

Funding

This work was supported by Volkswagen Foundation [grant number 86 057].

References

Bateman, S., R. L. Mandryk, C. Gutwin, A. Genest, D. McDine, and C. Brooks. 2010. "Useful Junk?: THE effects of Visual Embellishment on Comprehension and Memorability of Charts." Proceedings of the SIGCHI Conference on Human Factors in Computing Systems, 2573–2582. doi:10.1145/1753326.1753716.

Beck, U. 1992. *Risk Society: Towards a New Modernity.* London: Sage.

Beck, Ulrich, Anthony Giddens, and Scott Lash. 1994. "Reflexive modernization: Politics, tradition and aesthetics in the modern social order." Stanford, California: Stanford University Press.

Borkin, M. A., A. A. Vo, Z. Bylinskii, P. Isola, S. Sunkavalli, A. Olivia, and H. Pfister. 2013. "What Makes a Visualization Memorable?" *IEEE Transactions on Visualization and Computer Graphics.* http://vcg.seas.harvard.edu/files/pfister/files/infovis_borkin-128-camera_ready_0.pdf.

Böschen, S., K. Kastenhofer, L. Marschall, I. Rust, J. Söntgen, and P. Wehling. 2006. "Scientific Cultures of Non-knowledge in the Controversy Over Genetically Modified Organisms (GMO)." *The Cases of Molecular Biology and Ecology* 15 (4): 294–301.

Böschen, S., K. Kastenhofer, I. Rust, J. Söntgen, and P. Wehling. 2008. "Entscheidungen unter Bedingungen pluraler Nichtwissenskulturen." In *Wissensproduktion und Wissenstransfer. Wissen im Spannungsfeld von Wissenschaft, Politik und Öffentlichkeit,* edited by R. Mayntz, F. Neidhardt, P. Weingart, and U. Wengenroth, 197–220. Bielefeld: Transcript Verlag.

Böschen, S., K. Kastenhofer, I. Rust, J. Söntgen, and P. Wehling. 2010. "Scientific Nonknowledge and Its Political Dynamics: The Cases of Agri-biotechnology and Mobile Phoning." *Science, Technology & Human Values* 35 (6): 783–811. doi:10.1177/0162243909357911.

Brecht, B. 2001. *Stories of Mr. Keuner.* Translated by Martin Chalmers. San Francisco, CA: City Lights.

Christensen, J. 2008. "Smoking out Objectivity: Journalistic Gears in the Agnogenesis Machine." In *Agnotology: The Making and Unmaking of Ignorance,* edited by R. N. Proctor and L. Schiebeinger, 266–282. Stanford, CA: Stanford University Press.

Corbett, J. B., and J. L. Durfee. 2004. "Testing Public (un) Certainty of Science Media Representations of Global Warming." *Science Communication* 26 (2): 129–151. doi:10.1177/1075547004270234.

Fahnestock, Jean. 1986. "Accommodating Science: The Rhetorical Life of Scientific Facts." *Written Communication* 3 (3): 275–296. doi:10.1177/0741088386003003001.

Harrison, L., K. Reinecke, and R. Chang. 2015. "Infographic Aesthetics: Designing for the First Impression." Proceedings of the 33rd annual ACM Conference on Human Factors in Computing Systems, 1187–1190. doi:10.1145/2702123.2702545.

Jensen, J. D. 2008. "Scientific Uncertainty in News Coverage of Cancer Research: Effects of Hedging on Scientists' and Journalists' Credibility." *Human Communication Research* 34 (3): 347–369. doi:10.1111/j.1468-2958.2008.00324.x.

Knorr-Cetina, K. 1999. *Epistemic Cultures: How the Sciences Make Knowledge.* Cambridge, MA: Harvard University Press.

Lehmkuhl, M., and H. P. Peters. 2016. "Constructing (un-)certainty: An Exploration of Journalistic Decision-Making in the Reporting of Neuroscience." *Public Understanding of Science.* Advance online publication. doi:10.1177/0963662516646047.

Merton, R. K. 1987. "Three Fragments from a Sociologist's Notebooks: Establishing the Phenomenon, Specified Ignorance, and Strategic Research Materials." *Annual Review of Sociology* 13 (1): 1–29. doi:10.1146/annurev.so.13.080187.000245.

Oreskes, N., E. M. Conway, and M. Shindell. 2008. "From Chicken Little to Dr. Pangloss: William Nierenberg, Global Warming, and the Social Deconstruction of Scientific Knowledge." *Historical Studies in the Natural Sciences* 38 (1): 109–152. doi:10.1525/hsns.2008.38.1.109.

Parascandola, M. 2000. "Health in the News: What Happens When Researchers and Journalists Collide." *Research Practitioner* 1 (1): 1–29.

Pollack, H. 2003. *Uncertain Science ... Uncertain World.* Cambridge: Cambridge University Press.

Proctor, R. N. 1995. *Cancer Wars: How Politics Shapes What We Know and Don't Know About Cancer.* New York: Basic Books.

Proctor, R. N. 2008. "Agnotology: A Missing Term to Describe the Cultural Production of Ignorance (and its Study)." In *Agnotology. The Making and Unmaking of Ignorance*, edited by R. N. Proctor and L. Schiebinger, 1–33. Stanford, CA: Stanford University Press.

Ravetz, J. R. 1987. "Usable Knowledge, Usable Ignorance: Incomplete Implications." In *Sustainable Development of the Biosphere*, edited by W. C. Clark and R. E. Munn, 415–432. Cambridge: Cambridge University Press.

Schatz, Gottfried. 2012. "Freiheit schafft Wissen." *MaxPlanckForschung* 2: 14–18.

Singer, E., and P. M. Endreny. 1993. *Reporting on Risk.* New York: Russel Sage Foundation.

Smithson, M. 1985. "Toward a Social Theory of Ignorance." *Journal for the Theory of Social Behaviour* 15 (2): 151–172. doi:10.1111/j.1468-5914.1985.tb00049.x.

Smithson, M. 1989. *Ignorance and Uncertainty: Emerging Paradigms.* New York: Springer.

Stilgoe, J. 2007. "The (Co-)production of Public Uncertainty: UK Scientific Advice on Mobile Phone Health Risks." *Public Understanding of Science* 16 (1): 45–61. doi:10.1177/0963662506059262.

Stocking, S. H., and L. W. Holstein. 2008. "Manufacturing Doubt: Journalists' Roles and the Construction of Ignorance in a Scientific Controversy." *Public Understanding of Science* 18 (1): 23–42. doi:10.1177/0963662507079373.

Wehling, P. 2006. *Im Schatten des Wissens? Perspektiven der Soziologie des Nichtwissens.* Konstanz: UVK Verlagsgesellschaft.

Wehling, P. 2009. "Nichtwissen: Bestimmungen, Abgrenzungen, Bewertungen." *Erwägen – Wissen – Ethik* 20 (1): 95–106.

Wehling, P. 2015. *Vom Nutzen des Nichtwissens: Sozial- und kulturwissenschaftliche Perspektiven.* Bielefeld: Transcript.

Wehling, P., and S. Böschen. 2015. *Nichtwissenskulturen und Nichtwissensdiskurse. Über den Umgang mit Nichtwissen in Wissenschaft und Öffentlichkeit.* Baden-Baden: Nomos-Verlag.

Weiss, C. H., and E. Singer. 1988. *Reporting On Social Science in the National Media.* London: Russel Sage.

Wilson, K. M. 2000. "Drought, Debate, and Uncertainty: Measuring Reporters' Knowledge and Ignorance about Climate Change." *Public Understanding of Science* 9 (1): 1–13. doi:10.1088/0963-6625/9/1/301.

Zehr, S. C. 2000. "Public Representations of Scientific Uncertainty about Global Climate Change." *Public Understanding of Science* 9 (2): 85–103. doi:10.1088/0963-6625/9/2/301.

OBITUARY

A thank you note and a farewell to our colleagues to whom we owe our success

It all began in Cracow in the 1980s: Jan Jerschina, Professor of Sociology of Education at the Jagiellonian University of Krakow, was organizing an annual one week's event dedicated to current political developments. For this purpose, he became the founder of the "One Europe Research Group" to build bridges between the East and the West. Of course – it was still the Communist phase of Poland – he could not openly disclose the real topics discussed at these events, and the events did not take place in Cracow, but in holiday resorts around Cracow that belonged to the university, in Rabka and in Koniniki. The aim of the meetings was to bring together scholars from the East and the West of Europe to discuss current societal changes in the East and in the West by delivering papers of high academic standards. The idea of starting an academic journal was obvious. After the dissolution of the "One Europe Research Group" that has fulfilled its mission, the challenging journey, in the word of the late Martin Peterson, *to break down the rigors of orthodox academic boundaries* continued and brought us together with Routledge.

The first advisory board reflected the founding idea. Besides colleagues who were already then internationally collaborating with the ICCR, many members were participants of the Cracow workshops. Sadly enough, some of these eminent scholars have passed away in the meantime. In an anniversary issue it is the sad duty of the editor to commemorate gratefully those eminent scholars.

Already in 1990 *Friedrich R. Filippov, Member of the Russian Academy of Sciences,* was the first to pass away. He was among the first Soviet academic who were calling for reforms of the academic system and for opening up international cooperation for young researchers. He successfully encouraged them to participate at the deliberations of the "One Europe Research Group". One should not forget that this was at that time quite risky: in the Soviet Union totalitarianism was still prevailing (Jerschina and Pohoryles 1990).

Yngvar Løchen (31 May 1931–28 July 1998) was a quite renown academic in Norway and some even claim that he was one of the fathers of the modern Norwegian Sociology. He was among the founders both of the "One Europe Research Group" and of our journal. Yngvar was not only an eminent scholar, but an active citizen. He was among few scholars who has realized the potential for the transformation of the Communist Eastern Europe, and hence delivered not only intellectual input, but also contributed funding to the Cracow events. He was convinced that the social sciences have a mission to contribute to the further democratization. In his publications he called for a development from merely critical to constructive social sciences (Løchen 1990). As he could show, this depends on both urgent epistemological and structural changes. As he puts it:

> My attitude today is a combination of disillusioned realism and some form of romantic idealism. My expectations for the future are somewhat fearful – which might seem paradoxical in view of the success of sociology. (...) My perhaps thesis is that sociology cannot make significant

contributions to the process by which a society tries to understand itself without sustaining its most typical intellectual function or without letting larger parts of its total activity become significantly more intellectual in character. (Løchen 1994, 405)

This is for true in our contemporary society than it was at the time Yngvar has contributed his article to this journal: There is an obvious misunderstanding of what "applied social sciences" have to deliver. Mutual alignment between scientific communities and policy-makers – to paraphrase Lindblom (1977) – lead to processes of inclusion and inclusion, or, as Vadrot puts it "epistemic selectivities" (2017) inhibit the progress of the social science knowledge. Yngvar was aware of this challenge:

The question has been raised whether the conditions under which science is done, are conducive to cooperation between colleagues and healthy competition against the problems under investigation or whether these conditions on the contrary rather stimulate aggression and destructive conflicts among rivals and enemies on the battlefields of science. (Løchen 1990, 41)

In 2015 *Martin Peterson (1941–2015)* passed away. Martin was a quite knowledgeable historian by profession, but we would call him rather a general intellectual. Let the scientific communities judge about his academic reputation and his broad academic scope: when Martin was given the *emeritus* status in 2006 his assistants organized a *Festschrift* to honor his academic performance. Nearly all social science disciplines were represented and contributed to this book, called for good reasons: "A Case of Identities" (Hammarlund and Nilson 2006).

When Martin left us, we decided to publish to obituaries, one of the editorial team of Innovation (and the collaborators of the ICCR Foundation, a frequent research partner in social science projects) (Pohoryles 2015) and one of his Swedish collaborators (Hammarlund 2015). This respects the different frameworks, in which Martin was active and gave his relevant inputs.

It should be note here that like Yngvar, he not only had relevant intellectual inputs into the development of interdisciplinary social science research, but was one of the founding fathers of the "One Europe Research Group", but has joined the journal from its first issue onwards till his last days. And he was a very generous personality dedicated to the innovation of the social sciences and committed to the journal. His last contribution to our journal was a brief evaluation of *Innovation – The European Journal of Social Science Research*:

For someone with a background as much in the humanities as in the social sciences, involvement with Innovation has offered rare opportunities to break down the rigors of orthodox academic boundaries and reach across disciplines and faculties. (…) Innovation has always attracted those who wanted to try out new angles to established topics. Bold and nonconformist approaches could be tried out, often predating and predicting some major issue to come. (…) It has been an enormous privilege and pleasure to be part of the international editorial board of Innovation, where the most pertinent discussions about future paradigms and parameters take place. (Peterson 2012, 9)

In the course of a journal that is published for 30 years there are changes in both the editorial board and the advisory board. Among those, who joined the editorial board later and passed away in the meantime there were *John Rex,* who during his lifetime was not just one of the leading scholar in studying Max Weber, but studying migrant communities and fighting against the South African Apartheid regime; or *James Coleman,* well known for his methodological work in the social sciences. We do not keep full records of former members of the Advisory Board, so it could be that some of them might be left out of this commemorative article. To commemorate the colleagues whom we referred in this article shows our gratefulness to those who left us. We, of course, are indebted to all of those who served in the Advisory Board for some time, and those who are still with us and continue to support our journal.

Ronald J. Pohoryles
ICCR Foundation, Vienna, Austria

References

Hammarlund, K. G. 2015. "In Memory of Martin Peterson, 1941–2015." *Innovation: The European Journal of Social Science Research* 28 (4): 508–509. doi:10.1080/13511610.2015.1081811.

Hammarlund, K. G., and Tomas Nilson, eds. 2006. *A Case of Identities: Festschrift in Honour of Martin Petersen, June 22, 2006.* Gothenburg Studies in Modern History 2. Gothenburg: University Press.

Jerschina, Jan, and Ronald J. Pohoryles. 1990. "To Commemorate Our Colleague and Friend: Friedrich R. Filippov." *Innovation: The European Journal of Social Science Research* 3 (2): 418. doi:10.1080/13511610.1990.9968217.

Lindblom, Charles E. 1977. *Politics and Markets: The World's Political-Economic System.* New York: Basic Books.

Løchen, Yngvar. 1990. "From Critical to Constructive Sociology." *Innovation: The European Journal of Social Science Research* 3 (1): 41–60. doi:10.1080/13511610.1990.9968193.

Løchen, Yngvar. 1994. "Commitment and Imagination in the Social Sciences: A Concern for the Future State of Sociology." *Innovation: The European Journal of Social Science Research* 7 (4): 405–412. doi:10.1080/13511610.1994.9968420.

Peterson, Martin. 2012. "Innovation: One Step ahead of the Research Community." *Innovation: The European Journal of Social Science Research* 25 (1): 9–9. doi:10.1080/13511610.2012.655962.

Pohoryles, Ronald J. 2015. "Our Friend and Mentor Martin Peterson." *Innovation: The European Journal of Social Science Research* 28 (2): 99–100. doi:10.1080/13511610.2015.1056629.

Vadrot, Alice. 2017. "Knowledge, International Relations and the Structure-Agency Debate: Towards the Concept of 'Epistemic Selectivities'." *Innovation: The European Journal of Social Science Research* 30 (1).

Index

For Product Safety Concerns and Information please contact our EU representative GPSR@taylorandfrancis.com Taylor & Francis Verlag GmbH, Kaufingerstraße 24, 80331 München, Germany

T - #0295 - 270225 - C6 - 246/174/7 - PB - 9780367233921 - Gloss Lamination